Core Data iOS Essentials

A fast-paced, example-driven guide to data-driven iPhone, iPad, and iPod Touch applications

B.M. Harwani

BIRMINGHAM - MUMBAI

Core Data iOS Essentials

First published: April 2011

Production Reference: 1180411

Published by Packt Publishing Ltd.
32 Lincoln Road
Olton
Birmingham, B27 6PA, UK.

ISBN 978-1-849690-94-2

www.packtpub.com

Cover Image by Asher (a.wishkerman@mpic.de)

Credits

Author
B.M. Harwani

Reviewers
Fred McCann
Muhammad Adil

Acquisition Editor
David Barnes

Development Editor
Chris Rodrigues

Technical Editor
Aditi Suvarna

Copy Editor
Laxmi Subramanian

Indexer
Monica Ajmera Mehta
Rekha Nair

Editorial Team Leader
Aditya Belpathak
Vinodhan Nair

Project Team Leader
Lata Basantani

Project Coordinator
Vishal Bodwani

Proofreader
Aaron Nash

Graphics
Geetanjali Sawant

Production Coordinator
Alwin Roy

Cover Work
Alwin Roy

About the Author

B.M. Harwani is the founder and owner of Microchip Computer Education (MCE), based in Ajmer, India that provides computer education in all programming and web developing platforms. He graduated with a B.E. in computer engineering from the University of Pune, and also has a 'C' Level (Master's diploma in computer technology) from DOEACC, Government Of India. Having been involved in the teaching field for over 16 years, he has developed the art of explaining even the most complicated topics in a straightforward and easily understandable fashion. He has written several books on various subjects that include JSP, JSF, EJB, PHP, .NET, Joomla, jQuery, and Smartphones. He also writes articles on a variety of computer subjects, which can be seen on a number of websites. To know more, visit his blog, `http://bmharwani.com/blog`.

The list of books written by B.M. Harwani are Programming & Problem Solving through C (BPB, 2004), Learn Tally in Just Three Weeks (Pragya, 2005), Data Structures and Algorithms through C (CBC, 2006), Master Unix Shell Programming (CBC, 2006), Business Systems (CBC, 2006), Practical Java Projects (Shroff, 2007), Practical Web Services (Shroff, 2007), Java for Professionals (Shroff, 2008), C++ for Beginners (Shroff, 2009), Practical ASP.NET 3.5 Projects (Shroff, 2009), Java Server Faces — A Practical Approach for Beginners (PHI Learning, 2009), Practical JSF Project using NetBeans (PHI Learning, 2009), Foundation Joomla (Friends of ED, 2009), Practical EJB Projects (Shroff, 2009), Data Structures and Algorithms in C++ (Dreamtech Press, 2010), Developing Web Applications in PHP and AJAX (Tata McGraw Hill, 2010), and jQuery Recipes (Apress, 2010).

Acknowledgement

I owe a debt of gratitude to David Barnes, the Senior Acquisition Editor at Packt Publishing for his initial acceptance and giving me an opportunity to create this work. I am highly grateful to the whole team at Packt Publishing for their constant cooperation and contribution to create this book.

My gratitude to Chris Rodrigues, who as a Development Editor offered a significant amount of feedback that helped to improve the chapters. He played a vital role in improving the structure and the quality of information.

I must thank Muhammad Adil, the Technical Reviewer for his excellent, detailed reviewing of the work and the many helpful comments and suggestions he made.

Special thanks to Aditi Suvarna, the Technical Editor for first class structural and language editing. I appreciate her efforts in enhancing the contents of the book and giving it a polished look.

I also thank Alwin Roy, the Production Coordinator for doing excellent formatting and making the book dramatically better.

A big and ongoing thanks to Vishal Bodwani, the Project Coordinator for doing a great job and sincere efforts by the whole team to get the book published on time.

A great big thank you to the editorial and production staff and the entire team at Packt, who worked tirelessly to produce this book. I really enjoyed working with each one of you.

I am also thankful to my family — my small world; Anushka (my wife) and my two little darlings, Chirag and Naman for allowing me to work on the book even during the time that I was supposed to spend with them.

I should not forget to thank my dear students who have been a good teacher for me as they make me understand what basic problems they do face in a subject and enable me to directly hit at those topics. It is because of the endless interesting queries of my students that help me in writing the books with a practical approach.

About the Reviewers

Fred McCann is a co-founder of Zumisoft, an independent Mac software company. He started writing code at the tender age of eight on a TI-99a home computer and has since moved on to newer systems. His interests, outside of programming, include Judo, Yoga, Hiking, Kites, Amateur Robotics, Politics, and Meditation.

His websites include `http://www.duckrowing.com/` and `http://www.fredmccann.com/Home.html`.

Muhammad Adil graduated from the National University of Computer and Emerging Sciences in Pakistan, with a Bachelor's degree in Computer Science. He was a very active Freelance Software developer during his university years. So, after graduating, he kept working as a Freelance developer and has been working as an iOS developer for the past one and a half years.

www.PacktPub.com

Support files, eBooks, discount offers, and more

You might want to visit www.PacktPub.com for support files and downloads related to your book.

Did you know that Packt offers eBook versions of every book published, with PDF and ePub files available? You can upgrade to the eBook version at www.PacktPub.com and as a print book customer, you are entitled to a discount on the eBook copy. Get in touch with us at service@packtpub.com for more details.

At www.PacktPub.com, you can also read a collection of free technical articles, sign up for a range of free newsletters and receive exclusive discounts and offers on Packt books and eBooks.

http://PacktLib.PacktPub.com

Do you need instant solutions to your IT questions? PacktLib is Packt's online digital book library. Here, you can access, read, and search across Packt's entire library of books.

Why Subscribe?

- Fully searchable across every book published by Packt
- Copy and paste, print and bookmark content
- On demand and accessible via web browser

Free Access for Packt account holders

If you have an account with Packt at www.PacktPub.com, you can use this to access PacktLib today and view nine entirely free books. Simply use your login credentials for immediate access.

This book is dedicated to my mother Mrs. Nita Harwani and Mark Zuckerberg.

My mother is next to God for me and whatever I am today is because of the moral values taught by her.

It is because of Mark Zuckerberg's amazing development; Facebook that I could meet my school and Engineering college friends after a long break of 18 years.

Table of Contents

Preface

Since its invention, iPhone has been inspiring developers around the world to develop applications for it. Several applications can be built for iPhone, which include Web applications, Native iPhone applications, Games, Weather, News applications, Data driven applications, and so on.

Looking at the huge demand of developing data applications for iPhone inspired me to write a book on Core Data — a perfect framework for developing data-driven applications for iPhone. In this book, I have tried my level best to keep the code simple and easy to understand. I have provided step-wise instructions with screenshots at each step. Feel free to contact me at bmharwani@yahoo.com for any queries. Any suggestions for improving the book will be highly appreciated.

What this book covers

In *Chapter 1*, *Overview*, you will see a brief history of the Core Data and a small introduction to EOF and Xcode.

In *Chapter 2*, *Understanding Core Data*, you will have an introduction to the Core Data framework and its features. You will learn about the data model and how it defines the structure of data in terms of entities, properties, and their relationships. Also, you will get a brief idea of **Model View Controller** (**MVC**), the Core Data API and its main components. Besides this, the chapter includes an overview of the application (Sales Record System for a Store), which we will be building in the book along with its different views and the tasks performed when different controls in these views are selected.

Chapter 3, *Understanding Objective-C Protocol and Table View*, explains how an object collaborates with other objects through the delegation pattern. We will learn about the working of a protocol, that is, how a protocol and its methods are defined. We will also learn how an object adopts a protocol to act as a delegate and how a protocol establishes a contract for communication between two objects.

Chapter 4, *Designing a Data Model and Building Data Objects for Customers*, introduces the working of UITableView and explains step-by-step how information is displayed via the table view. The chapter explains the different methods used in displaying information through table view and also how to add more information to the existing information being displayed via table view. For instance, if four names are already being displayed in a table, this chapter will show how to add the newly entered name to the existing list of names in the table.

In *Chapter 5*, *Creating, Listing, and Deleting Names of Customers*, we will be learning how to design a data model for storing any customer's information, that is, we will define the Customer entity and its attributes. Also, we will learn to build the data object (classes) associated with the Customer entity.

Chapter 6, *Creating, Listing, Displaying, and Deleting Records of Customers*, focuses on explaining how a customer's information, which is stored in the Customer entity, is maintained. The chapter gives a step-by-step explanation of how to save, display, and delete the customer information that comprises customer's name, e-mail address, and contact number.

In *Chapter 7*, *Updating and Searching Records of Customers*, we will see how to modify the customer information, which is, unlike the "editing" feature in *Chapter 6* that was limited to the deletion of a record; we will see how to update (modify) the information of the existing customers. The chapter explains the procedure to add an **Edit** button to the view, which when selected will allow us to edit the information of the selected customer. This chapter also covers how to save the modified information back to the persistent store. In this chapter, we will also learn the application of NSPredicate to apply query facility to locate the desired customer quickly.

Chapter 8, *Entering, Saving, Listing, and Deleting the Records of the Products Sold to the Customers*, explains how to store the information of the products purchased by different customers, we will learn to add the Product entity to our existing data model and we will see how the relationship is established from the Customer entity to the Product entity. The chapter also explains how the **inverse relationship** is set from the Product entity to the Customer entity and finally, the procedure of building data objects for the modified data model. Also, we will learn how to maintain the product's information, that is, how to enter, save, display, and edit the information of the products that are sold to different customers. We will learn how to develop a view to enter the product's information, develop a product's menu to add, edit, and display the products sold to the selected customer and finally, to connect the product's menu to the rest of the application.

Chapter 9, *Entering, Displaying, and Deleting the Stock*, covers the creation of a Master Product entity, which will be used for storing the information of products that the vendor is dealing with. All the products available for sale are stored in this table. In order to store the image of the product, the chapter explains the concept of transformable data type that is used for creating custom data types. The chapter also explains how to enter, save, display, delete, and modify the information of the master products that the vendor deals with. It also covers the working of the **Image Picker** control—how it is used in selecting images of the products and the different methods to define the size of the image of the product. In all, the chapter explains how to develop a view to enter master product's information, develop a menu to add, delete, and display information of master products for the `MasterProduct`.

The information of the products entered in the `MasterProduct` entity is very different from the information of the product entered in the `Product` entity. The `Product` entity stores the information of the products that are sold to the customers, whereas the `MasterProduct` entity refers to the products that are available for sale.

Chapter 10, *Editing the Stock Information*, explains how to connect the menu meant for adding, deleting, and displaying the Master Product information to the rest of the application. Also, the chapter covers the step-by-step approach to develop a view to display and modify the selected master product's information.

In *Chapter 11*, *Displaying the Products for Sale and Updating the Stock*, we will learn how to implement query facility while entering the information of the products sold to the selected customer. Also, we will see how the quantity of the master product gets automatically reduced by the amount of quantity sold to the selected customer.

Chapter 12, *Appendix*, will give you a brief idea about the topics covered in this book.

What you need for this book

This book assumes that you have an Intel-based Macintosh running Snow Leopard (Mac OS X 10.6.2 or later). Why Snow Leopard? There are many new features in Xcode that are available only on Snow Leopard. Therefore, I highly recommend upgrading to Snow Leopard, if you are using an earlier release. We will be using Xcode, an integrated development environment used for creating applications for iPad, iPhone, core data, and other Mac applications. So, download the latest version of Xcode from the following link: `http://developer.apple.com/technologies/xcode.html`.

The latest version of Xcode that is available at the time of this writing is Xcode 3.2.5. I have used the same version for developing the core data application in this book.

Who this book is for

This book is mainly written for those who are familiar with iPhone SDK programming and are interested in developing data-driven applications using Core Data. For understanding the concept of Core Data better, knowledge of Objective C protocol and delegation pattern is required. Besides this, familiarity with the data source patterns, such as UITableView and UITableViewDataSource, for the purpose of displaying information is also required. But never mind if you are not aware of these two concepts, Chapters 3 and 4 of the book are focused on getting you acquainted with them.

Conventions

In this book, you will find a number of styles of text that distinguish between different kinds of information. Here are some examples of these styles, and an explanation of their meaning.

Code words in text are shown as follows: "The result may be either in the form of an NSArray (containing the fetched entities) or there may be an error."

A block of code is set as follows:

```
NSError *error;
NSArray *myArray = [myManagedObjectContext executeFetchRequest:
    fetchRequest error:&error]
```

When we wish to draw your attention to a particular part of a code block, the relevant lines or items are set in bold:

```
@property(nonatomic, retain) Customer *cust;
@property(nonatomic, retain) MasterProduct *mastprod;
@property(nonatomic, retain) Product *prod;
```

New terms and **important words** are shown in bold. Words that you see on the screen, in menus or dialog boxes for example, appear in the text like this: "The view contains a toolbar with three bar button item controls—**Customers List**, **Edit**, and **Add**."

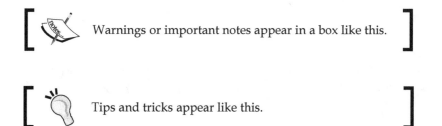

Warnings or important notes appear in a box like this.

Tips and tricks appear like this.

Reader feedback

Feedback from our readers is always welcome. Let us know what you think about this book—what you liked or may have disliked. Reader feedback is important for us to develop titles that you really get the most out of.

To send us general feedback, simply send an e-mail to feedback@packtpub.com, and mention the book title via the subject of your message.

If there is a book that you need and would like to see us publish, please send us a note in the **SUGGEST A TITLE** form on www.packtpub.com or e-mail suggest@packtpub.com.

If there is a topic that you have expertise in and you are interested in either writing or contributing to a book, see our' author guide on www.packtpub.com/authors.

Customer support

Now that you are the proud owner of a Packt book, we have a number of things to help you to get the most from your purchase.

Downloading the example code

You can download the example code files for all Packt books you have purchased from your account at http://www.PacktPub.com. If you purchased this book elsewhere, you can visit http://www.PacktPub.com/support and register to have the files e-mailed directly to you.

Errata

Although we have taken every care to ensure the accuracy of our content, mistakes do happen. If you find a mistake in one of our books—maybe a mistake in the text or the code—we would be grateful if you would report this to us. By doing so, you can save other readers from frustration and help us improve subsequent versions of this book. If you find any errata, please report them by visiting `http://www.packtpub.com/support`, selecting your book, clicking on the **errata submission form** link, and entering the details of your errata. Once your errata are verified, your submission will be accepted and the errata will be uploaded on our website, or added to any list of existing errata, under the Errata section of that title. Any existing errata can be viewed by selecting your title from `http://www.packtpub.com/support`.

Piracy

Piracy of copyright material on the Internet is an ongoing problem across all media. At Packt, we take the protection of our copyright and licenses very seriously. If you come across any illegal copies of our works, in any form, on the Internet, please provide us with the location address or website name immediately so that we can pursue a remedy.

Please contact us at `copyright@packtpub.com` with a link to the suspected pirated material.

We appreciate your help in protecting our authors, and our ability to bring you valuable content.

Questions

You can contact us at `questions@packtpub.com` if you are having a problem with any aspect of the book, and we will do our best to address it.

1
Overview

This book is a practical guide to help you in developing Data-Driven iPhone applications using Core Data. The tremendous success of iPhone has increased the demand of mobile applications. Besides the Game-based applications, there is a huge market for the data-driven mobile applications too. The focus of this book is to make you understand how the **Core Data**, Apple's persistence framework, is used for developing data-driven mobile applications.

Prerequisite

This book assumes that you have a basic understanding of the iPhone SDK and you also know the basics of iPhone SDK programming.

To better understand the concept of Core Data, you should:

- Have a good understanding of the Objective-C protocol and the delegation pattern
- Be familiar with data source patterns, such as `UITableView` and `UITableViewDataSource`, for the purpose of displaying information

Even if you're not aware of these two concepts, *Chapter 3, Understanding Objective-C Protocol and Table View* and *Chapter 4, Designing a Data Model and Building Data Objects for Customers* of the book are focused to get you acquainted with them. That is why the two chapters are self-contained and each chapter presents an individual application.

A brief history

The iPhone as we all know is an integrated cellular telephone and media player developed and marketed by Apple. It has become very popular in the past few years because of its amazing features. Looking at its huge number of users, developers around the world are attracted to develop applications for this unique device. Developers realized that besides games, there is a huge market of data applications for iPhone device. The attraction of creating data applications for iPhone device resulted into development of the Core Data framework. But the question is where did Core Data come from?

Core Data was first developed at NeXT Computer as the DBKit framework in 1992, which then became the **Enterprise Object Framework** (**EOF**) in 1994.

Enterprise Object Framework (EOF)

EOF is an **object-relational mapping** (**ORM**) framework that provides a mechanism for accessing the data as an object-oriented class structure. It is well-designed and encourages **Model View Controller** (**MVC**) design patterns. It also simplifies the tedious job of creating an application's data model. EOF is not just a framework, it is also a tool that helps in creating the application's data model visually — the task that was previously done by creating Objective-C classes. Besides this, the framework handles all the work involved in persisting the data to a SQL database, flat file, or any other data store. Based on object-oriented architecture, EOF is very flexible to use too. The roots of the Core Data framework come from the Enterprise Objects Framework (EOF).

Core Data

Core Data is part of the Cocoa API in Mac OS X first introduced with Mac OS X 10.4 Tiger and for the iOS with iPhone SDK 3.0. It is a powerful data model framework that was specifically designed to provide local data storage for Cocoa applications. The modeling functionality of Core Data is integrated right into XCode, so there's no need to switch back and forth between the IDE and modeler. With interface builder, it allows developers to quickly create a user interface (known as the views of the application in MVC terminology) without writing a single line of code. It is also the most effective solution to data persistence and allows us to persist our data to any number of different storage mediums, which includes storing data as XML, in binary files, or in an embedded SQLite database. The data modeling tool of Xcode allows us to define our application's data model graphically, which can be easily accessed through code. Instances of the entities defined in the data model are then managed by the Core Data framework and stored to a storage medium such as an XML file or SQLite database.

Now the question arises, what is Xcode and why we are using it for developing Core Data applications?

Why use Xcode?

Xcode is Apple's most comprehensive **Software Development Kit (SDK)**, and it provides an environment for developing the applications for iPhone. It is a highly customizable integrated development environment (IDE) that includes compilers and applications, together with an extensive set of programming libraries and interfaces. It is a powerful source editor and a graphic debugger too. While developing applications with XCode, it gives us an option to enable a checkbox for enabling Core Data support. On selecting the checkbox, Xcode automatically creates code for us that make the task of developing core data applications quite easy.

Source code

The source code of the book is available at the URL specified in the Preface of the book.

You'll find chapter-wise code bundle in the ZIP file. The book is so organized that it guides you to develop a data-drive application step-by-step. That is, by the end of the book, you'll be having a complete data-driven running application with you. In case, you want to run the end product directly, follow the below given steps:

1. Unzip the source bundle of the last chapter, *Chapter 11*, *Displaying the Products for Sale and Updating the Stock* on your local Mac.

2. Open Xcode, go to **File | Open** from the menu, and browse to the unzipped bundle of *Chapter 11*, *Displaying the Products for Sale and Updating the Stock*. In the `prob` folder, select the `prob.xcodeproj` file followed by clicking on the **Open** button.

3. Select the **Build and Run** icon from the Xcode project window to run the application. You'll get the main view of the application as shown in the following image. But the application is not yet ready to run until we define the photos of the master products (products that we are going to sell through application).

4. To define photos of the master products in iPhone Simulator, go to **Home** and then click on the **Photos** icon (refer to the given image (a)).

5. We get the **Albums** page as shown in image (b). Because we have not created any photo album yet, the figure displays the message, **No Photos**.

6. Drag the first image, IMG_0000.JPG provided in the code bundle of *Chapter 11, Displaying the Products for Sale and Updating the Stock* onto the simulator screen. Tap on the image and hold down the mouse on the image until the popover comes up, as shown in image (c). Click on the **Save Image** button to save the image.

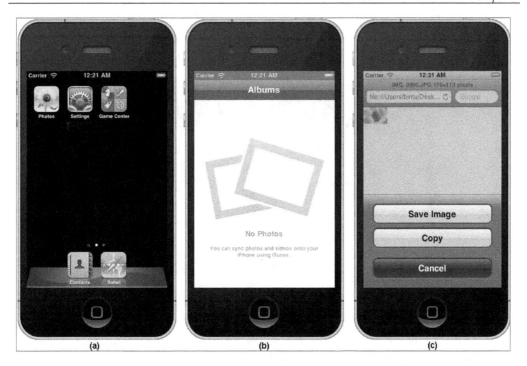

<table>
<tr><td>(a)</td><td>(b)</td><td>(c)</td></tr>
</table>

7. Repeat the procedure for the other three images (*IMG_0001.JPG, IMG_0002.
    JPG, IMG_0003.JPG*). After saving the four images, the simulator will display
    the images as shown in image (a).

8. On clicking back to **Photos**, we find that an album **Saved Photos** appears
    with one of the images considered as the icon of the photo album (image (b)).
    The number **(4)** in parenthesis represents that there are four images in this
    photo album.

9. Now, our application is completely ready for execution. For any guidance regarding operating the application, refer to the *An application output sample* section in *Chapter 2, Understanding Core Data.*

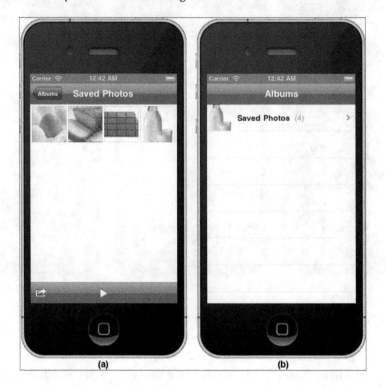

Shall we begin?

After following how our book will proceed, let us now get ready to dive in. Get ready for the introduction of Core Data and the step-by-step journey to understand its different concepts and applying them practically in developing a data-driven mobile application.

2
Understanding Core Data

In this book, we'll learn how to build a Sales Record Keeping System application using Core Data through a step-by-step approach. So, this chapter will give us an introduction to the following topics:

- Core Data framework and its features
- The data model and how it defines the structure of data in terms of entities, properties, and their relationships
- Model-View-Controller (MVC)
- Core Data API and its main components
- An overview of the application that we will be building in this book and a glance at the different application views and the tasks performed when different controls in these views are selected

Core Data

Core Data is Apple's persistence framework, which is used to *persist* — store our application's data in a persistent store, which may be memory or a flat file database. It helps us represent our data model in terms of an object graph, establish relationships among objects, and it can also store object graphs on the disk. It also allows us to use the entities of our data model in the form of objects, that is, it maps our data into a form that can be easily stored in a database, such as SQLite, or into a flat file. Also, the Core Data reduces a lot of coding. On using Xcode's templates for Core Data applications, we automatically get the boilerplate code that does several complex tasks such as generating XML files, binary files, SQLite files automatically for us without writing a single code, allowing us to focus on the business logic of our application.

Besides this, Core Data also provides several features that are required in data manipulation, which includes filtering data, querying data, sorting data, establishing relationships with other data, and persisting data in different repositories.

Core Data features

The Core Data framework provides lots of features that include the following:

- **Supports migrating and versioning**: It means we can modify our data model, that is, entities of the application, whenever desired. The Core Data will replace the older persistent store with the revised data model. This concept is nicely explained with figures in *Chapter 11, Displaying the Products for Sale and Updating the Stock*.

- **Supports Key-Value Coding** (KVC): It is used to store and retrieve data from the managed objects. Core Data provides the methods required for setting and retrieving attribute values from the managed object, respectively. We will be using this feature in our application to display the information of customers and the products sold to them through the table view.

- **Tracks the modifications**: Core Data keeps track of the modifications performed on managed objects thus allowing us to undo any changes if required. We will be using this feature in our application while modifying the information of a customer or product to know what the earlier value was and what the new value entered for it is.

- **Supports lazy loading**: It's a situation that arises when all the property values of a managed object are not loaded from the data store and the property values are accessed by the application. In such situations, faulting occurs and the data is retrieved from the store automatically.

- **Efficient database retrievals**: Core Data queries are optimized for this, though the execution of query is dependent on the data store.

- **Multi-threading**: Core Data supports multi-threading in an application, that is, more than one thread can be executed in parallel to increase performance. Even some tasks can be performed in the background using a separate thread.

- **Inverse relationship**: Core Data maintains an inverse relationship for consistency. If we add an object to a relationship, Core Data will automatically take care of adding the correct object to the inverse relationship. Also, if we remove an object from a relationship, Core Data will automatically remove it from the inverse relationship. In our application, we will be using an inverse relationship between the Customer and Product entities, so that if a customer is deleted, the information of all the products purchased by him/her should also be automatically deleted.

- **External data repositories**: Core Data supports storing objects in external data repositories in different formats.

Data Model

Core Data describes the data in terms of a data model. A **data model** is used to define the structure of the data in terms of entities, properties, and their relationships.

Entities

Because Core Data maintains data in terms of objects, an entity is an individual data object to represent complete information of the person, item, object, and so on. For example, customer is an entity, which represents information of customers, such as name, address, e-mail ID, contact number, products purchased, date of purchase, and so on. Similarly, the product is an entity, which represents the information of a product, such as name of the product, price, weight, and so on. An entity consists of properties that are a combination of attributes and relationships. An entity in Xcode's Data Model Editor may appear as shown in the following screenshot:

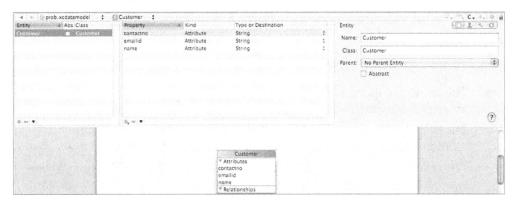

Properties

Properties of an entity give detailed information about it, such as what are its attributes and how it is related to other entities. A property of an entity refers to its attributes and relationships. Attributes are scalar values and relationships are pointers to or collections of other entities at the object level. A property is represented by a name and a type.

Attributes

Attributes are the variables within an object (entity). In fact, a collection of attributes makes an entity. In database language, they are known as columns of the table. For example, the customer's entity may consist of attributes such as name, address, contact number, items purchased, and so on. Similarly, the attributes in the products table may be item code, item name, quantity, and so on. While creating attributes of an entity, we have to specify its name and its data type to declare the kind of information (whether integer, float, string, and so on) that will be stored in the attribute. Also, we can define the constraints on the information that can be stored in the column. For example, we can specify the maximum, minimum value (range) that can be stored in that attribute, or whether the attribute can or cannot store certain special symbols, and so on. Also, we can specify the default value of an attribute.

Relationships

Besides attributes, an entity may also contain relationships (which define how an entity is related to other entities). The attributes and relationships of an entity are collectively known as properties. The relationships are of many types (*To-One*, *To-Many*, and *Many-to-Many*) and play a major role in defining connection among the entities and what will be the impact of insertion or deletion of a row in one entity on the connected entities.

Examples of relationship types:

- The relationship from a child entity to a parent entity is a *To-One* relationship as a child can have only one parent

- The relationship from a customer to a product entity is a *To-Many* relationship as a customer can purchase several products

- The relationship from an employee to a project entity is of *Many-to-Many* type as several employees can work on one project and an employee can work on several projects simultaneously

 To define a *many-to-many* relationship in Core Data, we have to use two *To-many* relationships. The first *To-many* relationship is set from the first entity to the second entity. The second *To-many* relationship is set from the second entity to the first entity.

In Xcode's Data Model Editor, the relationship from Customer to Product—a *To-Many* relationship—is represented by a line that appears pointing from the Customer entity to the Product entity with two arrows, (designating a *One-to-Many* relationship) as shown in the subsequent screenshot, whereas the *To-One* relationship is represented by a line with a single arrow:

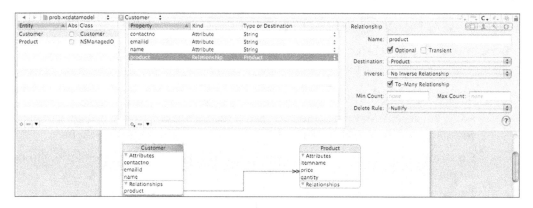

When defining relationships in Core Data we may use inverse relationships, though it's optional.

Inverse relationship

In Core Data, every relationship can have an inverse relationship. Like, if there is a relationship from Customer to Product, there will be a relationship from Product to Customer too. A relationship does not need to be the same kind as its inverse; for example, a *To-One* relationship can have an inverse relationship of type *To-Many*. Although relationships are not required to have an inverse, Apple generally recommends that you always create and specify the inverse, (even if you won't need) as it helps Core Data to ensure data integrity.

For example, consider a situation when a Customer entity has a relationship of the *To-Many* type to a Product entity and some information of a customer is changed or a row of a customer is deleted. Then it will be easier for Core Data to ensure consistency; that is, by inverse relationship, Core Data can automatically find the products related to the deleted customer and hence, delete them too. Inverse relationship is practically used in *Chapter 8, Entering, Saving, Listing, and Deleting the Records of the Products Sold to the Customers*.

Before we go further, let us have a quick look at the architecture that is used in iPhone application development: MVC.

Model View Controller (MVC)

iPhone application development uses MVC architecture where M stands for Model, V stands for View, and C for Controller.

- **Model** represents the backend data—data model
- **View** represents the user interface elements through which the user looks at the contents displayed by the application and can interact with them
- **Controller** represents the application logic that decides the type of view to be displayed on the basis of actions taken by the user

Core Data organizes the data model in terms of objects that are easy to handle and manipulate. The finalized objects are stored on a persistent storage. The usual way of representing data models is through classes that contains variables and accessor methods. We don't have to create classes by hand, (for our data models) as Core Data framework provides a special Data Model Design tool (also known as Data Model Editor) for quickly creating an entity relationship model. The terms that we will be frequently using from now onwards are Managed Object Model, Managed Objects, and Managed Object Context. Let us see what these terms mean:

- **Managed Object Model**: The data model created by the Data Model Design tool (Data Model Editor) is also known as Managed Object Model.
- **Managed Objects**: Managed objects are instances of the NSManagedObject class (or its subclass) that represent instances of an entity that are maintained (managed) by the Core Data framework. In a managed object model, an entity is defined by an entity name and the name of the class that is used at runtime to represent it. The NSManagedObject class implements all of the functionality required by a managed object.
- A managed object is associated with an entity description (an instance of NSEntityDescription) that describes the object; for example, the name of the entity, its attributes, relationships, and so on. In other words, an NSEntityDescription object may consist of NSAttributeDescription and NSRelationshipDescription objects that represent the properties of the entity. At runtime, the managed object is associated with a managed object context.
- **Managed Object Context**: The objects when fetched from the persistent storage are placed in managed object context. It performs validations and keeps track of the changes made to the object's attributes so that *undo* and *redo* operations can be applied to it, if required. In a given context, a managed object provides a representation of a record in a persistent store. Depending on a situation, there may be multiple contexts—each containing a separate managed object representing that record.

All managed objects are registered with managed object context.

For an application, we need the information represented by the Managed Object (instance of an entity) to be stored on the disk (persistent store) via managed object context. To understand the concepts of managed object context and its relation with data persistence, we need to understand the components of Core Data API, so let us go ahead and look at what Core Data API is all about.

Core Data API

The Core Data API, also called the stack, consists of three main components:

- NSPersistentStoreCoordinator
- NSManagedObjectModel
- NSManagedObjectContext

The PersistentStoreCoordinator plays a major role in storing and retrieving managed objects from the Persistent Store via ManagedObjectContext. We can see in the following figure how the three are related:

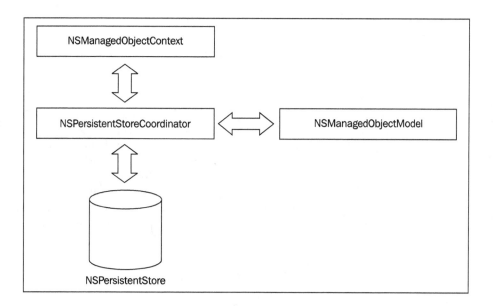

The Managed Object Model (an instance of NSManagedObjectModel class) is created from the data model of our application. If there is more than one data model in our application, the Managed Object Model is created by merging all of the data models found in the application bundle. The managed object (instance of the NSManagedObject class or its subclass) represents an instance of an entity that is maintained (managed) by the Core Data framework. A managed object is an instance of an Objective-C class, but it differs from other objects in three main ways:

- A managed object must be an instance of NSManagedObject or of a class that inherits from NSManagedObject
- The state of managed object is maintained by its managed object context
- A managed object has an associated entity description that describes the properties of the object

For working with a managed object, it is loaded into memory. The managed object context maintains the state of the managed object after it is loaded in memory. The Managed Object Context tracks in-memory changes that have yet to be persisted to the data store. Any changes made to the state of an NSManagedObject do actually affect the state of the object in memory, not just the persistent representation of that object in the data store. When we want to commit the modifications made to the managed object, we save the managed object context to the persistent store. In order to deal with persistent store, the managed object context needs a reference to a PersistentStoreCoordinator. In other words, a pointer to the PersistentStoreCoordinator is required for creating a Managed Object Context. Remember, the PersistentStoreCoordinator is the essential middle layer in the stack that helps in storing and retrieving the managed object model from the persistent store.

The managed object context is an object that plays a major role in the life cycle of managed objects. It handles all the aspects of managed object from faulting to validation including undo/redo. To modify managed objects, they are fetched from a persistent store through managed context. The modified managed objects are committed to the persistent store through context only. The managed objects represent data held in a persistent store. **Faulting** is considered to occur for an object whose property values have not yet been loaded from the external data store.

To access the objects (entity) in managed object context, FetchRequest, an instance of NSFetchRequest class, is used. To define the entity to be retrieved via NSFetchRequest, we pass the appropriate NSEntityDescription to the NSFetchRequest.

The result, that is, the set of entities retrieved from the managed object context (on the basis of `FetchRequest`) are managed by `FetchedResultsController`—an instance of `NSFetchedResultsController`.

In fact, `FetchRequest` is passed to the `FetchedResultsController` along with a reference to the managed object context. Once the `NSFetchedResultsController` class has been initialized, we can perform a fetch operation to load the entities (stored in it) into memory.

> The managed object context keeps track of all the changes made to the managed object since the last time it was loaded in memory and hence helps in undoing any changes made to the managed object (if required).The Persistent Store Coordinator helps in avoiding redundancy if multiple calls are made by different classes on the same file at the same time, that is, the multiple calls are serialized by the `NSPersistentStoreCoordinator` class to avoid redundancy.

Let us now get a detailed understanding of the terms used above.

Persistent Store

Persistent Store is a data store (repository) that handles mapping between data (in the store) and corresponding objects in a managed object context. The managed contexts can be stored in any of the following three formats—In-memory, Binary, and SQLite database format. In other words, the Persistence Store can be of three types—*In-memory store, Binary store*, and *SQLite store*.

- The In-memory store is used in caching mechanism
- Binary format stores information in a non-human-readable form but provides better performance
- SQLite database format is scalable and is the fastest

The drawback with the Binary and In-memory store contents is that they have to be entirely loaded in memory at startup and hence consume a lot of memory, whereas the SQLite store can be loaded and unloaded from memory as per requirements. SQLite is an open source embedded database that is highly preferred for Core Data.

> A persistent store is associated with a single data model.

Persistent Store Coordinator

The Persistent Store Coordinator is an instance of the
NSPersistentSoreCoordinator class that performs co-ordination between
managed object contexts and persistent store, that is, it helps in storing and retrieving
the managed object model from the Persistent Store. All the calls that require "reads"
or "writes" to the Persistent Store are serialized by the Persistent Store Coordinator
(so that multiple calls against the same file are not being made at the same time). The
Persistent Store Coordinator creates a path to a file (on disk drive) in the Documents
directory in our application's sandbox.

FetchRequest

FetchRequest is an instance of the NSFetchRequest class and is used to access
the objects in managed object context. There are two parts to the creation of an
NSFetchRequest:

- Deciding the entity to be retrieved
- Defining an NSPredicate to define the criteria (condition) to retrieve only
  the desired objects (this part is optional)

To define the entity to be retrieved via NSFetchRequest, we pass the appropriate
NSEntityDescription to the NSFetchRequest. Recall that NSEntityDescription
consists of the name of the entity, its attributes, relationships, and so on.

When NSFetchRequest is executed against the NSManagedObjectContext, the result
may be either in the form of an NSArray (containing the fetched entities) or there
may be an error. That is why, the execution of an NSFetchRequest accepts a pointer
to an NSError to describe the errors that may occur while execution. If the execution
of NSFetchRequest fails, then the pointer will be directed to an instance of NSError
that contains the reason of failure. The method signature will be as follows:

```
NSError *error;
NSArray *myArray = [myManagedObjectContext executeFetchRequest:
  fetchRequest error:&error]
```

FetchedResultsController

FetchedResultsController is an instance of the NSFetchedResultsController
class and as the name suggests, the NSFetchedResultsController class is meant for
managing the result—the set of entities from an NSManagedObjectContext that are
retrieved on the basis of FetchRequest. It helps with the following:

- Querying the retrieved result

- Arranging the result

- Notifying `UIViewController` in case any of the entities in the result set are modified (added, deleted, updated, and so on)

The `NSFetchedResultsController` requires an `NSFetchRequest` for its initialization. The `NSFetchRequest` contains the criteria of the entities that are accessed through the `NSFetchedResultsController`. The `NSFetchRequest` is passed to the `NSFetchedResultsController` along with a reference to the `NSManagedObjectContext`. Once the `NSFetchedResultsController` has been initialized, we can perform a fetch operation to load the entities into memory.

We have enough knowledge of Core Data and its different components. Let us see what kind of application we will be developing in this book using Core Data.

Overview of the application: Sales Record System for a Departmental Store

We are going to assume the end user of this app is a wholesale dealer who wants to track in-stock product quantities, sales, and customer information. In this application, the user can store and track information about customers, such as names, e-mail IDs, and phone numbers, as well as sales data and product information (name, quantity, price, photo, and inventory). Therefore, the application must store information about:

- Products

- Customer information

- Sales

 From now on, we will be referring to a vendor's product as Master Product and an item sold to customers as Product.

Entity Relationship Diagram

Our application consists of three entities:

- Customer
- Product
- MasterProduct

The **Entity Relationship Diagram (ERD)** of the application is as shown in the following figure:

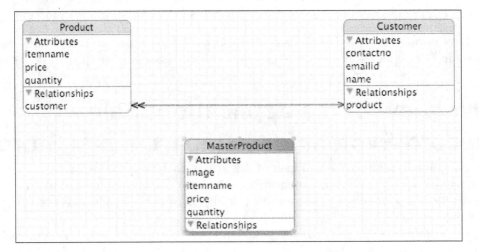

Let's have a quick look at the usage of the three entities displayed in the preceding figure:

- The **Product** table is used to store information about products sold to the selected customer. The table has three fields: **itemname**, **price**, and **quantity**. This table is related to the **Customer** table via a many-to-one relationship because many customers may purchase the same product.

- The **Customer** table is used to store information about the customer and has three data fields: name, e-mail ID, and contact number. This table is related to the **Product** table via a one-to-many relationship because a customer can purchase more than one product.

- The **MasterProduct** table is used to store information about the vendor's products. This table also shows the quantity on hand for each product. The table has four fields: **itemname**, **price**, **quantity**, and **image** (photo). This table is not related to any other table and works independently.

An application output sample

Let's take a look at how the application works. When the program is started, the initial view will appear, as shown in the following given *image (a)*. The top of the view holds a navigation bar with two bar button items: **Edit** and **+**. At the bottom of the view is a toolbar holding a bar button item called **Master Product Information**. The title in the navigation bar, **Customers List**, tells us that the two bar button items (**Edit** and **+**) are concerned with editing and adding customer information, respectively. The bar button item, **Master Product Information**, is used to store product data: name, price, quantity, and the product image.

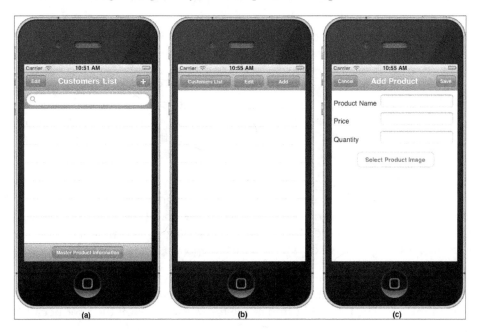

Entering Master Product Information

We begin by entering the product data, **Master Product Information**, which will include product name, price, quantity on hand, and a product photo. The product quantity is automatically adjusted after a sale.

When **Master Product Information** is selected, the view appears as shown in preceding *image (b)*. The view contains a toolbar with three bar button item controls — **Customers List**, **Edit**, and **Add**.

The functions of the three bar button item controls are as follows:

- **Customers List**: This button will take us back to the main view of the application where we can add or edit customer information.

- **Edit**: This button allows us to edit master product information. However, the button will work only when there actually are products in the database. Assuming at least one master product exists; the **Edit** button will show a deletion icon on the left of the master product. When the deletion icon on any master product is selected, a **Delete** button appears on the right for confirmation. When clicked, the master product is removed from the list.

- **Add**: This button lets us add new master products to the list. It displays a view as shown in the preceding *image (c)*. We have three text fields to fill: **Product Name**, **Price**, and **Quantity**. Below the text fields is a button to add a product photo. When we click on a text field, a keyboard for data entry appears. The keyboard covers the bottom half of the view, and covers the **Select Product Image** button. So, a method is added to the application that makes the keyboard disappear if the user presses the Return key after entering value in the **Quantity** text field. After the keyboard has disappeared, our view will appear, as shown in the subsequent *image (a)*.

When the **Select Product Image** button is tapped, the Image Picker view displays the **Photo Albums**, as shown in the next *image (b)*. The category **Saved Photos** is created by us to contain the master product photos. We'll talk about the steps for creating our own photo category later. When the **Saved Photos** category is selected, we are shown all of the images that we have copied into this category as shown in the next *image (c)*.

Let's select the image that represents a sample product, as shown in the subsequent *image (d)*. We can now save the product information by tapping the **Save** button in the navigation bar. The **Cancel** button at the top is used to stop the product addition process.

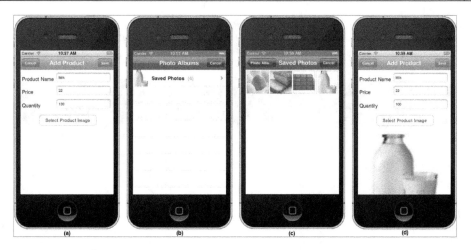

After the product data has been saved, we are returned to the **Master Product** list view. We'll now see the product **Milk** in the table view, as shown in the next *image (a)*. The black **>** sign is used to navigate to the product's information page, as shown in *image (b)*. Here, we can modify the information of the chosen master product by selecting the **Edit** button from the navigation bar. Additionally, we can change the product's image by clicking on the **Change Product Image** button.

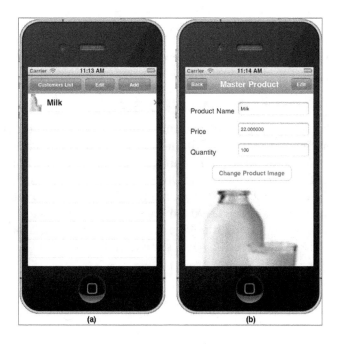

Let's add three more products: **Chocolate** shown in the next given *image (a)*; **Eggs** shown in *image (b)*; and **Bread** shown in *image (c)*. And, to keep things simple, let's use **100** as the beginning inventory quantity.

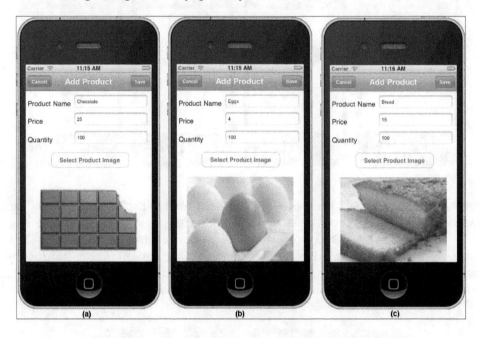

After adding four master products, our table view will look like the subsequent *image (a)*. The master products are automatically sorted in alphabetical order.

Modifying the Master Product

The black **>** indicates that selecting a product item will take us to the product editing view, as shown in the next *image (b)*. All the text fields showing master product information are in **disabled** mode; we cannot modify their content until we select the **Edit** button from the navigation bar. Once the **Edit** button is clicked, the button text changes to **Save**, the text fields are enabled, and we can modify the field data. After updating the master product's information, we save the changes by clicking on the **Save** button. After tapping the **Save** button, we will be returned to the view displaying the entire Master Products list, shown in the *image (a)*.

Deleting the Master Product

The **Edit** button in the navigation bar shown in the next *image (a)* is used to remove an existing Master Product. When the **Edit** button is selected, a deletion icon appears to the left of each master product, as shown in *image (c)*. Note that the **Edit** button's text changes to **Done**, which we'll use once we have finished with the deletion(s).

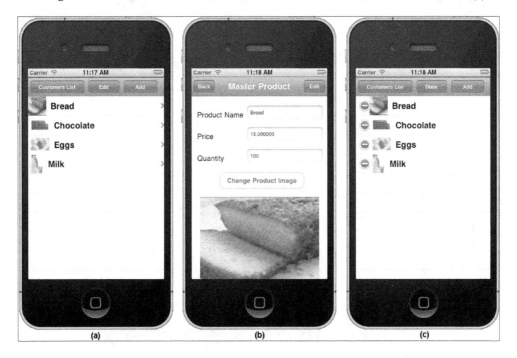

(a)   (b)   (c)

Selecting the deletion icon on any master product displays a **Delete** button to reconfirm that we really, really want to remove the item. For example, let's say we want to remove the product named **Chocolate** from the list. We tap on its deletion icon, which brings up a **Delete** button, as shown in the following *image (a)*. If we tap this button, **Chocolate** disappears from the list, as shown in the subsequent *image (b)*. The deletion icon will disappear when the **Done** button is pressed.

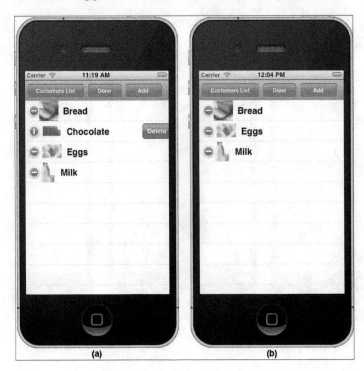

Entering customer information and order details

If we press the + button in the main view—the first view of the application—we'll see a view to enter customer information—name, e-mail address, and phone number—as shown in the next *image (a)*. The information is saved by selecting the **Save** button from the navigation bar. The **Cancel** button discards the new entry. After entering information for three customers, the table view will appear as shown in the next *image (b)*. We can see that the customers' names are automatically sorted in alphabetical order. The search bar in the navigation bar can be used to search the desired customer. For example, entering a character *C* in the search bar will display only those customer names that contain character *C* as shown in the next given *image (c)*.

The black **>** to the right of each customer can be used for two purposes:

- To modify a customer's information
- To enter the selected customer's purchases

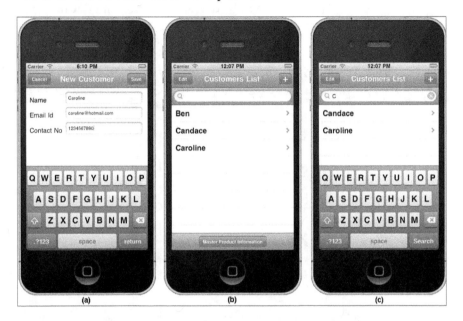

(a)   (b)   (c)

Deleting customer information

The next given *image (a)* displays a more specific search on entering more characters in the search bar. We can see that on entering characters **Can** *in the search bar*, we get the list of customer names that contain characters **Can**. We can select the customer name from the table view to edit information or enter the details of purchased products. For example, if we select a customer, say **Candace**, we'll see her information in the view, as shown in the next *image (b)*. In this view, there are two bar button items — **Edit** (at the top) and **Products Information** at the bottom. The **Edit** button is used to modify customer information and the **Products Information** button is used to display the view for adding or editing the customer's purchasing data. The **Customers List** button returns us to the table view displaying the complete list of customers.

If the **Edit** button in the **Customers List** view is tapped, a deletion icon appears to the left of the customer's name. The **Edit** button changes to **Done** when we are finished editing the data. Tapping the deletion icon of any customer displays a **Delete** button for confirmation, as shown in the next given *image (c)*. If that button is pressed, the information of the selected customer will be deleted, and pressing **Done** (from the navigation bar), returns us to the Customer List.

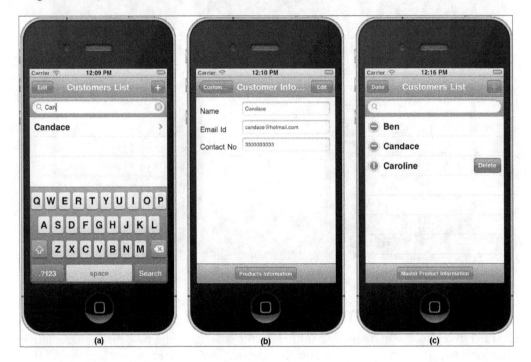

(a)   (b)   (c)

Searching for specific customers

The search bar at the top of the view can be used to search for a particular customer. For example, to search for customer names that contain the character *C*, we enter *C* in the search bar. The customer list in the table view will be filtered and only customer names containing *C* will be displayed. We can make the search more precise by entering more characters in the search bar. For example, if we enter Can, we'll see the customer name(s) containing that set of characters, as shown in the preceding *image (a)*.

Searching and modifying customer information

To modify customer information, we first select a customer. The next view displays the customer's data, as shown in the given *image (b)*. The text fields are initially in **disabled** mode. To enable the text fields, click on the **Edit** button from the navigation bar. The **Edit** button changes to **Done**, as shown in *image (b)*. Let's change Ben to David and save it by selecting the **Done** button. The customer names are alphabetically sorted, so we'll now see that David (previously Ben), appears after Candace, as shown in the given *image (c)*.

Entering Customer Sales Information

Let's enter information about products sold to Candace. On selecting her name, we'll see her information being displayed in the view, as shown in the next *image (a)*. At the bottom of the view is the **Products Information** button, used to add and edit information about the products sold to the selected customer. When we tap this button, we'll see a view with three buttons—**Back**, **Edit**, and **Add**, as shown in the next *image (b)*.

- **Back** returns us to the view displaying the customer's information (as shown in *image(a)*).

- **Edit** is used to delete an entry. This view shows deletion icons to the left of the products sold.

- **Add** takes us to a view that displays the list of products available for sale, as shown in *image (c)*.

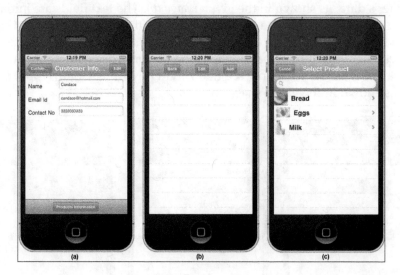

The search bar at the top of the view can be used to search for the desired product. Typing text in the search bar will filter the products and display only those containing the characters typed into the search bar. After a product is selected, its name, price, and image will appear and we will be asked to enter the quantity of the selected product sold to the customer. For example, if we select **Bread** from the list, we'll be asked to enter its quantity as shown in *image (a)*. Let's suppose that Candace bought three loaves of bread, so we enter **3** in the **Quantity** text field as shown in *image (b)*, then select the **Save** button from the navigation bar. We will be returned to the table view, which is shown in *image (c)*. Note that the value **3** is displayed to the right of **Bread**, which tells us that the quantity of the bread sold to Candace was three.

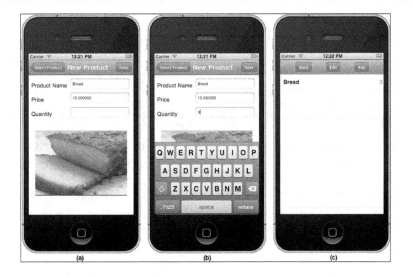

We can again select the **Add** button to add additional products sold to the customer. The next given *image (a)* displays the view when **Eggs** is selected from the available products list. The next given *image (b)* shows how the name, price, and product image automatically appear, asking the user to fill in the quantity sold.

 The quantity entered here will be deducted from the product inventory in the Master Products entity. After selecting the **Save** button, all products sold to the customer are displayed, as shown in the next *image (c)*. The products will be displayed in sorted alphabetical order.

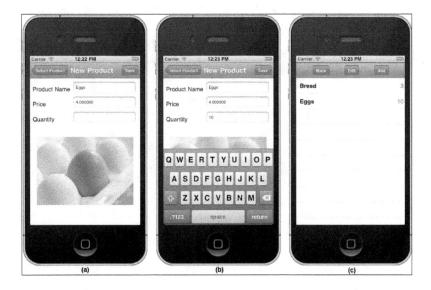

The **Edit** button shown in the preceding *image (c)* is used to delete a product entry sold to the customer. When the **Edit** button is tapped, we'll see a deletion icon to the left of the items as shown in the next *image (a)*. Note that if we delete a customer, the list of products sold is automatically deleted as well.

Automatic Master Product Update

The quantity sold to a customer is automatically deducted from the master product's quantity in hand. To see if the stock has been updated, first click on the **Master Product Information** button from the toolbar at the bottom of the main view (the first view of the application); we'll see the list of products we saved earlier, as shown in the given *image (b)*. After selecting a master product, we'll see the page that displays the master product information, as shown in next given *image (c)*. And we'll find that the quantity of the master product has been adjusted accordingly.

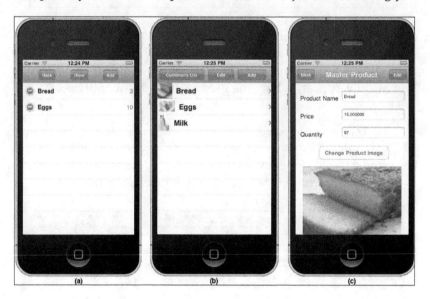

(a)   (b)   (c)

Summary

- In this chapter, we had an introduction of what Core Data is and its features that make it a preferred framework used for persisting information.

- We also had a brief idea of the Data Model and how it is related to entities, properties, attributes, relationships, inverse relationships, and so on.

- We have also learned about the concept of MVC and the role of the terms: Managed Object Model, Managed Object, and Managed Object Context. Finally, we saw the Core Data API and Persistent Store, Persistent Store Coordinator, Fetch Request, and FetchedResultsController.

- Also, we took a detailed look at the different functions that can be performed by the application we will develop in this book.

- We saw different screenshots the variety of application views, along with their respective controls. Also, we saw the tasks performed when different view controls are selected.

In the next chapter, we'll talk about protocols—what they are, how the methods are declared in a protocol, and the role of the delegate that conforms to the protocol. The next chapter explains how protocol works and how information is displayed via the table view control.

3
Understanding Objective-C Protocol and Table View

In the previous chapter, we had a fair enough introduction of the Core Data framework and its components. We also learnt about the Data Model and its different terms including Entities, Properties, Attributes, Relationships, Inverse Relationships, and so on. We also explored the concepts of the Managed Object Model, Managed Object, and Managed Object Context. Finally, we saw the relationships among different components of Core Data API: Persistent Store, Persistent Store Coordinator, Fetch Request, and FetchedResultsController. Besides this, we also had a quick overview of the entire application that we will be building in this book from chapters 4 through 11.

As said in *Chapter 1, Overview*, for a better understanding of the Core Data, we need to have a good knowledge of two important concepts: How classes can adopt various protocols in Objective-C and knowledge of how information is displayed via Table View control. So, before we begin developing our application—Sales Record System for Departmental Store—we need to learn the first concept, which is about Protocols—what they are, how the methods are declared in a protocol, and the role of the delegate that conforms to the protocol. In other words, we can say that we're going to learn how a class receives tasks performed by another class via the *Delegation Pattern*.

You might be thinking, why it is necessary to understand the concept of protocol for developing our Core Data application. The answer is simple. While developing our application (which will begin from *Chapter 5, Creating, Listing, and Deleting Names of Customers*), we will realize that the main class of the application is the implementation file: RootViewController.m and its objects will adopt protocols, so that they can be used by other objects in a well-defined manner. That is, the main implementation file, RootViewController.m, will implement the methods of the protocols defined in other classes of the application.

This chapter will help you to better understand what we mean by the terms protocol, delegate, methods, and so on, through a running application.

Before we begin with the protocols, let's get a quick idea of the two patterns, Delegation pattern and Strategy pattern:

- The Delegation pattern is usually used to allow reuse of objects by allowing a helper object, or delegate, to assume the responsibility of customizing the behavior of the existing object without modifying its code. That is, a delegate is usually used to take some action at a defined hook. This is an alternative to customizing the behavior of a class via subclassing.

- In Strategy pattern, we have a few operations that will perform a calculation as per the strategy of the class that adopts the protocol. Regardless of how this is implemented, the implementation will only ever return a calculated value. The calculated values will not alter or customize the behavior of the object that is making use of the delegate.

Let's see how we can declare and enforce the behavior of delegate objects through protocols.

Protocol

A protocol is not itself a class. Rather, it's an interface that declares methods. Only the methods are declared, that is, there is no body of the method defined in the protocol. The reason that format protocols are used for the delegation pattern is two fold:

1. The protocol acts as a documentation of the delegate interface and it allows for the compiler to check adherence.

2. At runtime you can interrogate an object in a single call to see if a protocol has been adopted rather than checking on a per method basis to see if an object will respond to a message.

The delegates are responsible for implementing the methods of the confirming protocol.

Implementing the Strategy pattern

To work with a protocol, we need to:

1. Define the protocol
2. Create the delegate property
3. Declare the protocol methods

Defining the protocol

A protocol is defined by using the `@protocol` compiler directive, combined with an `@end` directive. In between the two directives, we must declare the protocol method:

```
@protocol protocolname
method declarations;
@end
```

Creating a delegate property

The delegate property is created in the class definition of the object that will utilize a delegate, not in the protocol nor in the class that adopts the protocol. A delegate property is created by defining an instance variable in the header file and synthesizing it in the implementation file. In the following example, we define an instance variable called *delegate* of type *<protocolname>*:

```
id <protocolname> delegate;
```

We also define the instance variable as a property with the attributes *retain* and *nonatomic*, used for generating the accessor and mutators:

```
@property (nonatomic, retain) id <protocolname> delegate;
```

The instance variable must be synthesized in the implementation file with the following command:

```
@synthesize delegate
```

 The methods implemented in the delegate class are invoked by using this delegate property.

Declaring protocol methods

Protocol methods are defined between the `@protocol` and `@end` directives. The methods can be of two types: optional and required.

The format of the defining methods in the protocol is:

```
@protocol protocolname
-(void) method1: (data type) parameter1 secondparam: (data type)
parameter2;
@optional
-(void) method2: (data type) parameter1 secondparam: (data type)
parameter2;
@end
```

Now the class that adopts to this protocol, that is, the class declared as a delegate of this protocol, must implement the protocol methods.

 By default, all methods declared in a protocol are considered to be required, and the class adopting the protocol must implement all its methods. We can, of course, declare optional methods in a protocol by using the @optional compiler directive.

Creating a sample application using a protocol and a delegate

We will begin developing our actual application, Sales Record System for Departmental Store from *Chapter 5, Creating, Listing, and Deleting Names of Customers*. In this chapter, we will develop a small application that is meant for making you better understand the concept of protocol and delegate. The application that we are going to develop is a nice example of a class adopting a protocol. Here, we'll define a protocol called SecondViewControllerDelegate, which has two methods: *sum* and *multiply*. These two methods are used to calculate the sum and product of two numbers. The class that will conform to this protocol is called demodelegateViewController. It will implement the two protocol methods, *sum* and *multiply*. We will see how the delegate methods are invoked to calculate the sum and product of two numbers entered by the user:

1. Launch Xcode and select the **New Project** option from the **File** menu. The **New Project Assistant** window appears, prompting us to select a template for the new project.

2. Let's select the **View-based application** template. A dialog box prompts us to save the new project.

3. Let's assign it the name demodelegate and then select the **Save** button. Xcode will generate the project files and the project opens in the **Xcode Project** window.

Every project template provided in Xcode automatically generates project files containing default code. Our View-based application, *demodelegate*, automatically generates four files: demodelegateAppDelegate.h, demodelegateAppDelegate.m, demodelegateViewController.h, and demodelegateViewController.m. Files with the suffix *AppDelegate* are application delegate files. Files with the suffix *ViewController* are *RootViewController* files that display the first View of the application when it is launched.

The job of application delegate files is handling and generating responses to the application messages passed to it. The files are in the form of a header and an implementation file; we won't be altering the code of these autogenerated files. The default code of the application delegate header file, demodelegateAppDelegate.h, is shown next:

```
//  demodelegateAppDelegate.h
//  demodelegate
#import <UIKit/UIKit.h>
@class demodelegateViewController;
@interface demodelegateAppDelegate : NSObject <UIApplicationDelegate>
{
    UIWindow *window;
    demodelegateViewController *viewController;
}
@property (nonatomic, retain) IBOutlet UIWindow *window;
@property (nonatomic, retain) IBOutlet demodelegateViewController
*viewController;
@end
```

> **Downloading the example code**
>
> You can download the example code files for all Packt books you have purchased from your account at http://www.PacktPub.com. If you purchased this book elsewhere, you can visit http://www.PacktPub.com/support and register to have the files e-mailed directly to you.

The default code of the application implementation file, demodelegateAppDelegate.m is shown next:

```
//  demodelegateAppDelegate.m
//  demodelegate

#import "demodelegateAppDelegate.h"
#import "demodelegateViewController.h"

@implementation demodelegateAppDelegate

@synthesize window;
@synthesize viewController;

- (BOOL)application:(UIApplication *)application didFinishLaunchingWit
hOptions:(NSDictionary *)launchOptions {
[self.window addSubview:viewController.view];
    [self.window makeKeyAndVisible];
    return YES;
}
```

```
- (void)dealloc {
    [viewController release];
    [window release];
    [super dealloc];
}

@end
```

There are seven main steps for creating our sample application. We will be dealing with each of these steps in the following sections.

Adding the ViewController class for entering numerical values

The first step is adding a `ViewController` class that will display a View prompting the user to enter two numerical values. The View will also display two text buttons, *Add* and *Multiply*, which, when selected, will invoke the respective delegate methods.

 The View Controllers are used for managing the view and the class used for controlling the views is called `UIViewController` (provided by UIKit). We must create a subclass of `UIViewController` to manage our application view.

To create a subclass of the UIViewController, follow these steps:

1. Right-click on the **Classes** group in the **Xcode Project** window and select **Add | New File** option.

2. A dialog box appears, asking us to select a template for the new file. Choose **Cocoa Touch Class** under the **iOS** section in the left pane. Then select the **UIViewController subclass** as the template for the new file.

3. Select the **With XIB for user interface** checkbox, followed by the **Next** button (refer to the following screenshot).

4. A dialog box appears, asking us to specify the name of the View Controller. Let's assign the name `SecondViewController.m`.

5. Select the **Also create SecondViewController.h** checkbox (which will create the header file), and click the **Finish** button.

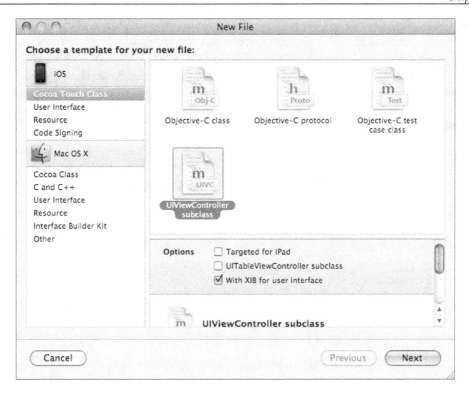

Both the header and implementation files SecondViewController.h and
SecondViewController.m are created for us, along with the .xib file. The files are
placed in the Classes group default location of our Xcode Project window. Select the
SecondViewController.xib file in the Xcode Project window's Classes group and
drag it to the Resources group—the default location for all Interface Builder files.

Defining the protocol, outlets, and action methods in the SecondViewController.h header file

After a user enters two numbers in the SecondViewController class view and
presses the *Add* or *Multiply* button, a calculation should be performed by the
demodelegateViewController class (the application's RootViewContoller class).
This operation will be carried out when the demodelegateViewController class is
declared as delegate of the protocol defined in the SecondViewController class.

So, in the header file of the new `SecondViewController.h` View Controller class, we define a protocol called `SecondViewControllerDelegate`. In the protocol, we declare two methods: *sum* and *multiply*. The sum method is declared as a *required* type by default and the multiply method is declared as an *optional* type by using the *@optional* directive. Thus, the class conforming to this protocol must implement the *sum* method; the *multiply* method is optional. *Sum* and *multiply* accept two arguments of data type *int*.

In addition to defining a protocol, the `SecondViewController` class header file will also contain outlets, properties, and action methods. The code that we will write in the header file of the `SecondViewController.h` view controller class is as shown next:

```
//  SecondViewController.h
//  demodelegate

#import <UIKit/UIKit.h>

@protocol SecondViewControllerDelegate
-(void) sum: (int) val1 secondparam: (int) val2;
@optional
-(void) multiply: (int) x secondvalue: (int) y;
@end

@interface SecondViewController : UIViewController {
    IBOutlet UITextField *value1;
    IBOutlet UITextField *value2;
    id <SecondViewControllerDelegate> delegate;
}

@property (nonatomic, retain) UITextField *value1;
@property (nonatomic, retain) UITextField *value2;
@property (nonatomic, retain) id <SecondViewControllerDelegate>
delegate;

-(IBAction) add:(id)sender;
-(IBAction) multiply:(id)sender;
@end
```

In this code block, we also define two `UITextField` class instance variables: value1 and value2 and mark them as outlets. These two outlets, value1 and value2, will be connected to the two Text Field controls that we will be adding to the View.

A delegate property is also created by defining an instance variable called delegate of type `<SecondViewControllerDelegate>`. All instance variables are defined as properties with the two attributes: *retain* and *nonatomic*, so that their accessors and mutators are generated automatically when synthesized. We also see that the previous code block includes two action methods: *add* and *multiply*, which will be connected to the two Round Rect Button controls that we will be placing in the View. After adding this code, save the header file.

Defining the SecondViewController class and connecting controls

The next step is to add two *Label* controls, two *Text Field* controls, and two *Round Rect Button* controls to the View of `AddNameController` class. Follow these steps:

1. Open the `SecondViewController.xib` file in the Interface Builder.

2. Drag the controls from the **Library** window and drop them into the **View** window.

3. Double-click the two *Label* controls and change the text to **First value** and **Second value**.

4. Double-click the two *Round Rect Button* controls and change the button text to **Add** and **Multiply**.

5. To connect the **value1** outlet to the *Text Field* control in the View, select the **File's Owner** icon in the **Documents** window and open the **Connections Inspector** window. All the outlets and action methods we defined in the header file will be visible in the **Connections Inspector** window under the headings **Outlets** and **Received Actions** respectively.

6. Select the circle to the right of the *value1* outlet: Keeping the mouse button pressed, drag it to the *Text Field* control in the View. Repeat the procedure for connecting the *value2* outlet with the other *Text Field* control.

7. To connect the *multiply* action method to the *Round Rect Button* control, select the circle to the right of the **multiply** action method. Keeping the mouse button pressed, drag it to the **Multiply** *Round Rect Button* control in the View window and release the mouse button.

8. Select the **Touch Up Inside** from the menu that appears, as shown in the following screenshot. Repeat the procedure to connect the **add** action method to the **Add Round Rect Button control**.

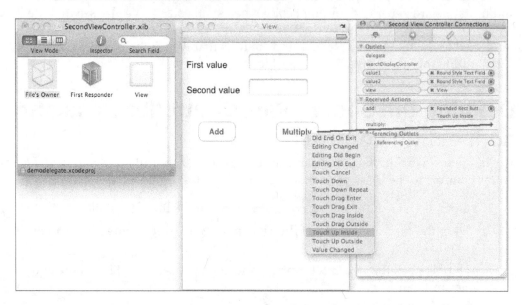

Invoking delegate methods from the SecondViewController.m implementation file

We need to add code to the SecondViewController.m file that invokes the correct action method when the **Add** or **Multiply** control is pressed. The following shows the code that we will write in the ViewController class implementation file:

```
//   SecondViewController.m
//   demodelegate

#import "SecondViewController.h"

@implementation SecondViewController

@synthesize value1,value2,delegate;

-(IBAction) add:(id)sender
{
   [delegate sum: [value1.text intValue] secondparam:[value2.text
intValue]];
   [self dismissModalViewControllerAnimated:YES];
```

```
}

- (IBAction) multiply: (id) sender
{
    [delegate multiply: [value1.text intValue] secondvalue: [value2.text
intValue]];
    [self dismissModalViewControllerAnimated:YES];
}


-  (void) didReceiveMemoryWarning {
    // Releases the view if it doesn't have a superview.
      [super didReceiveMemoryWarning];

    // Release any cached data, images, etc that aren't in use.
}

-  (void) viewDidUnload {
[super viewDidUnload];
    // Release any retained subviews of the main view.
    // e.g. self.myOutlet = nil;
}

-  (void) dealloc {
    [super dealloc];
}


@end
```

Our first action is to generate the value1, value2, and delegate IBOutlets, which generate their respective accessor and mutator methods. In the **Add** action method, we have added code that invokes the sum method of the demodelegateViewController delegate class. We then pass the user-entered numerical values to the appropriate method. The two Text Fields in the View are connected to the value1 and value2 outlets.

We then dismiss the modal View of the SecondViewController class, so that the View of the demodelegateViewController root view controller appears at the top of the display. Similarly, the **Multiply** action method invokes the multiply method of the delegate class and the values entered in the Text Field controls are passed to this method via outlets value1 and value2.

 The numerical values entered in the Text Field controls are converted into integer format when passed to the *sum* and *multiply* methods.

Finally, we release the reference to the outlets through using the `dealloc` method.

Declaring the delegate, outlet, and action methods in the demodelegateViewController.h header file

At this point, it's time to declare the `SecondViewController` class delegate and implement its methods. To do this, we set the `demodelegateViewController` class as a delegate of the `SecondViewControllerDelegate` protocol. The following code snippet shows the `demodelegateViewController` header file:

```
//   demodelegateViewController.h
//   demodelegate

#import <UIKit/UIKit.h>
#import "SecondViewController.h"

@interface demodelegateViewController : UIViewController
<SecondViewControllerDelegate>{
   IBOutlet UILabel *result;
}

@property(nonatomic,retain) UILabel *result;
-(IBAction) gotoSecondView:(id)sender;
@end
```

The first step is to declare the file as a delegate for the `SecondViewControllerDelegate` protocol.

An instance of the `UILabel` class – result – is created, which will be used to display the result of addition or multiplication. The instance variable result is defined as a property with the two attributes, *retain* and *nonatomic*. Result is used to generate the accessors and mutators without synchronization and to keep the objects retained by the mutators without being flushed from memory.

An action method called `gotoSecondView` is declared. It will be used to invoke the View of the `SecondViewController` class, which prompts the user to enter two numerical values and then select either the *Add* or *Multiply* button.

Defining the demodelegateViewController and connecting controls

Let us design the view of demodelegateViewController class and connect its controls with the outlet and action methods defined in its header file. The steps are as follows:

1. Open the demodelegateViewController.xib file in the Interface Builder.

2. Drag a **Label** and a **Round Rect Button** control from the **Library** window and drop them in the View.

3. Double-click the **Round Rect Button** control and change the text to **Go to Second View**.

4. To connect the **result** outlet with the **Label** control in the View, select the **File's Owner** icon in the **Documents** window and open the **Connections Inspector** window. All the outlets and action methods we defined in the demodelegateViewController.h header file will be visible in the **Connections Inspector** window under the headings **Outlets** and **Received Actions**, respectively.

5. To connect the **result** outlet to the **Label** control, select the circle to the right of the **result** outlet. Keeping the mouse button pressed, drag the circle to the **Label** control in the View. Release the mouse button.

6. To connect the **gotoSecondView** action method to the **Round Rect Button** control, select the circle to the right of the **gotoSecondView** action method. Keeping the mouse button pressed, drag the circle to the **Round Rect Button** control in the View window. Release the mouse button.

7. Select the **Touch Up Inside** option from the menu that appears, as shown in the following screenshot:

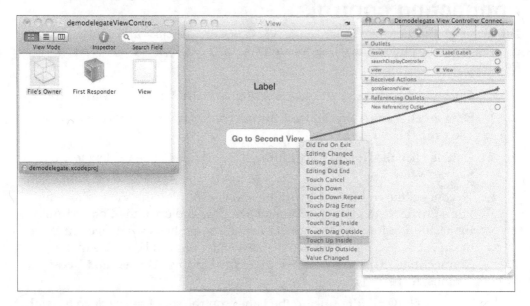

Implementing the protocol methods in the demodelegateViewController.m file

The `demodelegateViewController` View is supposed to do tasks such as:

- To navigate to the `SecondViewController` View that prompts the user to enter numerical values
- To display computation results

To perform the preceding tasks, we will implement the protocol methods in the `demodelegateViewController` class, as shown next:

```
//   demodelegateViewController.m
//   demodelegate

#import "demodelegateViewController.h"

@implementation demodelegateViewController

@synthesize result;

-(IBAction) gotoSecondView:(id)sender
```

```
{
    SecondViewController *secondvw=[[SecondViewController alloc] initWit
hNibName:@"SecondViewController" bundle:nil];
    secondvw.delegate=self;
    UINavigationController *navController =[[UINavigationController
alloc] initWithRootViewController:secondvw];
    [self presentModalViewController:navController animated:YES];
    [secondvw release];
    [navController release];
}

-(void) sum: (int) val1 secondparam: (int) val2
{
    int a;
    a=val1+val2;
    result.text=[NSString stringWithFormat:@"Sum is %d",a];
}

-(void) multiply: (int) x secondvalue: (int) y
{
    int a;
    a=x*y;
    result.text=[NSString stringWithFormat:@"Multiplication is %d",a];
}

- (void)didReceiveMemoryWarning {
    // Releases the view if it doesn't have a superview.
    [super didReceiveMemoryWarning];

    // Release any cached data, images, etc that aren't in use.
}

- (void)viewDidUnload {
    // Release any retained subviews of the main view.
    // e.g. self.myOutlet = nil;
}

- (void)dealloc {
    [result release];
    [super dealloc];
}

@end
```

The first step is synthesizing the *result* property to generate its `accessor` and `mutator` methods.

The `gotoSecondView` method is invoked when the user selects the **Go to Second View** Round Rect Button control. This method displays a View that prompts the user to enter two numerical values. We then create and initialize an instance of the `SecondViewController` class called `secondvw`, because the View that prompts the user to enter two numerical values is built into this View.

We use *alloc* to create the view controller object and initialize it. The *init* method specifies the name of the NIB file that has to be loaded by the `SecondViewController` controller, followed by the bundle where the NIB file is expected to be found. The *bundle* parameter is set to *nil*, as we want the method to look for the NIB file in the main bundle. The `initWithNibName` method allows the `UIViewController` view to be initialized from a NIB file rather than from code. This method is preferred when the View of the view controller exists in the NIB file and we want to load it from there.

Next, we declare the current view controller file, `demodelegateViewController.m`, as the delegate of the *secondvw* instance of the `SecondViewController` class. That is, we will implement the methods declared in the protocol, *SecondViewControllerDelegate* that were defined in the `demodelegateViewController.m` file's `SecondViewController` class.

The *sum* is the method of the *SecondViewControllerDelegate* protocol that the current class, `demodelegateViewController`, conforms to, and hence, implements this method. *Sum* is invoked by the *add* action method. Similarly, the *multiply* method of the `demodelegateViewController` class will be invoked by the *multiply* action method. The *add* action method, defined in the `SecondViewController.m` file, calls the *sum* method of the delegate with two parameters of data type *int* representing the values entered in the Text Field controls. The *multiply* action method calls the *multiply* method of the delegate, passing the numerical values entered by the user in the Text Field controls. The result of the computation – sum or multiply – is displayed via the *Label* control.

Running the project

We are ready to run the project. Let's select the Build and Run icon from the Xcode Project window. Initially, we get the view shown in the following given *image (a)*, with a **Label** and a **Go to Second View** Round Rect Button control. When we tap this button, the View of the `SecondViewController` class will appear, prompting the user to enter two numerical values, as shown in the following given *image (b)*.

This view also displays the **Add** and **Multiply** buttons. When we enter values in the Text Field controls and tap the **Add** button, the *add* action method in the `SecondViewController.m` file is invoked. The *sum* method, defined in the `demodelegateViewController.m` delegate is subsequently invoked, displaying the calculation result, as shown in the following given *image (c)*:

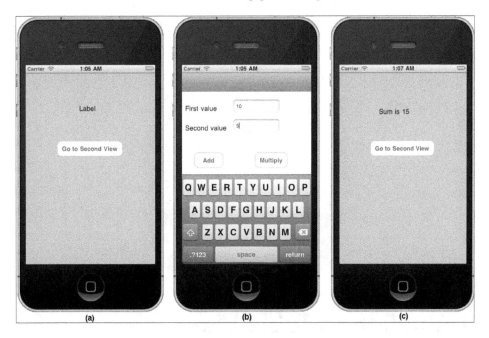

Similarly, when we enter values in the Text Field controls and tap the **Multiply** button, the *multiply* action method in the `SecondViewController.m` file is invoked. The multiply method, defined in the `demodelegateViewController.m` delegate is subsequently invoked, displaying the calculation result, as shown in the following given image:

Introduction to Table View

We just saw how protocols are created and defined through a running example. We also saw the creation of the delegate property, methods, and the implementation of those methods. The second important concept that we will understand before developing Core Data application is the working of *TableView* control. The `UITableView` class is very useful and has support for core data operations out of the box. It is very popularly used to display information and to edit, delete, and insert new information too. As it is very important to have a sound knowledge of *TableView* control and its different methods that are used for displaying information, let us go ahead and look at the working of *TableView* control.

Table View plays a major role in iPhone applications because it's a primary choice for displaying lists, for example, available options, products, and so on. From lists displayed in a table view, users choose a selection and jump to another page for further information. Table View is not only a popular way to display data, but is also preferred for maintaining databases, because items may be added, deleted, or updated in a specific table. Tables display information in multiple rows and a single column.

[The table view is usually linked to a navigation controller.]

In this chapter, we are going to see how table views are created and how the items displayed through it can be edited. The following section will help you understand the concepts related to Table View.

The class responsible for displaying information in a table view in an iPhone application is known as the UITableView class. UITableView is a subclass of UIScrollView, which, in turn, is a subclass of UIView. A table includes two important components: *sections* and *cells*. A section refers to a group of rows. Each table row is represented by a cell that's an instance of the UITableViewCell class. The UITableView class uses two external objects:

- The first object adopts the UITableViewDataSource protocol and provides the data to be displayed through Table View.

- The second object adopts the UITableViewDelegate protocol and controls the table's appearance.

The table's data source is an object that provides information to the table view and must implement the UITableViewDataSource protocol. There is a special view controller associated with Table View, called UITableViewController, which handles events such as rotations and navigations.

There are three common methods for displaying information in a table:

- The numberOfSectionsInTableView method is used to specify the number of unique groups within the table. By default, a standard table consists of only one section.

- The numberOfRowsInSection method is used to specify the number of rows that will be displayed in each section of the table.

- The cellForRowAtIndexPath method is used to return a UITableViewCell object that contains information to be displayed in the given table cell.

Creating an application to display Table View cells

The application that we are going to create in this chapter is focused on understanding the working of Table View control and has nothing to do with the actual application: Sales Record System for Departmental Store. From the next chapter, we will start developing the actual application. In this application, we'll learn how to display a list of names in a table view. The steps are as follows:

1. Create a new project by selecting the **File | New Project** option.

2. The **New Project Assistant** window appears, prompting us to select a template for the new project. Select the **Navigation based Application** template and click the **Choose** button.

3. A dialog box appears, asking us to assign a name and location for the new project. The default location is the Documents folder on our local drive, but we can specify a different location if we wish. Let's assign the name **demotable** to our new project and select the **Save** button.

Xcode will generate the project files and the project opens in the Xcode Project window, as shown in the following screenshot. The *Navigation-based project* template creates two classes for us: RootViewController and demotableAppDelegate.

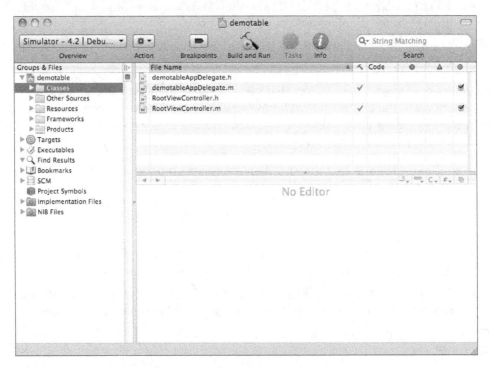

If we select **Build and Run** and run it on the iPhone simulator, we'll see a blank Table View, as shown in the following image, because we haven't yet entered any data:

To display information in the Table View, we will use array as a data source. So, let's go ahead and declare an array.

Declaring an array in the header file

To display table rows, we will declare an array in the header file of the RootView controller and implement several methods of the UITableViewDataSource protocol.

From the Classes folder, select the RootViewController.h header file to open it in an Editor pane. We will declare a mutable array called nameslist in this header file, which is used to display a collection of items.

```
//   RootViewController.h
//   demotable
#import <UIKit/UIKit.h>
#import <CoreData/CoreData.h>
```

```
@interface RootViewController : UITableViewController
<NSFetchedResultsControllerDelegate> {
NSMutableArray *nameslist;
@private
    NSFetchedResultsController *fetchedResultsController_;
    NSManagedObjectContext *managedObjectContext_;

}
@property (nonatomic, retain) NSManagedObjectContext
*managedObjectContext;
@property (nonatomic, retain) NSFetchedResultsController
*fetchedResultsController;
@property(nonatomic, retain) NSMutableArray *nameslist;

@end
```

After declaring an array, the next step is to define its array elements. It is the array elements that will appear as table rows in Table View control.

Implementing UITableViewDataSource protocol methods

We'll be using the `RootViewController.m` implementation file to define array elements. The code that we will write in the implementation file is as shown next:

```
//   RootViewController.m
//   demotable

#import "RootViewController.h"

@implementation RootViewController

@synthesize nameslist;

- (void)viewDidLoad {
  [super viewDidLoad];
  nameslist=[[NSMutableArray alloc] initWithObjects: @"Brian",
    @"David",@"Charles", @"Mike", nil];
  [self setTitle:@"Names List"];
}

#pragma mark Table view methods

 - (NSInteger)numberOfSectionsInTableView:(UITableView *)tableView {
```

```
        return 1;
}


// Customize the number of rows in the table view.
- (NSInteger)tableView:(UITableView *)tableView
      numberOfRowsInSection:(NSInteger)section {
  return [nameslist count];
}



// Customize the appearance of table view cells.
- (UITableViewCell *)tableView:(UITableView *)tableView
      cellForRowAtIndexPath:(NSIndexPath *)indexPath {
      static NSString *CellIdentifier = @"Cell";
      UITableViewCell *cell = [tableView
        dequeueReusableCellWithIdentifier:CellIdentifier];
      if (cell == nil) {
          cell = [[[UITableViewCell alloc]
            initWithStyle:UITableViewCellStyleDefault
            reuseIdentifier:CellIdentifier] autorelease];
      }

      cell.textLabel.text=[nameslist objectAtIndex:indexPath.row];
      return cell;
}

- (void)dealloc {
      [super dealloc];
}

@end
```

The sequence of events is as follows:

1.   In the `viewDidLoad` method, we assign elements to the declared array `nameslist` with the values `Brian`, `David`, `Charles`, and `Mike`.

2.   We mark the end of the array with the keyword `nil`.

3.   The `[NSMutableArray alloc]` code sends an alloc message to the `NSMutableArray` class to allocate memory for the new `NSMutableArray` object.

4.   The `initWithObjects` method initializes the newly created `NSMutableArray` object `nameslist` with the NSString values of `@"Brian"`, `@"David"`, and so on.

5. The second statement sets the title of the Navigation Bar to `Names List`. An NSString object is created, containing the value `Food List`, and is assigned to the Navigation bar title.

 The `viewDidLoad` method is called after the controller's view is loaded into memory. We use this method to perform initialization tasks required for views that will be loaded from NIB files.

6. The `numberOfSectionsInTableView` method is set to return 1, as we assume that this table has only one group by default.

7. In a Table View, the information can be categorized in sections. The `numberOfRowsInSection` method is used by the table to find the number of rows in a section. We set this method to return the count of the number of elements in the `nameslist` array because we want to display all the names in the `nameslist` array.

8. The `cellForRowAtIndexPath` method is called for each table row. Basically, the method fills the table cells one at a time. This method returns a `UITableViewCell` object containing the information to be displayed in a given table cell. The argument to this method is an NSIndexPath instance used to represent indices, that is, it wraps the section and row into a single object. We can get the row or the section number from an NSIndexPath instance by using its row or section method, respectively. Each table row is represented by an instance of `UITableViewCell`.

9. All the cells are maintained in a table queue for caching purposes, so that the cells created earlier need not be recreated and can be quickly displayed. For efficient memory use, the Table View cells that scroll off the screen may be removed from the queue to create space for cells scrolling onto the screen.

10. We ask for a lookup in the table queue cell. If the table queue doesn't have the cell (it's nil), we create a new Table View cell.

11. We keep the default cell style, `UITableViewCellStyleDefault`, to display only the text in the cell.

12. The text displayed with the `textLabel` property is considered the primary text of the cell.

13. The parameter sent to the message, `indexPath.row`, is the index of each table row. The index number sends an `objectAtIndex` message to the `nameslist` array to set the text of the row or cell equal to the value of the element, which is the name found at the index location of the `nameslist` array.

14. All the names in the `nameslist` array are displayed in the Table View, as shown in the following image:

The index path contains both a row and a section number.

Adding names to the Table View

To add more names to the table view, we need to add a View Controller class that displays a navigation bar with two items: *Save* and *Cancel*. This View Controller class also displays a View that prompts the user to enter a name to be added. We also need to add code to the RootView controller implementation file, so that when the user selects the **Save** button after entering the new name, it's added to the Table View for display.

The sequence is as follows:

1. Add a View Controller class called AddNameController.
2. Define a protocol, outlets, and action methods in the AddNameController.h header file.

3. Define the View of the `AddNameController` class and the connecting controls.

4. Add code to the `AddNameController.m` implementation file to invoke delegate methods.

5. Invoke the newly added *AddNameController* View and implement the protocol methods.

6. Place a Bar Button Item Control in the *RootViewController* and connect it.

Adding the AddNameController View controller

View controllers are used for managing a view. The class used for controlling the views is called `UIViewController` and is provided by UIKit. To manage the view, we'll create a `UIViewController` subclass:

1. Right-click on the **Classes** group in the **Xcode Project** window.

2. Select the **Add | New File** option. Select the **UIViewController** subclass as the new file template.

3. Select the **With XIB for user interface** checkbox, because the XIB file will be used to create the View that prompts the user to enter a new name.

4. Click the **Next** button.

5. We'll see a dialog box asking for the name of the View Controller. Let's use `AddNameController.m`.

6. Select the **Also create "AddNameController.h"** checkbox, as shown the following screenshot, and click the **Finish** button:

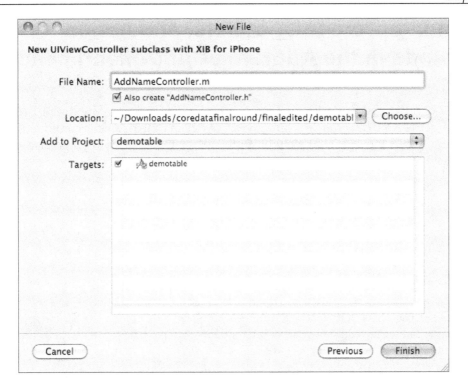

7. `AddNameController.h`, `AddNameController.m`, and an `.xib` file are created and added to our project. The files will be placed in the default location, the application folder's `Classes` subfolder.

8. Let's select the `AddNameViewController.xib` file in the **Classes** folder and drag it to the **Resources** folder, the default location of Interface Builder files.

We're going to define a delegate protocol in the header file of the new View Controller class `AddNameController.h`. A delegate protocol must declare several methods, and the classes conforming to a delegate protocol must implement the methods declared in it. The classes that conform to a delegate protocol are known as delegates. The delegates are the classes responsible for implementing the methods of the confirming protocol. Let's go ahead and define the delegate protocol.

Defining protocols, outlets, and action methods in the AddNameController.h header file

A protocol is defined using the *@protocol* compiler directive combined with an *@end* directive. Between the two directives, we declare the protocol methods. The following shows the code that we will write in the View controller class header file, AddNameController.h:

```objc
//   AddNameController.h
//   demotable

#import <UIKit/UIKit.h>
@protocol AddNameControllerDelegate;

@interface AddNameController : UIViewController {
  id <AddNameControllerDelegate> delegate;
  IBOutlet UIBarButtonItem *cancelbutton;
  IBOutlet UIBarButtonItem *savebutton;
  IBOutlet UITextField *newname;
}

@property(nonatomic, retain) id <AddNameControllerDelegate>
    delegate;
@property(nonatomic, retain) IBOutlet UIBarButtonItem *cancelbutton;
@property(nonatomic, retain) IBOutlet UIBarButtonItem *savebutton;
@property(nonatomic, retain) UITextField *newname;

-(IBAction) cancel:(id) sender;
-(IBAction) save:(id)sender;

@end

@protocol AddNameControllerDelegate
   -(void) addnameController:(AddNameController *)controller
     selectedsave:(BOOL) save name:(NSString *) newname;
@end
```

We can see that an AddNameControllerDelegate protocol is defined, called delegate. The method declared in the AddNameControllerDelegate is addnameController. A class conforming to this protocol must implement this method.

By default, all the methods declared in a protocol are considered *required*, that is, the class adopting the protocol must implement all its methods. We can also declare optional protocol methods by using the *@optional* compiler directive.

Besides defining a delegate protocol, we also define three outlets: *cancelbutton*, *savebutton*, and *newname*. The two outlets, `cancelbutton` and `savebutton`, will be connected to the two Bar Button Items that we will soon drag-and-drop onto the View. The outlets will be titled *Save* and *Cancel* respectively. The `newname` outlet will be connected to the Text Field control of the View in which the user enters the new name to be added to the Table View.

The header file includes two action methods, `cancel` and `save`, which will be connected to the `Cancel` and `Save` Bar Button Items.

The next step is to add two Bar Button Item controls to the AddNameController's View and connecting them with the outlets and action methods defined in the preceding header file.

Defining the AddNameController class View and connecting controls

The steps for adding Bar Button Item controls to the view and for connecting them with the respective outlet and action methods are given as follows:

1. Let's open the **AddNameController.xib** file in the Interface Builder.

2. Drag two **Bar Button Item** controls from the **Windows, Views & Bars** category and drop them into the **Documents** window, as shown in the following screenshot:

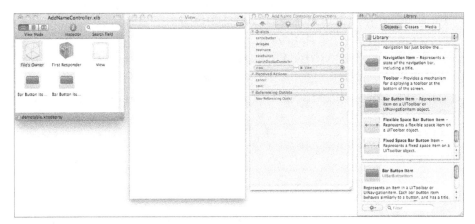

3. Select the two **Bar Button Item** controls one by one in the **Documents** window and with the help of the **Attributes Inspector**, set the **Titles** to **Save** and **Cancel**.

4. Drag-and-drop a **Label** and a **Text Field** control onto the View.

5. Double-click the **Label** control and change its text to **Enter Name**, as shown in the following screenshot:

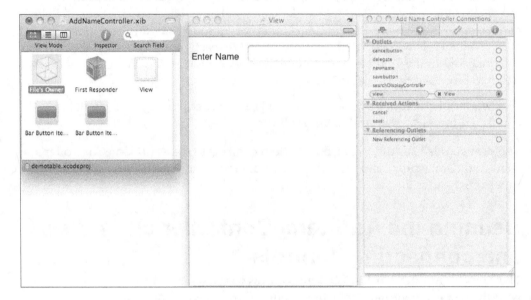

To connect the `cancelbutton` and `savebutton` outlets defined in the header file with the Bar Button Item controls in the **Documents** window, follow these steps:

1. Select the **File's Owner** icon in the **Documents** window and open the **Connections Inspector** window. The outlets and action methods defined in the header file will be visible in the **Connections Inspector** window under the headings **Outlets** and **Received Actions**.

2. Select the circle to the right of the **savebutton** outlet and drag it to the **Bar Button Item** control in the **Documents** window, as shown in the following screenshot.

3. Repeat the procedure to connect the **cancelbutton** outlet with the other **Bar Button Item** control.

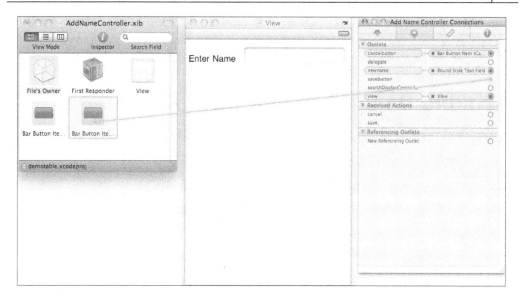

To connect the **save** and **cancel** action methods with the **Bar Button Item** controls, follow these steps:

1. Select a **Bar Button Item** control in the **Documents** window and open the **Connections Inspector** window.

2. In the **Connections Inspector** window, select the circle to the right of the selector under the **Sent Actions** heading and keeping the mouse button pressed, drag it to the **File's Owner** icon in **Documents** window.

3. Two action methods will pop up. Select the one to be connected to this **Bar Button Item** control.

The following screenshot shows the process for `cancelbutton`. When we select the **Bar Button Item** control in the **View** window, the `cancel` method code – we will be writing in the implementation file – will be executed.

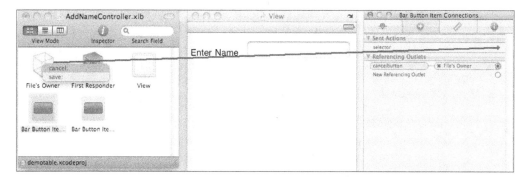

Repeat this procedure to connect **save** to the other **Bar Button Item** control. These Bar Button Item controls will be useless if they don't result in some action when clicked. So, let's make ground for these Bar Button Item controls to initiate action.

Invoking Delegate methods in the AddNameController.m implementation file

We need to write code in the AddNameController.m implementation file to invoke the delegate methods when Bar Button Item controls are pressed. The following code fragment also includes code that places the Bar Button items on the left and right side of the navigation bar. The following is the code that we write in the implementation file:

```
//   AddNameController.m
//   demotable

#import "AddNameController.h"

@implementation AddNameController

@synthesize savebutton;
@synthesize cancelbutton;
@synthesize delegate;
@synthesize newname;

-(IBAction) cancel:(id) sender
{
   [delegate addnameController: self selectedsave:NO
      name:newname.text];
}

-(IBAction) save:(id)sender{
   [delegate addnameController: self selectedsave:YES
       name:newname.text];
}

// Implement viewDidLoad to do additional setup after loading the
view, typically from a nib.
- (void)viewDidLoad {
   [super viewDidLoad];
    self.title=@"New Name";
    self.navigationItem.rightBarButtonItem=savebutton;
    self.navigationItem.leftBarButtonItem=cancelbutton;
```

```
}

- (void)didReceiveMemoryWarning {
    // Releases the view if it doesn't have a superview.
    [super didReceiveMemoryWarning];
    // Release any cached data, images, etc. that aren't in use.
}

- (void)viewDidUnload {
    [super viewDidUnload];
    // Release any retained subviews of the main view.
    // e.g. self.myOutlet = nil;
}

- (void)dealloc {
    [savebutton release];
    [cancelbutton release];
    [newname release];
     [super dealloc];
}

@end
```

The sequence of events is as follows:

First we synthesize the IBOutlets `savebutton`, `cancelbutton`, `delegate`, and `newname`, so we can generate their accessor and mutator methods.

In the `cancel` action method, invoke the `addnameController` method and set the value of `selectedsave` to NO.

- The value of the name parameter is set to the *name* entered in the Text Field control. Recall that the Text Field placed on the View is connected to the *newname* outlet.

- Similarly, in the `save` action method, we invoke the `addnameController` method and set the value of `selectedsave` to YES and `name` to the *name* entered in the Text Field control by the user.

- In the `viewDidLoad` method, we set the Navigation Item's title to **New name** and its right bar button item to **savebutton** — an instance variable of the **Save** Bar Button Item.

- The navigation bar's left button is set to **cancelbutton** — an instance variable of the **Cancel** Bar Button Item control.

- Finally, through dealloc method, we release the reference to the Outlets.

So far, we've defined a View that prompts the user to enter the name to be added to the Table View. The next task is to write code for invoking the AddNameController view from the main page of the application, that is, from the RootViewController view. Also we need to write code for displaying the entered name in the Table View. Let's go ahead and do that now.

Invoking the AddNameController View and implementing the protocol methods

We need to invoke this *AddNameController* View from the Root View Controller and implement the *AddNameController* delegate protocol methods. The *RootView Controller* class will be the class conforming to the *AddNameControllerDelegate* delegate protocol defined in the AddNameController.h header. Thus, the following shows the code that we will write in the RootViewController class:

```
//  RootViewController.h
//  demotable

#import <UIKit/UIKit.h>
#import <CoreData/CoreData.h>
#import "AddNameController.h"

@interface RootViewController : UITableViewController
<NSFetchedResultsControllerDelegate, AddNameControllerDelegate> {
NSMutableArray *nameslist;
IBOutlet UIBarButtonItem *addbutton;

@private
    NSFetchedResultsController *fetchedResultsController_;
    NSManagedObjectContext *managedObjectContext_;
}

@property (nonatomic, retain) NSManagedObjectContext
*managedObjectContext;
@property (nonatomic, retain) NSFetchedResultsController
*fetchedResultsController;
@property(nonatomic, retain) NSMutableArray *nameslist;
@property(nonatomic, retain) IBOutlet UIBarButtonItem *addbutton;

-(IBAction)addname:(id)sender;
@end
```

To make the `RootViewController` class adopt the delegate protocol – so that it implements the methods declared in the protocol – we first add the protocol's name. We can see `AddNameControllerDelegate` in angle brackets, which declares that the `RootViewController` class conforms to the *AddNameControllerDelegate* protocol and guarantees that the class implements the methods declared in the protocol. We also add an `addbutton` IBOutlet, called UIBarButtonItem, which will be connected to the Bar Button Item control. When this control is selected, the `addname` action method is invoked. In turn, this action method invokes the View of the *AddNameController* class that prompts the user to enter the name to be added to the Table View. The next step is to add a Bar Button Item controller to the view of the `RootViewController` class and connect it with the outlet and action method defined in the preceding header file. So, let's do it.

Placing and connecting the Bar Button Item control in the RootViewController

Let's open the `RootViewController.xib` file in Interface Builder and drag a Bar Button Item control from the **Windows, Views & Bars** category of the **Library** window and drop it into the **Documents** window, as shown in the following screenshot. With the help of the **Attributes Inspector**, set the **Title** property of the Bar Button Item control to **Add**.

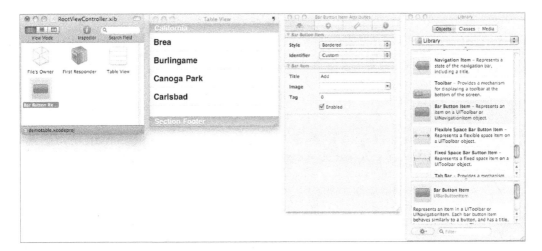

Then follow this series of steps:

1. Select the **File's Owner** control in the **Documents** window and open the **Connections Inspector**.

2. Under the heading **Outlets,** select the circle to the right of the **addbutton** outlet, and, keeping the mouse button pressed, drag it to the **Bar Button Item** control in the **Documents** window.

3. To connect the Bar Button Item control to the **addname** action method, select the **Bar Button Item** control in the **Documents** window and open the **Connections Inspector.**

4. Select the circle to the right of the selector under the **Sent Actions** heading and, keeping the mouse button pressed, drag it to the **File's Owner** icon in the **Documents** window. The action method **addname** pops up.

5. Select the **addname** action to connect it with the **Bar Button Item** control, as shown in the following screenshot:

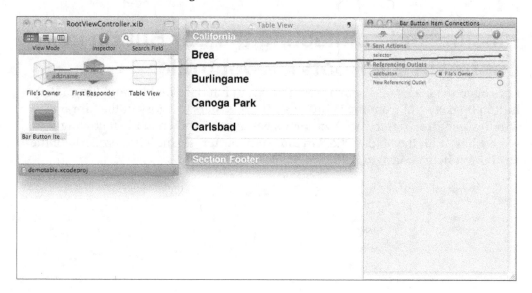

Now we need to write the code in the Root View Controller implementation file to invoke the AddNameController View and implement the addnameController method declared by *AddNameControllerDelegate*. The following shows the code that we will write in the RootViewController.m file:

```
// RootViewController.m
// demotable

#import "RootViewController.h"

@implementation RootViewController
@synthesize fetchedResultsController=fetchedResultsController_, manage
dObjectContext=managedObjectContext_;
@synthesize nameslist;
```

```
@synthesize addbutton;

- (void)viewDidLoad {
  [super viewDidLoad];
    nameslist=[[NSMutableArray alloc] initWithObjects: @"Brian",
      @"David",@"Charles", @"Mike", nil];
  [self setTitle:@"Names List"];
  self.navigationItem.rightBarButtonItem=addbutton;
}

-(IBAction)addname:(id)sender
{
  AddNameController *addnameController=[[AddNameController alloc]
      initWithNibName:@"AddNameController" bundle:nil];
  addnameController.delegate=self;
  UINavigationController *navController=[[UINavigationController
      alloc] initWithRootViewController:addnameController];
  [self.navigationController
       presentModalViewController:navController animated:YES];
  [addnameController release];
  [navController release];
}

-(void) addnameController:(AddNameController *)controller
    selectedsave:(BOOL) save name:(NSString *)newnme{
  if(save)
  {
      [nameslist addObject:newnme];
      [self.tableView reloadData];
  }
  [self dismissModalViewControllerAnimated:YES];
}

#pragma mark Table view methods

- (NSInteger)numberOfSectionsInTableView:(UITableView *)tableView {
    return 1;
}

// Customize the number of rows in the table view.
- (NSInteger)tableView:(UITableView *)tableView
    numberOfRowsInSection:(NSInteger)section {
  return [nameslist count];
}
```

```objc
// Customize the appearance of table view cells.
- (UITableViewCell *)tableView:(UITableView *)tableView
    cellForRowAtIndexPath:(NSIndexPath *)indexPath {

    static NSString *CellIdentifier = @"Cell";
    UITableViewCell *cell = [tableView
        dequeueReusableCellWithIdentifier:CellIdentifier];
    if (cell == nil) {
        cell = [[[UITableViewCell alloc]
            initWithStyle:UITableViewCellStyleDefault
            reuseIdentifier:CellIdentifier] autorelease];
    }

    cell.textLabel.text=[nameslist objectAtIndex:indexPath.row];
    return cell;
}

- (void)dealloc {
    [nameslist release];
    [addbutton release];
    [super dealloc];
}

@end
```

Here's what's happening in the code:

1. In the `viewDidLoad` method, we create the **Add** Bar Button Item control. The Button will appear on the right side of the Navigation bar.

2. When the **Add** Bar Button Item is selected, it will invoke the `addname` action method. The **addname** action method contains the code to initialize and create the instance of `addnameController`, which displays the user-input view.

3. The `RootViewController` class is set to act as a delegate of the `AddNameController` class.

4. The `addnameController` method is implemented in `AddNameController`.

5. The `save` parameter will contain a Boolean `Yes`/`No` value, depending on whether the **Save** or **Cancel** button is selected in the View.

6. The `newname` parameter contains the new name entered by the user in the input field. If the parameter `Save` contains the value `YES`, that is, if the **Save** button is selected in the View, then the new name is added to the `nameslist` array and the table view is refreshed to display the newly added name.

7. Let's select **Build and Run** to run the application. Initially, we get the Table View containing the contents of the `nameslist` array, as shown in the following given *image (a)*:

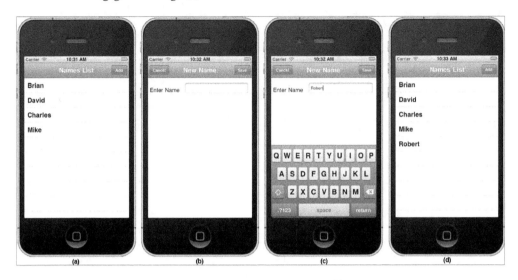

When the **Add** button is selected, the AddNameController View appears, as shown in the preceding *image (b)*, which prompts the user to enter a new name. When the user enters a name and selects the **Save** button (shown in the preceding *image (c)*), the new name will appear in the Table View, as shown in preceding *image (d)*.

Summary

In this chapter, we examined the steps required for working with protocols — definition, creation, delegate property creation, methods, delegate declaration, and implementation methods. Also, we saw how Table View controls can be used to display array data. We also took a look at common methods for adding information to Table Views. In the next chapter, we are going to start building our application: Sales Record System for a Departmental Store. We will begin with the first step: Design Data Model for keeping the customer's information, that is, we will learn to define Customer entity and its attributes. Also, we will learn to build data object (classes) associated with the Customer entity.

4

Designing a Data Model and Building Data Objects for Customers

In the previous chapter, we saw how the contents of an array can be used to display information through the Table View control. Also, we have seen the different methods that play a major role in displaying contents in the Table View control. We have also seen the steps involved in adding more information to the existing information being displayed in the Table View control. Assuming that we want to create an application "Sales Record System of a Store" where we want to keep the information of the customers along with the product details sold to each of them, we will gradually create this application step-by-step, that is, in each chapter, we will add a building block to the application.

In this chapter, we will design a data model for keeping the customer's information, that is, we will define a Customer entity and its attributes. After designing data model, we build data object (classes) associated with the Customer entity.

To design data model, we need to create a new project. So, let's start with.

Creating a new project

To create a new project, perform the following steps:

1. Launch Xcode and create a new project by selecting the **File** | **New Project** option.

2. The **New Project Assistant** window will appear, prompting us to select a template for the new project, as shown in the next screenshot. We will select the **Navigation-based Application** template.

3. Ensure that the **Use Core Data for storage** checkbox is checked and click on the **Choose…** button.

4. On selecting the **Choose…** button, we will get a dialog box to specify the name and the location of the project. Let us keep the location the same as default (**Documents** folder) and assign the project name as: **prob** (any name).

5. Click on **Save**. Xcode will then generate the project files and the project gets opened in the **Xcode** project window.

> The checkbox **Use Core Data for storage** will ask Xcode to provide all the default code that is required for using Core Data. This option is visible with only two project templates: **Navigation-based Application** and **Window-based Application** templates.

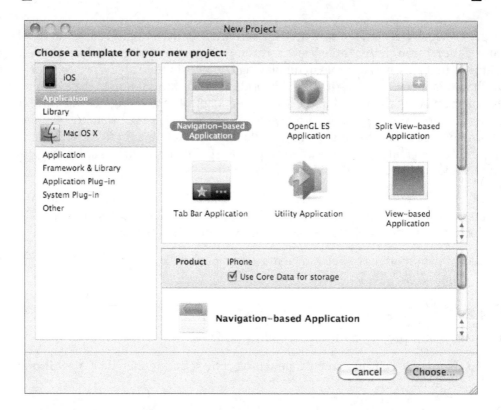

Designing the data model

Designing a data model means defining entities, attributes, and relationships for our application using a special tool. Xcode includes a data modeling tool (also known as Data Model Editor or simply a modeler) that facilitates the creation of entities, defining attributes, and the relationships among them.

Data Model Editor

The **Data Model Editor** is a data modeling tool provided by Xcode that makes the job of designing a data model quite easy. It displays the browser as well as a diagram view of the data model. The Browser view displays two panes, the **Entity** pane and the **Properties** pane, for defining entities and their respective properties. The diagram view displays rounded rectangles that designate entities and lines to show relationships among the entities.

Adding an entity

To add an entity to our data model, perform the following steps:

1. Invoke the data modeling tool by double-clicking the `prob.xcdatamodel` file in the **Resources** group found in the **Xcode Project** window.

2. Xcode's data modeling tool will open and we will find that an entity by default is already created for us by the name: **Event** (as shown in the next image) with an attribute: **timeStamp**.

3. We can delete or rename the default entity **Event** as desired. Let us select the default **Event** entity and delete it by clicking on the minus **(-)** button in the **Entity** pane followed by either choosing plus **(+)** button in the **Entity** pane or by choosing **Design | Data Model | Add Entity** option from the menu bar. This will add a blank entity (by the name **Entity**) to our data model, which we can rename as per our requirements. Let us set the name of the new entity as: **Customer**.

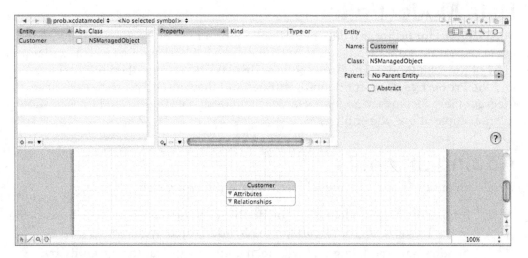

4. Automatically, an instance of **NSManagedObject** will be created to represent our newly created **Customer** entity. The next step is to add attributes to this entity.

Adding an attribute property

We want to add three attributes by name—**name**, **emailid**, and **contactno**—to the **Customer** entity. Let's follow the steps mentioned next for the same:

1. Select the entity and choose the **Design | Data Model | Add Attribute** option from the menu bar or select the **+ (plus)** button in the **Property** pane. A menu with several options such as **Add Attribute**, **Add Fetched property**, **Add Relationship**, and **Add Fetch Request** will pop up.

2. We select the **Add Attribute** option from the popped up menu. We see that a new attribute property is created for our **Customer** entity by a default name: **newAttribute** in the inspector.

3. Let us rename our new attribute as: **name** (as we will be using this attribute to store the names of the customers).

4. Then, we set the **type** of the name attribute to **String** as shown in the next screenshot (as names consists of strings):

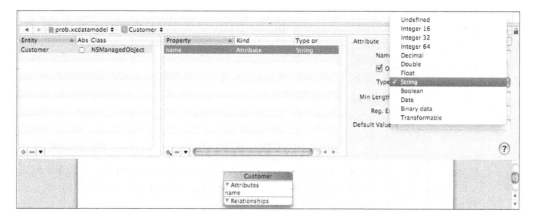

5. Below the **Name** field are three checkboxes: **Optional, Transient**, and **Indexed**. Though we will be using the **Optional** checkbox for the **name** attribute, let us see the usage of all three:

   ° **Optional**: If this checkbox is checked, it means the entity can be saved even if the attribute is nil (empty). If this checkbox is unchecked and we try to save the entity with this attribute set to nil, it will result in a validation error. When used with a relationship, if the checkbox is checked it means that the relationship can be empty. Suppose that we create one more entity say: **Credit Card** (where information of the customer's credit card is kept). In that case, the relationship from customer to the credit card will be optional (we have to leave this checkbox checked) as a customer may or may not have a credit card. And if we create an entity say: **Product** – in that case, the relationship from the **Customer** to the **Product** cannot be empty as a customer will definitely buy at least a single product (the checkbox has to be unchecked).

   ° **Transient**: This checkbox, if checked, means that the attribute or the relationship is of a temporary nature and we don't want it to be stored (persist) in the persistent store. This checkbox must be unchecked for the attributes or relationship that we want to persist (to be stored on the disk).

   ° **Indexed**: This checkbox has to be checked to apply indexing on the attribute. It is used when we want to perform sorting or searching on some attribute. By checking this checkbox, an index will be created on that attribute and the database will be ordered on that attribute.

Types of attributes

Using the **Type** drop-down list control, we select the data type (that is, numerical, string, date, and so on) of the attribute to specify the kind of information that can be stored in the attribute. The following is the list of data types:

- `Integer 16`, `Integer 32`, and `Integer 64` data types are for storing signed integers. The range of values that these types are able to store is as follows:

    - Integer 16:-32,768 to 32, 767
    - Integer 32:-2,147,483,648 to 2,147,483,647
    - Integer 64:-9,223,372,036,854,775,808 to 9,223,372,036,854,775,807

- `Decimal`, `Double`, and `Float` data types are for storing fractional numbers. The `Double` data type uses 64 bits to store a value while the `Float` data type uses 32 bits for storing a value. The only limitation with these two data types is that they round off the values. To avoid any rounding of values, the `Decimal` data type is preferred. The `Decimal` type uses fixed point numbers for storing values, so the numerical value stored in it is not rounded off.

- `String` data type is used for storing text contents.

- `Boolean` data type is used for storing YES or NO values.

- `Date` data type is used for storing dates as well as timestamps.

- `Binary` data type is used for storing binary data.

- Transformable data type works along with **Value Transformers** that help us create attributes based on any Objective-C class, that is, we can create custom data types other than the standard data types. This data type can be used to store an instance of `UIColor`, `UIImage`, and so on. It archives objects to instances of `NSData`. We will learn more about it in detail in *Chapter 9, Entering, Displaying, and the Deleting Stock*.

Below the **Type** drop-down menu, we will see a few more fields in the **detail** pane, as shown in the next screenshot:

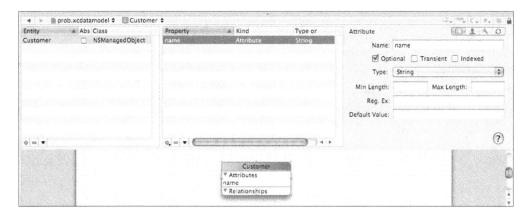

Fields applying constraints

Min Length: and **Max Length:** fields are for applying constraints of minimum and maximum number of characters to an attribute. If we exceed the range supplied in these fields, we get a validation error. Meaning, if we enter the string of fewer characters than the value supplied in **Min Length:** or the string has more characters than the value supplied in **Max Length:** field, this will result in a validation error while saving managed objects.

Reg. Ex: field stands for regular expression and is used for applying validation checks on the data entered in the attribute by making use of regular expressions.

Default Value: field is for specifying default value of the attribute. If we create a new managed object, the attribute will automatically be set to the default value specified in this field.

Let us add two more attributes to the **Customer** entity: **emailid** and **contactno** (for storing a customer's e-mail address and contact number, respectively). These two attributes will also be of type: `String` as shown in the next screenshot. Now, save the `.xcdatamodel`.

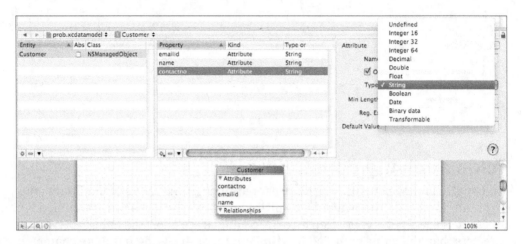

Building data objects for the Customer entity

To build the data objects (classes) for the entity defined in the data model, perform the following steps:

1. Click on the entity in Data Model Editor and then go to **File | New File**.

2. We get a dialog box to choose a template for the new file. Select **Cocoa Touch Class** from under the **iOS** heading in the left pane and select the **Managed Object Class** template, as shown in the next screenshot followed by **Next** button. This template is visible only when the editing pane is currently showing a Core Data model and is the active pane.

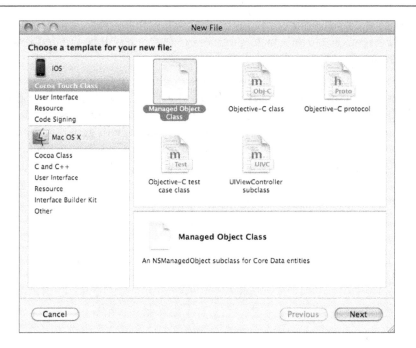

3. We get a dialog box that prompts for the location of generating managed object class, as shown in the following screenshot. The name of the subclass is based on the Entity name, so we will not be prompted to provide name for the subclass. Keeping the values as default, let's click on the **Next** button.

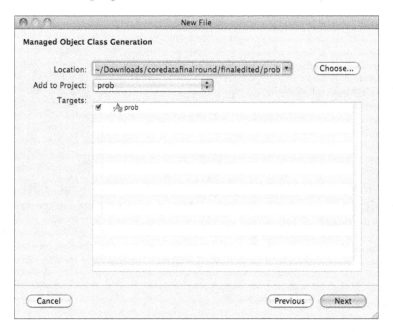

4. Check the **Customer** entity in the dialog box that appears, as shown in the next screenshot (a subclass of NSManagedObject will be created for our **Customer** entity).

5. We find two checkboxes that are already checked: **Generate accessors** and **Generate Obj-C 2.0 Properties** (these checkboxes will create properties for all the attributes in the new class). We also find one unchecked checkbox: **Generate validation methods**, which if checked, will generate method stubs for validating the attributes of our entity (but we leave it unchecked for the time being). Keeping only the two checkboxes checked, click on **Finish**.

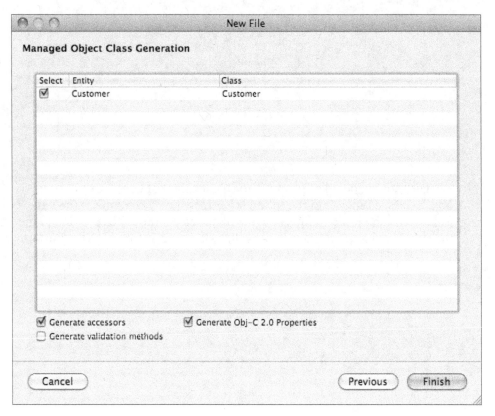

We find two files: Customer.h and Customer.m generated for our entity in the Classes folder of *Xcode Project window*. The code in header file, Customer.h, will appear as shown next:

```
//   Customer.h
//   prob

#import <CoreData/CoreData.h>
```

```
@interface Customer :  NSManagedObject
{
}


@property (nonatomic, retain) NSString * name;
@property (nonatomic, retain) NSString * emailid;
@property (nonatomic, retain) NSString * contactno;


@end
```

We can see that three properties are defined, `name`, `emailid`, and `contactno`, one for each attribute that we defined in the model editor. These properties are not declared in the header, as they will be created dynamically at runtime.

The code in the implementation file, `Customer.m`, will appear as shown next:

```
//  Customer.m
//  prob


#import "Customer.h"


@implementation Customer


@dynamic name;
@dynamic emailid;
@dynamic contactno;


@end
```

In the implementation file, we find that the properties are marked as *dynamic* to inform the compiler not to generate accessors and mutators for the property and will be provided (generated) by the super class at runtime and hence, not to display any warning message related to them. The getter/setter implementations that Core Data provides are KVO compliant.

Understanding code of autogenerated files

On creating a new application through Xcode, it simplifies the task of the developer by generating several files for us that are required for successful execution of the application. The two important files that are autogenerated by Xcode are **application delegate files**. The question is what is the usage of application delegate files? The answer is quite simple: there are several important events that happen in the life of an application. The two most important events are *launching* and *termination* of the application. The application needs to know when these events happen or are about to happen. The iPhone OS notifies about these events through Application Delegate by calling its appropriate methods. iPhone OS calls the `applicationDidFinishLaunching` method when it finishes the launch procedure and calls `applicationWillTerminate` when the application is terminated, so as to close any open files.

Let's have a look at the code of the autogenerated files. We begin with the header file of Application Delegate:

Header file of Application Delegate

The header file of Application Delegate, `progAppDelegate.h` contains some default code, as shown in the following code listing:

```
//   probAppDelegate.h
//   prob

#import <UIKit/UIKit.h>
#import <CoreData/CoreData.h>

@interface probAppDelegate : NSObject <UIApplicationDelegate> {

    UIWindow *window;
    UINavigationController *navigationController;

@private
    NSManagedObjectContext *managedObjectContext_;
    NSManagedObjectModel *managedObjectModel_;
    NSPersistentStoreCoordinator *persistentStoreCoordinator_;
}

@property (nonatomic, retain) IBOutlet UIWindow *window;
```

```
@property (nonatomic, retain) IBOutlet UINavigationController
*navigationController;

@property (nonatomic, retain, readonly) NSManagedObjectContext
*managedObjectContext;
@property (nonatomic, retain, readonly) NSManagedObjectModel
*managedObjectModel;
@property (nonatomic, retain, readonly) NSPersistentStoreCoordinator
*persistentStoreCoordinator;

- (NSURL *)applicationDocumentsDirectory;
- (void)saveContext;

@end
```

The preceding file declares instance variables of the NSManagedObjectModel, NSManagedObjectContext, and the NSPersistentStoreCoordinator class. Also, all of the variables including an NSString instance are defined as properties with the two attributes: retain and nonatomic. The retain attribute informs the compiler to retain (keep) the instance variable and not to flush from memory while being used. The nonatomic attribute informs the compiler that when it will be asked to generate the accessor and mutator methods of the outlets (synthesized), it should generate them without any additional code of implementing multithreading. The nonatomic attribute is used for simple applications.

Let us also see the autogenerated code in Application Delegate's implementation file: probAppDelegate.m.

Implementation file of Application Delegate

The implementation file of Application Delegate, progAppDelegate.m, contains some default code, as shown in the following code listing:

```
//    probAppDelegate.m
//    prob

#import "probAppDelegate.h"
#import "RootViewController.h"

@implementation probAppDelegate

@synthesize window;
@synthesize navigationController;

- (void)awakeFromNib {
```

```objc
    RootViewController *rootViewController = (RootViewController *)
      [navigationController topViewController];
    rootViewController.managedObjectContext = self.
managedObjectContext;
}


- (BOOL)application:(UIApplication *)
   application didFinishLaunchingWithOptions:(NSDictionary *)
   launchOptions {
       [self.window addSubview:navigationController.view];
       [self.window makeKeyAndVisible];
       return YES;
}
```

In `awakeFromNib` method, the root view controller of the application
is set equal to the top view controller of the navigation controller. In
`applicationDidFinishLaunching` method, the view of the navigation controller is
set as a subview of the content view and hence is displayed to the user.

```objc
- (void)applicationWillTerminate:(UIApplication *)application {
    [self saveContext];
}


- (void)saveContext {

    NSError *error = nil;
    NSManagedObjectContext *managedObjectContext = self.
managedObjectContext;
      if (managedObjectContext != nil) {
        if ([managedObjectContext hasChanges] &&
           ![managedObjectContext save:&error]) {
              NSLog(@"Unresolved error %@, %@", error, [error
userInfo]);
              abort();
        }
      }
}
```

applicationWillTerminate method

The `applicationWillTerminate` method is invoked just before exiting from the application and is usually used for saving the modifications applied to the managed object via managed object context. That is, the managed object context (containing the modifications applied to the managed object) is saved to the persistent store. The `save action` method is used for saving the managed object context to the persistent store, that is, the changes made to the managed object context are committed through this method. An error will be displayed if there occurs some problem while saving the managed object context.

```
- (NSManagedObjectContext *)managedObjectContext {
    if (managedObjectContext_ != nil) {
        return managedObjectContext_;
    }
    NSPersistentStoreCoordinator *coordinator =
        [self persistentStoreCoordinator];
    if (coordinator != nil) {
        managedObjectContext_ = [[NSManagedObjectContext alloc] init];
        [managedObjectContext_ setPersistentStoreCoordinator:coordina
tor];
    }
    return managedObjectContext_;
}
```

managedObjectContext method

Every application has at least one managed object context. The managed object context maintains the state of the managed object after it is loaded in memory. All modifications that we apply to the managed object are actually applied to the managed object context. It keeps track of all the changes made to the managed object since the last time it was loaded in memory and hence helps in undoing any changes made to the managed object (if required). When we want to commit the modifications made to the managed object, we save the managed object context to the persistent store.

The managed contexts are not thread-safe, which means there are many chances of faults when managed object contexts are shared between threads or are accessed from multiple threads simultaneously. To avoid any conflicts, we need to apply the **Locking mechanism**. In other words, contexts in general should not be shared between threads. Apple's advice is to use one context per thread and to merge changes.

In the preceding method, a check is made to see if the instance variable, managedObjectContext, already exists or not (nil value means the instance variable does not exist). If the instance variable exists, it is returned, else it is created. In order to deal with persistent store, the managed object context needs a reference to a PersistentStoreCoordinator. Recall that the PersistentStoreCoordinator is the essential middle layer in the stack that helps in storing and retrieving the managed object model from the persistent store (in the form of managed object context). So, to create the managedObjectContext instance variable, we check for a pointer to the NSPersistentStoreCoordinator. If the pointer to PersistentStoreCoordinator exists, we create a new managedObjectContext and after linking it with the pointer to the PersistentStoreCoordinator, return it.

```
- (NSManagedObjectModel *)managedObjectModel {
    if (managedObjectModel_ != nil) {
        return managedObjectModel_;
    }
    NSString *modelPath = [[NSBundle mainBundle]
pathForResource:@"prob"
        ofType:@"momd"];
    NSURL *modelURL = [NSURL fileURLWithPath:modelPath];
    managedObjectModel_ = [[NSManagedObjectModel alloc]
        initWithContentsOfURL:modelURL];
    return managedObjectModel_;
}
```

managedObjectModel method

This method first checks if the instance variable managedObjectModel (of NSManagedObjectModel class) already exists or not (nil value means the instance variable does not exist). If the instance variable exists, it is returned, or else it is created by merging all the data models found in the application bundle. It also means that we can have several data models (created in separate .xcdatamodelfiles) in an application. All the data models (entities and their relationships) contained in different files will be merged (combined) into a single managed object model.

```
- (NSPersistentStoreCoordinator *)persistentStoreCoordinator {
    if (persistentStoreCoordinator_ != nil) {
        return persistentStoreCoordinator_;
    }
    NSURL *storeURL = [[self applicationDocumentsDirectory]
     URLByAppendingPathComponent:@"customersdata.sqlite"];
    NSError *error = nil;
```

```
      persistentStoreCoordinator_ = [[NSPersistentStoreCoordinator
alloc]
         initWithManagedObjectModel:[self managedObjectModel]];
      if (![persistentStoreCoordinator_ addPersistentStoreWithType:NSSQL
iteStoreType configuration:nil URL:storeURL options:nil error:&error])
      {
          NSLog(@"Unresolved error %@, %@", error, [error userInfo]);
          abort();
      }
      return persistentStoreCoordinator_;
}
```

persistentStoreCoordinator method

The NSPersistentStoreCoordinator class is meant for storing and retrieving the managed object model from the persistent store. It also helps in avoiding redundancy if multiple calls are made by different classes on the same file at the same time. The multiple calls are serialized by the NSPersistentStoreCoordinator class to avoid redundancy.

The preceding code first checks whether the instance variable, persistentStoreCoordinator, exists or not. If it exists, it is returned, or else it is created. Because we want to store the names of the customers in the file: customersdata.sqlite, we define a path to the file in the Documents directory of our application's sandbox.

We want the format of the persistent store to be of SQLite type, hence the parameter NSSQLiteStoreType is passed to the method to specify the type of the persistent store. NSSQLiteStoreType is a constant that tells Core Data to use a SQLite database for its persistent store. If we want to store the information in binary format, we may use the constant, NSBinaryStoreType for the persistent store. If anything goes wrong while creating the instance variable persistentStoreCoordinator, an error will be displayed:

```
- (NSURL *)applicationDocumentsDirectory {
    return [[[NSFileManager defaultManager] URLsForDirectory:NSDocumen
tDirectory inDomains:NSUserDomainMask] lastObject];
}
```

applicationDocumentsDirectory method

This method is for finding the location to store the persistent store file. In Xcode, each application has its own sandboxed Documents directory designed for the storage of files. So, we retrieve a list of the cache directories from the SearchPathForDirectoriesInDomains method and write code to find the Documents folder specific to our application.

```
- (void)dealloc {
    [managedObjectContext_ release];
    [managedObjectModel_ release];
    [persistentStoreCoordinator_ release];
    [navigationController release];
    [window release];
    [super dealloc];
}

@end
```

The dealloc method is for releasing the memory assigned to different instance variables.

As seen in the previous code we specify the file: customersdata.sqlite for storing the names of the customers in the NSURL statement of the persistentStoreCordinator method.

Summary

In this chapter, we saw how the Xcode's Data Model Editor can be used for creating Entity, defining its attributes and how its Data Model (class) associated with the Entity can be automatically generated. We also had a brief idea of different fields that appear while defining attributes of an Entity. In the next chapter, we will learn how to save, display, and delete customer's information. The information of the Customer will comprise the customer's name, his e-mail address, and contact number and will be stored in the Customer entity.

5
Creating, Listing, and Deleting Names of Customers

In the previous chapter, we created a Data Model and Data objects for the *Customer* entity. In this chapter, we will learn how to save, display, and delete a customer's information. The information of the customer will comprise of the customer's name, his/her e-mail address, and contact number, and will be stored in the *Customer* entity.

Recall that we created a project with the name *prob* in the last chapter and used the *Navigation-based Application* project template for doing so. The project template, as we know, provides default code in the form of auto-generated files that are required in developing the application. Let us now use the knowledge that we have gained so far to do something practical. Let us see how to create, read, update, and delete records of a customer entity.

Splitting the task into two modules

To make it easier for us to understand the procedure of maintaining the customer's information, which consists of fields such as name, emailid, and contactno, we split this task into two modules:

- Module to save and delete customer name (that is, instead of dealing with all the three fields (name, emailid, and contactno) together, we will first learn how to handle a single field, that is, name of the customer

- Module to save, display, and delete the complete information of the customer, that is, name, emailid, and contactno

This means that we will first learn how to handle a single attribute: *customer's name*. When we properly understand the procedure of saving and deleting a customer's name, we will go ahead with developing a second module that stores complete information of the customer; that includes name, e-mail ID, contact number, and so on.

Creating a module to save and delete a customer's name

In this module, we will learn how to save and edit the name of the customer.

The following are the steps involved in developing this module:

1. Adding a `ViewController` class: `AddNameController` class for adding the name of the customer.

2. Defining protocol, outlets, and action methods in header file: `AddNameController.h`.

3. Defining View of the `AddNameController` class and connecting controls.

4. Invoking delegate methods from an implementation file: `AddNameController.m` file.

5. Declaring delegate and implementing methods for storing name of the customers.

Using the ViewController class for adding the name of the customer

To enter the name of the customer, we need to add a `View Controller` class that will display a View that has a navigation bar with two navigation bar items: *Save* and *Cancel*. The View will also prompt the user to enter the customer's name to be stored in the `customersdata.sqlite` file (persistent store).

The View Controllers are used for managing the view and the class used for controlling the views is called `UIViewController` (provided by UIKit). To manage the view of our application, we create its subclass. To create a subclass of `UIViewController`, follow the given steps:

1. Right-click on the **Classes** group in the **Xcode Project** window and select the **Add** | **New File** option. We will get a dialog box to select the template for the new file.

2. Select **Cocoa Touch Class** from under the **iPhone OS** heading in the left pane and select the **UIViewController** subclass as the template of the new file.

3. Select the checkbox **With XIB for user interface** (we will be using the XIB file for creating the View for the View Controller that will prompt the user to enter the name of the customer) followed by the **Next** button. We get a dialog box to specify the name of the View Controller.

4. Assign the name as: AddNameController.m and select the checkbox **Also create "AddNameController.h"** (for creating the header file also) followed by the **Finish** button, as shown in following screenshot:

 Now our application has two View Controller classes: RootViewController (automatically created by default by the *Navigation-based Application* template) and AddNameController.

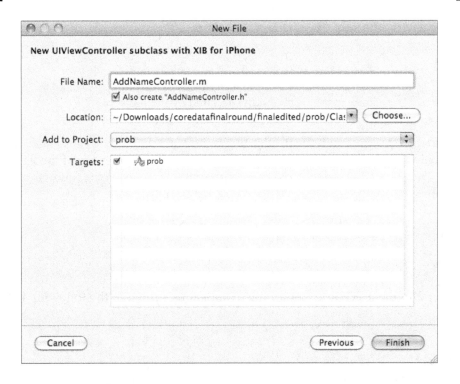

Both the header and implementation files, AddNameController.h and AddNameController.m, will be created for us along with the .xib file and are added to our project. The files will be placed at the default location: the **Classes** group of our **Xcode Project** window. Let us select the AddNameViewController.xib file in the **Classes** group in the **Xcode Project** window and drag it to the **Resources** group, which is the default location for all Interface Builder (.xib) files.

Defining protocol, outlets, and action methods in the header file

We want it so that after entering the customer's name in the View of the AddNameController class, when a user selects the **Save** or **Cancel** button from the navigation bar, the task of saving or discarding the customer's name should be performed by the RootViewController class. This is possible when the RootViewController class is declared as the delegate of the protocol defined in the AddNameController class). So, in the header file of the new View Controller class AddNameController.h, we define a protocol with the name AddNameControllerDelegate, and in the protocol, we declare a method with the name addnameController. Then, we will make the RootViewController class conform to that protocol (that is, the RootViewController class will be declared as the delegate of the AddNameControllerDelegate protocol). As a result, the method addnameController, declared in AddNameControllerDelegate, will be implemented by the RootViewController class.

 Protocols are not classes, but an interface that declares methods and the class that conforms to the protocol needed to implement the method(s) declared by the protocol.

Besides defining a protocol, the header file of the AddNameController class will also contain outlets, properties, and action methods. The header file of the View controller class AddNameController.h originally appears as the following code shows:

```
#import <UIKit/UIKit.h>
@interface AddNameController : UIViewController {
}
@end
```

Let us modify the preceding header file to appear as shown in the following listing:

```
//   AddNameController.h
//   prob

#import <UIKit/UIKit.h>
#import "Customer.h"

@protocol AddNameControllerDelegate;

@interface AddNameController : UIViewController {
   Customer *cust;
   id <AddNameControllerDelegate> delegate;
   IBOutlet UIBarButtonItem *cancelbutton;
```

```
    IBOutlet UIBarButtonItem *savebutton;
    IBOutlet UITextField *newname;
}
@property(nonatomic, retain) Customer *cust;
@property(nonatomic, retain) id <AddNameControllerDelegate> delegate;
@property(nonatomic, retain) IBOutlet UIBarButtonItem *cancelbutton;
@property(nonatomic, retain) IBOutlet UIBarButtonItem *savebutton;
@property(nonatomic, retain) UITextField *newname;

-(IBAction) cancel:(id) sender;
-(IBAction) save:(id)sender;

@end


@protocol AddNameControllerDelegate
-(void) addnameController:(AddNameController *)controller
    selectedsave:(BOOL) save;
@end
```

Besides defining a protocol, we also define an object of the Customer class by the name cust and three instance variables, namely, cancelbutton, savebutton, and newname. The three instance variables are marked as outlets. The two outlets cancelbutton and savebutton will be connected to the two Bar Button Items (that we will soon be adding to the View) Save and Cancel respectively, and the outlet newname will be connected to the Text Field control of the View in which the user will enter the name of the customer. We also see that the preceding file includes two action methods, namely, cancel and save that will be connected to the two respective Bar Button Items, namely, Cancel and Save. We also see that the three instance variables (cancelbutton, savebutton, and newname) along with the object cust (of Customer entity) are defined as *properties* with the two attributes, *retain* and *nonatomic*, for generating the accessor and mutators without any overhead code (when synthesized). After adding the preceding code, we save the preceding header file.

The cust object of the Customer class will be used to handle the name entered by the user in the Text Field control in the View of the AddNameController class (which we are going to design in the next step). Soon we will declare the RootViewController class as the delegate of the AddNameControllerDelegate protocol so that the method addnameController (declared in the protocol) can be implemented in it.

Defining the View of the AddNameController class and connecting controls

The next step is to add two Bar Button Item controls to the View of the `AddNameController` class. We will follow the given steps for doing so:

1.   Open the `AddNameController.xib` file in the **Interface Builder** and drag two Bar Button Item controls from the **Windows, Views & Bars** category of the **Library** window and drop them in the **Documents** window.

2.   Select the two Bar Button Item controls one at a time in the **Documents** window, and with the help of **Attributes Inspector**, set their **Title** to **Save** and **Cancel** respectively.

3.   Drag and drop a **Label** and a **Text Field** control on the View.

4.   Double-click the **Label** control and edit its text to **Enter name**, as shown in the following screenshot:

To connect the outlet **newname** (instance of UITextField defined in the header file `AddNameController.h`) with the Text Field control in the View, select the **File's Owner** icon in the **Documents** window and open the **Connections Inspector** window. All the outlets and action methods that we defined in the header file will be visible in the **Connections Inspector** window under the headings **Outlets** and **Received Actions** respectively. To connect the outlet **newname** with the TextField control, select the circle to the right of the outlet **newname** and, keeping the mouse button pressed, drag it to the Text Field control in the View.

Similarly, to connect the outlets of the Bar Button Items, **cancelbutton** and **savebutton**, with the Bar Button Item controls dropped in the **Documents** window, select the circle to the right of the outlet **savebutton** and, keeping the mouse button pressed, drag it to the **Bar Button Item** control (with the Title **Save**) in the **Documents** window and release the mouse button, as shown in the following screenshot. Repeat the procedure to connect the **cancelbutton** outlet with the other Bar Button Item control.

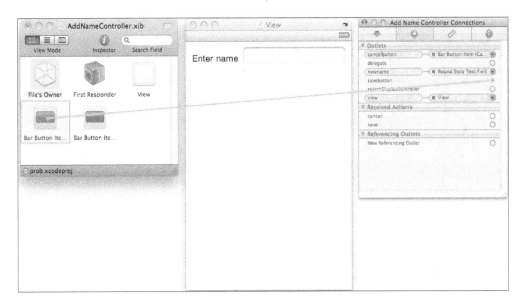

As we want the **Save** and **Cancel** Bar Button Item controls to invoke the action methods, namely, **save** and **cancel** declared in the header file (`AddNameController.h`), we need to connect them. To connect the **save** and **cancel** action methods with the Bar Button Item controls, follow the given steps:

1.   Select one Bar Button Item control (say, the one with the Title **Cancel**) in the **Documents** window and open the **Connections Inspector** window.

2.   In the **Connections Inspector** window, select the circle to the right of **selector** (under the **Sent Actions** heading) and keeping the mouse button pressed, drag it to the **File's Owner** icon in the **Documents** window. Two action methods will pop up (that are defined in header file – `AddNameController.h`).

3.   Select the action method that we want to connect to this Bar Button Item control. As the selected Bar Button Item control is the one with Title **Cancel**, we select the action method **cancel** to connect it with the selected Bar Button Item control, as shown in the following screenshot.

Now, if we select the **Cancel** Bar Button Item control in the View, the code (that we are going to write in the implementation file AddNameController.m) in the action method **cancel** will be executed.

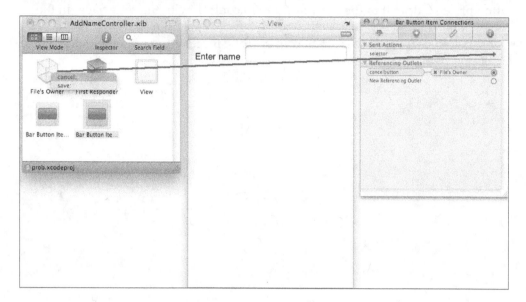

Repeat the procedure to connect the action method **save** to the other Bar Button Item control.

Invoking delegate methods from the implementation file

We need to write the code in the implementation file of the ViewController class, AddNameController.m, to invoke the respective action method when either Bar Button Item control is pressed and also we write the code to place the Bar Button items on the left and right side of the navigation bar. The implementation file contains the default code, as shown next:

```
#import "AddNameController.h"

@implementation AddNameController

/*
 // The designated initializer.  Override if you create the controller
 programmatically and want to perform customization that is not
 appropriate for viewDidLoad.
 - (id)initWithNibName:(NSString *)nibNameOrNil bundle:(NSBundle *)
 nibBundleOrNil {
```

```objc
    self = [super initWithNibName:nibNameOrNil bundle:nibBundleOrNil];
    if (self) {
      // Custom initialization.
    }
    return self;
}
 */


/*
// Implement viewDidLoad to do additional setup after loading the
view, typically from a nib.
- (void)viewDidLoad {
    [super viewDidLoad];
}
*/


/*
// Override to allow orientations other than the default portrait
orientation.
- (BOOL)shouldAutorotateToInterfaceOrientation:(UIInterfaceOrientati
on)interfaceOrientation {
  // Return YES for supported orientations
  return (interfaceOrientation == UIInterfaceOrientationPortrait);
}
*/

- (void)didReceiveMemoryWarning {
    [super didReceiveMemoryWarning];
}

- (void)viewDidUnload {
    [super viewDidUnload];
}

- (void)dealloc {
    [super dealloc];
}

@end
```

Let us modify the implementation file to appear as shown in the following code listing:

```
// AddNameController.m
// prob

#import "AddNameController.h"

@implementation AddNameController

@synthesize savebutton;
@synthesize cancelbutton;
@synthesize delegate;
@synthesize newname;
@synthesize cust;

-(IBAction) cancel:(id) sender
{
    [delegate addnameController: self selectedsave:NO];

}
-(IBAction) save:(id)sender{
    cust.name=newname.text;
    [delegate addnameController: self selectedsave:YES ];

}

// Implement viewDidLoad to do additional setup after loading the
view, typically from a nib.
- (void)viewDidLoad {
    [super viewDidLoad];
    self.title=@"New Name";
    self.navigationItem.rightBarButtonItem=savebutton;
    self.navigationItem.leftBarButtonItem=cancelbutton;
}

- (void)dealloc {
    [savebutton release];
    [cancelbutton release];
    [newname release];
    [cust release];
    [super dealloc];
}
@end
```

In the code, first of all, we see that we synthesize the IBOutlets (`savebutton`, `cancelbutton`, `delegate`, `newname`, and `cust`) for generating the accessor and mutator methods for them. In the `cancel` action method, we write code to invoke the `addnameController` method of the delegate class (the `RootViewController` class) and pass the parameter `selectedsave` set to the value `NO` to it. Similarly, in the `save` action method, we invoke the `addnameController` method of the delegate and pass the parameter `selectedsave` set to the value `YES` to it. Also, in the save action method, we assign the name entered by the user in the Text Field control to the name attribute of the cust object (of the `Customer` class).

In the `viewDidLoad` method, we set the Navigation Item's title to **New Name** and its right bar button item to **savebutton** (Instance variable of Bar Button Item with the title **Save**) so that the Save Bar Button appears on the right of the navigation bar. Similarly, to make the Cancel Bar Button appear on left of the navigation bar, we set the left bar button item of the navigation bar to `cancelbutton` – the instance variable of Bar Button Item control with the Title **Cancel**. Finally, through dealloc method, we release the reference to the Outlets.

Declaring delegate and implementing methods for storing the name of the customers

It's time to declare the delegate of the `AddNameController` class and implement its methods. We also need to implement the methods of the `NSFetchedResultsControllerDelegate` protocol. We set the `RootViewController` class as delegate of both the protocols `NSFetchedResultsControllerDelegate` and `AddNameControllerDelegate`. The header file of the `RootViewController` file may be modified to appear as shown in the following code listing:

 In the following given file, only the highlighted code is modified. Rest of the code is the default code that is automatically generated for us by the *Navigation-based Application project* template.

```
//  RootViewController.h
//  prob

#import <UIKit/UIKit.h>
#import <CoreData/CoreData.h>
#import "AddNameController.h"
```

```
@interface RootViewController : UITableViewController
<NSFetchedResultsControllerDelegate, AddNameControllerDelegate> {

  @private
    NSFetchedResultsController *fetchedResultsController_;
    NSManagedObjectContext *managedObjectContext_;
}
@property (nonatomic, retain) NSManagedObjectContext
*managedObjectContext;
@property (nonatomic, retain) NSFetchedResultsController
*fetchedResultsController;

@end
```

The preceding file is declared as delegate for two protocols, namely, `NSFetchedResultsControllerDelegate` and `AddNameControllerDelegate`, that is, it will implement the methods of both the protocols. Also, the file declares instance variables of `NSFetchedResultsController` and `NSManagedObjectModel` by the names `fetchedResultsController` and `managedObjectContext`. Also, all the instance variables are defined as *properties* with the two attributes *retain* and *nonatomic* for generating the accessor and mutators without any overhead code (when synthesized) and for keeping the objects retained to the mutators without being flushed from memory.

The implementation file of the `RootViewController` class will carry the default code that is automatically generated for us by the *Navigation-based Application project* template. We will add the code to this file. The highlighted code that appears in the following code listing is the added code. The complete file is provided in the code bundle of this chapter. The code that needs explanation is shown next:

```
//  RootViewController.m
//  prob

#import "RootViewController.h"

@interface RootViewController ()
- (void)configureCell:(UITableViewCell *)cell atIndexPath:(NSIndexPath
*)indexPath;
@end


@implementation RootViewController

@synthesize fetchedResultsController=fetchedResultsController_, manage
dObjectContext=managedObjectContext_;
```

Synthesizing the `fetchedResultsController` and `managedObjectContext` properties, that is, generating the accessor and mutator methods for the properties (instance variable: `fetchedResultsController` and `managedObjectContext`).

```
- (void)viewDidLoad {
    [super viewDidLoad];

    // Set up the edit and add buttons.
    self.navigationItem.leftBarButtonItem = self.editButtonItem;

    UIBarButtonItem *addButton = [[UIBarButtonItem alloc]
        initWithBarButtonSystemItem:UIBarButtonSystemItemAdd target:self
        action:@selector(addCustomer)];
    self.navigationItem.rightBarButtonItem = addButton;
    [addButton release];

    NSError *error = nil;
    if (![[self fetchedResultsController] performFetch:&error]) {
        NSLog(@"Unresolved error %@, %@", error, [error userInfo]);
        abort();
    }
}
```

The `viewDidLoad` method calls its super class. After that, two Bar Button Item buttons are set to appear on the left and right side of the navigation bar respectively. The button displayed on the left side of the navigation bar is the **Edit** button that is displayed by using the `editButtonItem` property of the UIViewController. For the right side, we create an `addButton` using the alloc method and make it appear on the right side of the navigation bar. The `RootViewController` inherits from `UIViewController`, which provides a property named `editButtonItem`, which in turn returns an **Edit** button. Using dot notation, we retrieve `editButtonItem` and pass it to the mutator for left Bar Button Item. The title of the **Edit** button automatically changes to **Done** when selected. To the **Add** button, we attach an `addCustomer` action (method that will be executed when the **Add** button is selected by the user). After the creation and initialization of the left and right side Bar Button Items of the navigation bar, the `performFetch:` message is invoked on an object returned by the method `fetchedResultsController` to display the result retrieved in `fetchedResultsController`. Recall that the `fetchedResultsController` contains the entities specified by the fetch request, arranged on the attribute specified by the sort descriptor.

```
- (void)configureCell:(UITableViewCell *)cell atIndexPath:(NSIndexPath
*)indexPath {
    NSManagedObject *managedObject = [self.fetchedResultsController
        objectAtIndexPath:indexPath];
```

```
    cell.textLabel.text = [[managedObject valueForKey:@"name"]
    description];
}
```

In the cell `atIndexPath` method, we retrieve the managed object
from the `fetchedResultsController` instance. Recall that the
`NSFetchedResultsController` stores the set of entities from an
`NSManagedObjectContext` that are retrieved on the basis of FetchRequest. Then, by
making use of KVC, the value stored in the `name` attribute of the managed object is
assigned to the table cell for display. The concept of KVC is explained in detail after
this program.

```
- (NSInteger)numberOfSectionsInTableView:(UITableView *)tableView {
    return [[fetchedResultsController sections] count];
}
```

The `numberOfSectionsInTableView` method defines the number of sections for the
table view. The section's message is passed to the `fetchedResultsController` (as it
contains the entities retrieved on the basis of fetch request) and its count is returned.

```
- (NSInteger)tableView:(UITableView *)tableView numberOfRowsInSection:
(NSInteger)section {
    id <NSFetchedResultsSectionInfo> sectionInfo =
      [[self.fetchedResultsController sections] objectAtIndex:section];
      return [sectionInfo numberOfObjects];
}
```

The `numberOfRowsInSection` method is for returning the count of the rows (number
of objects) in the concerned section. The section selected is the one that is returned by
the fetched results controller (the section returned by calling `objectAtIndexPath:`
on the `fetchedResultsController` instance and passing in the section parameter to
it). Then, we request a reference to the `NSFetchedResultsSectionInfo` instance for
the specified section. We then return the count of the objects in the current section.

```
// Customize the appearance of table view cells.
- (UITableViewCell *)tableView:(UITableView *)tableView cellForRowAtIn
dexPath:(NSIndexPath *)indexPath {
    static NSString *CellIdentifier = @"Cell";
    UITableViewCell *cell = [tableView
      dequeueReusableCellWithIdentifier:CellIdentifier];
    if (cell == nil) {
        cell = [[[UITableViewCell alloc]
          initWithStyle:UITableViewCellStyleDefault
          reuseIdentifier:CellIdentifier] autorelease];
    }

    // Configure the cell.
    [self configureCell:cell atIndexPath:indexPath];
```

```
        return cell;
    }
```

The `cellForRowAtIndexPath` method invokes the cell `atIndexPath` method to display the value stored in the name attribute of the managed object.

```
// Override to support editing the table view.
- (void)tableView:(UITableView *)tableView commitEditingStyle:(UITabl
eViewCellEditingStyle)editingStyle forRowAtIndexPath:(NSIndexPath *)
indexPath {

if (editingStyle == UITableViewCellEditingStyleDelete) {
        // Delete the managed object for the given index path
        NSManagedObjectContext *context = [self.
fetchedResultsController
            managedObjectContext];
        [context deleteObject:[self.fetchedResultsController
          objectAtIndexPath:indexPath]];

        // Save the context.
        NSError *error = nil;
        if (![context save:&error]) {
          NSLog(@"Unresolved error %@, %@", error, [error userInfo]);
          abort();
        }
    }
}
```

The `commitEditingStyle` method is used for editing the table cells (and hence the managed objects). In the preceding code, we are deleting current table cell contents (that is, the managed object in the current row of the table view). We first confirm whether we want to initiate the delete operation. If yes, then we retrieve the managed object context from the `fetchedResultsController` and the object is deleted from the context. The object deleted is the one that is returned by the `fetchedResultsController` (the object returned by calling `objectAtIndexPath:` on the `fetchedResultsController` and passing in the `indexPath` parameter to it). Finally, the managed object context's `save:` method is called to commit the changes into the persistent store.

```
- (BOOL)tableView:(UITableView *)tableView canMoveRowAtIndexPath:(NSIn
dexPath *)indexPath {
    // The table view should not be re-orderable.
    return NO;
}
```

The `canMoveRowAtIndexPath:` method confirms the data source whether a given row can be moved to another location in the table view or not. The method returns YES if the row indicated by index path can be moved.

```
- (IBAction) addCustomer
{
AddNameController *addnameController=[[AddNameController alloc] initWi
thNibName:@"AddNameController" bundle:nil];
  addnameController.delegate=self;

  addnameController.cust= (Customer *) [NSEntityDescription
    insertNewObjectForEntityForName:@"Customer"
    inManagedObjectContext:managedObjectContext_];

  UINavigationController *navController=[[UINavigationController
alloc]
    initWithRootViewController:addnameController];
  [self.navigationController presentModalViewController:navController
    animated:YES];
  [addnameController release];
  [navController release];


}
```

The `addCustomer` method is invoked when the user selects the plus (+) button in the navigation bar. This method displays a View that prompts the user to enter the name of the customer. On selecting the **Save** button (after entering name of the customer), a new managed object is created and stored in the persistent store. We create and initialize an instance of the `AddNameController` class by the name `addnameController`, as the View that prompts the user to enter the name of the customer is built into this View. We make use of alloc to create the view controller object and initialize it. The init method specifies the name of the NIB file that has to be loaded by the controller (`AddNameController`) followed by the bundle where the NIB file is expected to be found. The bundle parameter is set to nil as we want the method to look for the NIB file in the main bundle. The `initWithNibName` method allows initializing a UIViewController's view from a NIB file rather than from code. This method is preferred when View of the view controller exists in the NIB file and we want to load it from the NIB file.

Also, we set the current View Controller file `RootViewController.m` as the delegate of the `addnameController` instance (of the `AddNameController` class). That is, we will implement the methods declared in the protocol (defined in the `AddNameController` class) in the `RootViewController.m` file.

Then we insert a new managed object into the managed context using the class method on the NSEntityDescription. Also, we return the instance of class that represents the entity (Customer) and assign it to the cust object of addnameController (instance of the AddnameController class).

To display a navigation bar in the View of AddNameController, we create and initialize an instance of the UINavigationController class with the name navController and set its root view controller to be the View of the AddNameController class. Then we display the View of the AddNameController class modally using the presentModalViewController:animated: method. The view controller animates the appearance of the view and creates a parent-child relationship between the current view controller and the modal view controller.

```
- (void) addnameController: (AddNameController *) controller
  selectedsave: (BOOL) save {
    if(!save)
    {
       [managedObjectContext_ deleteObject:controller.cust];
    }

    NSError *error=nil;
    if(![managedObjectContext_ save:&error])
    {
       NSLog(@"Unresolved error %@, %@", error, [error userInfo]);
       abort();
    }
  [self dismissModalViewControllerAnimated:YES];
}
```

The addnameController is the method of the protocol AddNameControllerDelegate that the current class (RootViewController) conforms to and hence implements this method. It is invoked by the cancel and save action methods (defined in the implementation file of the AddNameController class). Recall that the cancel action method (defined in the AddNameController.m file) calls the addnameController method with a parameter: selectedsave set to value NO and the save action method calls the same method with the selectedsave parameter set to the value YES. The value of the selectedsave parameter is assigned to the argument: save.

In the addnameController method, we check that if the value of the variable save is false, then we delete the cust object (of the Customer entity class that we inserted in the addCustomer method) from the managed object context, and save the context in the persistent store. Finally, we dismiss the modal view of the AddNameController class and the View of Root View Controller appears to display the updated table view.

```
- (void)tableView:(UITableView *)tableView didSelectRowAtIndexPath:(NS
IndexPath *)indexPath {
    // Navigation logic may go here -- for example, create and push
      another view controller.


}
```

The didSelectRowAtIndexPath method is for displaying the detailed information of the selected row from the table view:

```
- (NSFetchedResultsController *)fetchedResultsController {

  if (fetchedResultsController_ != nil) {
    return fetchedResultsController_;
  }

NSFetchRequest *fetchRequest = [[NSFetchRequest alloc] init];
NSEntityDescription *entity = [NSEntityDescription
entityForName:@"Customer"
  inManagedObjectContext:self.managedObjectContext];
    [fetchRequest setEntity:entity];

[fetchRequest setFetchBatchSize:20];

NSSortDescriptor *sortDescriptor = [[NSSortDescriptor alloc]
  initWithKey:@"name" ascending:YES];
    NSArray *sortDescriptors = [[NSArray alloc]
      initWithObjects:sortDescriptor, nil];

  [fetchRequest setSortDescriptors:sortDescriptors];

NSFetchedResultsController *aFetchedResultsController =
[[NSFetchedResultsController alloc] initWithFetchRequest:fetchRequest
managedObjectContext:self.managedObjectContext sectionNameKeyPath:nil
cacheName:@"Root"];
    aFetchedResultsController.delegate = self;
    self.fetchedResultsController = aFetchedResultsController;

  [aFetchedResultsController release];
```

```
    [fetchRequest release];
    [sortDescriptor release];
    [sortDescriptors release];

    NSError *error = nil;
    if (![fetchedResultsController_ performFetch:&error]) {
      NSLog(@"Unresolved error %@, %@", error, [error userInfo]);
        abort();
    }
    return fetchedResultsController_;
}
```

The fetchedResultsController method creates a FetchedResultsController.
We first check whether the fetchedResultsController already exists (non
nil). If it exists, we return it, or else we create it. We already know that the
fetchedResultsController contains the entities specified by the criteria applied in
fetch request, so the first step is to create a fetch request.

In the fetch request, we specify the entity to be retrieved along with an optional
criterion (filter condition) to retrieve only the desired entities. In the preceding
code, we set the entity as Customer to be retrieved (using fetch request) from the
managed object context. The entity to be fetched is specified using an instance of
the NSEntityDescription class). To get the retrieved entities organized on the
basis of key or the attribute of the entity, we create and add a sort descriptor to the
fetch request. We specify the attribute name of the Customer entity to arrange the
fetched results on the ascending order on the name of the customer. After that, an
array of sort descriptors is created. As we want to sort the result only on the basis of
the name attribute, we will pass sortDescriptor (for sorting on name) to the array
(of sortDescriptors) and terminate the array with nil. Finally, the fetch request and
managed object context are used to create a fetched results controller which is then
returned by the function. The cacheName is used for assigning the name of the cache
(Root−any name) that can be used by the NSFetchedResultsController objects.

```
- (void)didReceiveMemoryWarning {
    // Releases the view if it doesn't have a superview.
    [super didReceiveMemoryWarning];

    // Relinquish ownership any cached data, images, etc that aren't
      in use.
}
```

The `didReceiveMemoryWarning:` method is for handling the warning received by an Operating System when excessive memory is consumed by an application.

```
- (void)viewDidUnload {
    // Relinquish ownership of anything that can be recreated in
viewDidLoad
      or on demand.
    // For example: self.myOutlet = nil;
}
```

In the `viewDidUnload` method, the `fetchedResultsController` instance is set to nil to release the memory allocated to it.

```
- (void)dealloc {
    [fetchedResultsController_ release];
    [managedObjectContext_ release];
    [super dealloc];
}
```

The dealloc method releases the memory allocated to different instances.

```
@end
```

Key value coding (KVC)

The Core Data uses KVC to store and retrieve data from its managed objects. `NSManagedObject` supports the key value methods `valueForKey:` and `setValue:forKey:` for setting and retrieving attribute values from the managed object respectively.

Key value methods

The two key value methods that are widely used for setting and retrieving values of the attributes of the managed object are explained in the following sections.

The -valueForKey: method

The method `-valueForKey:` is a generic accessor to retrieve the specified attribute value from a managed object.

For example, let's say we have a managed object (`Customer`) and it has an attribute called `name`; we can obtain the value of the name attribute with the following:

```
NSString *custName = [managedObject valueForKey:@"name" ];
```

The value of the attribute `name` is retrieved from the managed object and is assigned to the NSString instance `custName`.

Similarly, the code used in the `cellForRowAtIndexPath` method in the `RootViewController.m` file is as follows:

```
cell.textLabel.text = [[managedObject valueForKey:@"name"]
description];
```

The `valueForKey:@"name"` retrieves the value of the attribute *name* of the managed object and assigns it to the table cell for display.

The -setValue:forKey: method

It dynamically sets the properties (attributes) on an object.

For example, to set the value of the name attribute of the managed object to the string `John`, we use following statement:

```
[managedObject setValue: @"John" forKey:@"name"];
```

The preceding statement will first search for the `setName:` method. If the method is not available, it will look for the `name` attribute and use it directly to set its value. If the name attribute is also not available, then the `setValue:forUndefinedKey:` method is called on the managed object.

That is, we can manipulate managed objects dynamically using KVC without writing their accessors or mutators.

  Using KVC, we can access all the properties of an `NSManagedObject` protocol.

Keypath

KVC also includes the concept of a keypath that helps in iterating through object hierarchies using a single string. For example, let's say there are two entities, `Customer` and `Product`, and their relationship is established from the Customer to Product entity by the name `products`. We want to access the attribute `prodname` of the `Product` entity from the `Customer` entity. We can do so by using a keypath as follows:

```
NSString *productname = [managedObject valueForKeyPath:@"products.
prodname"];
```

We can see that the value of the keypath is `@"products.prodname"`. When this value is parsed by KVC, it will be divided into two separate values, namely, `products` and `prodname`. The products relationship will return a managed object instance that represents the Customer's product, that is, product entity, and the second part of the `prodname` keypath will retrieve the value of the prodname attribute from the managed object that represents the product entity.

Implementing the methods of the NSFetchedResultsControllerDelegate protocol

The classes that are declared as delegate of the `NSFetchedResultsControllerDelegate` protocol have to implement its methods, as these methods take the necessary actions (like updating the table view) when some changes are applied to the managed object. Let us get an idea of all the four methods declared in the said protocol:

- controllerWillChangeContent
- controllerDidChangeContent
- controller:didChangeObject
- controller:didChangeSection

These four methods are defined in the protocol: `NSFetchedResultsControllerDelegate`. The fetched results controller monitors its managed object context and calls its delegates as changes are made to its context. These methods help in updating the table view or take other actions on the basis of modifications applied to the context.

The controllerWillChangeContent method

When the object managed by fetchedResultsController is modified, that is, if it is deleted, updated, or a new object is added to it, a notification is sent to its delegate (using the method `controllerWillChangeContent`) before it makes any changes. As the results are usually displayed via tableView, this delegate method is used to inform the table view that updates are supposed to occur soon. So, the usual code written in this delegate method is somewhat as follows:

```
- (void)controllerWillChangeContent:(NSFetchedResultsController *)
controller {
[self.tableView beginUpdates];
}
```

The controllerDidChangeContent method

When the changes made to the managed object context are over, the `fetchedResultsController` sends the notification to its delegate using this method. This delegate method is mostly used to inform the table view that the updates are over. So, the usual code written in this delegate method is somewhat as follows:

```
- (void)controllerDidChangeContent:(NSFetchedResultsController *)
controller {
  [self.tableView endUpdates];
}
```

The preceding statement informs the table view that the updates are now complete.

The controller:didChangeObject method

When some changes are made to an object (of managed object context), the fetched results controller sends a notification to its delegate using the method `controller:didChangeObject:`. This method is very important as, here, we update the table view to reflect the modifications (insertion, deletion, changing of contents, and so on) made to the objects (managed by the fetched results controller). The code of this method may appear as follows:

```
- (void)controller:(NSFetchedResultsController *)controller
didChangeObject:(id)anObject
  atIndexPath:(NSIndexPath *)indexPath
    forChangeType:(NSFetchedResultsChangeType)type
  newIndexPath:(NSIndexPath *)newIndexPath {

UITableView *tableView = self.tableView;
switch(type) {
  case NSFetchedResultsChangeInsert:
    [tableView insertRowsAtIndexPaths:[NSArray
      arrayWithObject:newIndexPath]
      withRowAnimation:UITableViewRowAnimationFade];
    break;

  case NSFetchedResultsChangeDelete:
    [tableView deleteRowsAtIndexPaths:[NSArray
      arrayWithObject:indexPath]
      withRowAnimation:UITableViewRowAnimationFade];
    break;

  case NSFetchedResultsChangeUpdate:
```

```
            [self configureCell:[tableView cellForRowAtIndexPath:indexPa
th]
               atIndexPath:indexPath];
         break;

         case NSFetchedResultsChangeMove:
           [tableView deleteRowsAtIndexPaths:[NSArray
             arrayWithObject:indexPath]
             withRowAnimation:UITableViewRowAnimationFade];
           [tableView insertRowsAtIndexPaths:[NSArray
             arrayWithObject:newIndexPath]withRowAnimation:
             UITableViewRowAnimationFade];
         break;
    }
}
```

The controller:didChangeSection method

When we modify the object so that it results in a change in the number of sections in the table, the fetchedResultsController sends the notification to its delegate using the method controller:didChangeSection.

In this method, the code for handling the addition and deletion of sections in the table view is written, which may appear as shown in the following piece of code:

```
- (void)controller:(NSFetchedResultsController *)controller
didChangeSection:(id <NSFetchedResultsSectionInfo>)sectionInfo
  atIndex:(NSUInteger)sectionIndex
    forChangeType:(NSFetchedResultsChangeType)type {

    switch(type) {
      case NSFetchedResultsChangeInsert:
        [self.tableView insertSections:[NSIndexSet
        indexSetWithIndex:sectionIndex]
        withRowAnimation:UITableViewRowAnimationFade];
      break;

      case NSFetchedResultsChangeDelete:
        [self.tableView deleteSections:[NSIndexSet
        indexSetWithIndex:sectionIndex]
        withRowAnimation:UITableViewRowAnimationFade];
      break;
    }
}
```

We have implemented only one delegate method, `controller:didChangeObject`, in the implementation file of the `RootViewController` class. `RootViewController.m` does the job of updating the table view contents.

A standard implementation of the delegate method that updates the table view is as follows:

```
- (void)controller:(NSFetchedResultsController*)controller
didChangeObject:(id)anObject atIndexPath:(NSIndexPath*)indexPath
forChangeType:(NSFetchedResultsChangeType)type
newIndexPath:(NSIndexPath*)newIndexPath
{

UITableView *tableView = self.tableView;

NSIndexSet *section = [NSIndexSet indexSetWithIndex:[newIndexPath
section]];

switch (type) {
case NSFetchedResultsChangeInsert:
[tableView insertRowsAtIndexPaths:[NSArray
arrayWithObject:newIndexPath]
withRowAnimation:UITableViewRowAnimationFade];
break;
case NSFetchedResultsChangeDelete:
[tableView deleteRowsAtIndexPaths:[NSArray
arrayWithObject:newIndexPath]
withRowAnimation:UITableViewRowAnimationFade];
break;
case NSFetchedResultsChangeMove:
[tableView deleteRowsAtIndexPaths:[NSArray
arrayWithObject:newIndexPath]
withRowAnimation:UITableViewRowAnimationFade];
[tableView reloadSections:section
withRowAnimation:UITableViewRowAnimationFade];
break;
case NSFetchedResultsChangeUpdate:
[self modifyCell:[tableView cellForRowAtIndexPath:indexPath]
objectAtIndexPath:indexPath]];
break;
}
}
```

When any change occurs to an object, the "type" of change is received and accordingly actions are taken. The type is an argument that receives the value that designates the kind of changes made to the managed object. Like, when a row is inserted, we receive the type NSFetchedResultsChangeInsert, and as a consequence, we insert a new row into the table. Similarly, if a row is deleted, we receive the type NSFetchedResultsChangeDelete and we delete the specified row in the table. When a row of the table is moved, we receive the type NSFetchedResultsChangeMove and we delete the row from the old location and insert it at the location specified by newIndexPath.

When the contents of the row are updated, we invoke our custom method modifyCell and pass the table view cell to it for performing updation.

Running the project

Now, we are ready to run the project. Let us select the Build and Go icon from the **Xcode Project** window. Initially, we get a blank table view (the following *image (a)*) with **Edit** and **+** (plus) button on the left and right side of the navigation bar respectively. On selecting the **+** button, the View of the AddNameController class will appear, which prompts the user to enter the name of the customer, as shown in the following given *image (b)*. We can also see the two Bar Button Item Controls with titles **Cancel** and **Save** respectively in the navigation bar of the View of the AddNameController class. On selecting the **Save** button, after entering a name in Text Field control, the name will be stored in the persistent store and the table view will be refreshed (reloaded) to display the new name added, as shown in the following given *image (c)*:

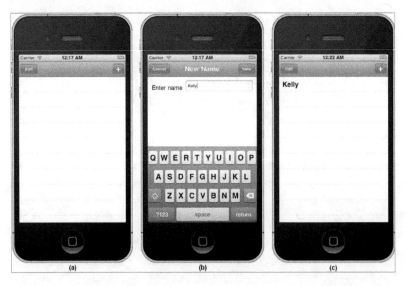

After entering a few names, our table view may appear, as shown in the following *image (a)*. We can delete any name by selecting the corresponding **Edit** icon of the table cell. A **Delete** button appears on selecting the **Edit** icon of a table cell, as shown in the following *image (b)*. The name will be deleted from the table view on selecting the **Delete** button and the table view is refreshed to show the modification applied, as shown in the following *image (c)*:

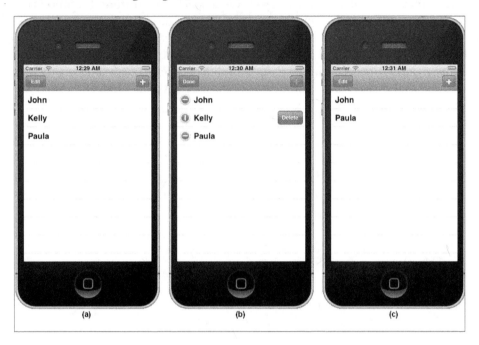

In the preceding application, we have made use of a single managed object context. In the next chapter, we will modify the preceding application to have multiple managed object context.

In the preceding module, we used a single instance of the Managed Object Context by the name `managedObjectContext` and all the modifications (insert, delete, and so on) were implemented on the same instance. In the next chapter, we will see what changes we have to do in the module if we plan to maintain more than one instance of Managed Object Context.

Summary

In this chapter, we first saw the meaning of the code that is automatically generated for us by Core Data in the Application Delegate files. Then, we saw the step-by-step procedure of saving, listing, and deleting customer names. We have also learnt about the concept of KVC and its methods used in setting and retrieving attribute values from the managed object. We also saw the different methods of the NSFetchedResultsControllerDelegate protocol. In the next chapter, we will see how to implement the concept of multiple managed object contexts to our application and also how to merge the information in different managed object contexts. We will also learn how to apply the knowledge gained in this chapter to maintain a customer's information, that is, we will see step-by-step how to save, display, and delete the customer's information.

6

Creating, Listing, Displaying, and Deleting Records of Customers

In the previous chapter, we understood the meaning of the code that is automatically generated for us by Core Data in the Application Delegate files. We also developed the application that saves, lists, and deletes customer names. In this chapter, we will enhance the same application to save, list, display, and delete the information of a customer. But before we do so, we will learn to implement the concept of multiple managed object contexts to our application and also how to merge the information in different managed object contexts. We will also learn to apply the knowledge gained so far such as the concept of KVC, its methods used in setting and retrieving attribute values from the managed object, different methods of the NSFetchedResultsControllerDelegate protocol, and so on, to our application.

Understanding multiple managed object context

In **multiple managed object context** concept, we make several instances of managed object context and each instance works independently without having knowledge of what modifications are implemented in other instances. In order to keep all instances informed of different modifications performed in each context, a notification is broadcasted by a managed object context when any save or delete operation is performed on it. Like, if a managed object context completes a save operation, it broadcasts an NSNotification with the NSManagedObjectContextDidSaveNotification key.

The benefit of this notification is that any managed object context that listens to the notification NSManagedObjectContextDidSaveNotification can update its contents by invoking the method mergeChangesFromContextDidSaveNotification:. This method updates the contents of managed object context (with the managed object context that broadcasted the notification) and will also notify any *observers* of those changes.

> The notification that is broadcasted when a delete operation is performed on a managed object is: NSManagedObjectContextObjectsDidChangeNotification notification.

So, broadcasting notification is a technique to synchronize different managed objects. Every view maintains an observer to a specific key. When a notification with that key is broadcasted, the view invokes a method to handle the notification.

NSNotification

NSNotification is an object that is broadcasted by an NSNotificationCenter object to other objects. The NSNotification object, also known as *notification*, is received by the observers of that notification. The notification consists of a *name* and an *object* where name is a tag that identifies the notification and the object is the object that posted the notification.

> The methods of NSNotificationCenter that are used for posting the notification are postNotificationName:object and postNotificationName:object:userInfo.

Applying the concept of multiple managed object context in our application

To apply the concept of multiple managed object context in our application, we will create a separate instance of managed object context with the name `custcontext` and associate it with the View of the `AddNameController` class. That is, the name of the customer added by the user in the View of `AddNameController` class will be stored in this separate context (`custcontext`) and not in the application's main context: `managedObjectContext`. When the **Save** button is selected (in the View of `AddNameController` class), a NSNotification with the `NSManagedObjectContextDidSaveNotification` key will be broadcasted that invokes a method, which consequently invokes the `mergeChangesFromContextDidSaveNotification` on the main managed object of the application: `managedObjectContext`, so that it incorporates all the changes (new customer names added) to the managed object context: `custcontext`.

To implement the multiple managed object context, coding of all the files (`probAppDelegate.h`, `probAppDelegate.m`, `AddNameController.h`, and `AddNameController.m`) will be the same except for the header and implementation files of the `RootViewController` class. The header file of the `RootViewController` class may be modified to appear, as shown in the following code listing. The statements in bold are the new statements that are added, while the rest of the code is the same as we saw in the *Declaring delegate and implementing methods for storing the name of the customers* section of *Chapter 5, Creating, Listing, and Deleting Names of Customers*:

```
//  RootViewController.h
//  prob

#import <UIKit/UIKit.h>
#import <CoreData/CoreData.h>
#import "AddNameController.h"

@interface RootViewController : UITableViewController
<NSFetchedResultsControllerDelegate, AddNameControllerDelegate> {

@private
  NSFetchedResultsController *fetchedResultsController_;
  NSManagedObjectContext *managedObjectContext_;
  NSManagedObjectContext *custcontext;
}

@property (nonatomic, retain) NSManagedObjectContext
*managedObjectContext;
```

```
@property (nonatomic, retain) NSFetchedResultsController
*fetchedResultsController;
@property (nonatomic, retain) NSManagedObjectContext *custcontext;

@end
```

We can see in the preceding code that an instance: custcontext of managed object context is added to the header file of the RootViewController class file.

The implementation file of RootViewController will also be modified. The following code listing is just a snippet from the RootViewController.m file and the complete listing can be found in the code bundle for this chapter from the packtpub site.

```
//   RootViewController.m
//   prob

(...)
@synthesize fetchedResultsController=fetchedResultsController_, manage
dObjectContext=managedObjectContext_,  custcontext;
    (...)
- (IBAction)addCustomer
{
   AddNameController *addnameController=[[AddNameController alloc] init
WithNibName:@"AddNameController" bundle:nil];
   addnameController.delegate=self;

   self.custcontext=[[NSManagedObjectContext alloc] init];
   [custcontext setPersistentStoreCoordinator:[[fetchedResultsControll
er_ managedObjectContext] persistentStoreCoordinator]];
   addnameController.cust= (Customer *) [NSEntityDescription insertNewO
bjectForEntityForName:@"Customer" inManagedObjectContext:custcontext];

   UINavigationController *navController=[[UINavigationController
alloc] initWithRootViewController:addnameController];
   [self.navigationController  presentModalViewController:navController
animated:YES];
   [addnameController release];
   [navController release];
}

- (void) addnameController:(AddNameController *)controller
   selectedsave:(BOOL) save {
     if(save)
     {
```

```
        NSNotificationCenter *noticenter =[NSNotificationCenter
defaultCenter];
        [noticenter addObserver:self selector:@selector(newnamecontextD
idSave:)
        name:NSManagedObjectContextDidSaveNotification
object:custcontext];
        NSError *error;
        if(![custcontext save:&error])
        {
          NSLog(@"Unresolved error %@, %@", error, [error userInfo]);
          abort();
        }
        [noticenter removeObserver:self name:NSManagedObjectContextDidSa
veNotification object:custcontext];
    }
    self.custcontext=nil;

    [self dismissModalViewControllerAnimated:YES];
    }


-(void) newnamecontextDidSave:(NSNotification *)savenotice{
NSManagedObjectContext *context=[fetchedResultsController_
managedObjectContext];
   [context mergeChangesFromContextDidSaveNotification:savenotice];
}
(...)

  - (void)dealloc {
  [fetchedResultsController_ release];
  [managedObjectContext_ release];
  [custcontext release];
  [super dealloc];
}
@end
```

The idea is that we want to keep the new name of Customer to be associated with the AddNameController's managed object context: custcontext. Hence, the application's main managed object context: managedObjectContext will have no idea of the new name added until we merge the modifications.

In the `addCustomer` method, we can see that a new managed object context is created by the name: `custcontext`. Then, we set the persistent store coordinator of the new managed object context, `custcontext`, to be the same as of the `fetchedResultsController`'s context. We also assign a valid `NSEntityDescription` to the `cust` object of the `AddNameController` class and this *cust* object (of the `Customer` entity class) is inserted in the managed object context: `custcontext` (the context made of the `AddNewNameController` class).

On selection of the **Save** button in the View of the `AddNameController` class, as shown in the following *image (b)*, the preceding implemented delegate method (`addnameController`) will be invoked, which will broadcast an NSNotification with the `NSManagedObjectContextDidSaveNotification` key. We have added an observer to the View that listens for notifications and invokes the method: `newnamecontextDidSave` (any name) and the `NSManagedObjectContextDidSaveNotification` notification is passed to it that is consequently assigned to its `savenotice` parameter.

Recall from the last chapter that the `RootViewController` class initially displays a blank table view (*image (a)*) and after adding a name, the table view displays the new name added (*image (c)*).

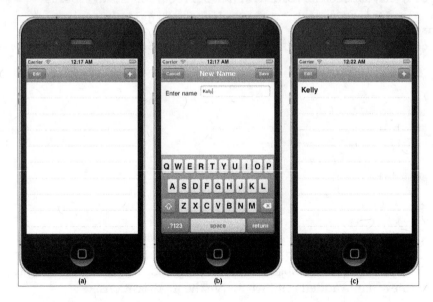

(a)   (b)   (c)

In the `newnamecontextDidSave` method, we invoke the `mergeChangesFromContextDidSaveNotification` on the main managed object of the application: `managedObjectContext`, so that it incorporates all the changes that have been applied (new customer names added) in the managed object context: `custcontext`.

As working on single instances will help us towards working on multiple instances, we will continue to use single instances of managed object context in the examples that we will create.

Enhancing our application to save, list, display, and delete customer information

As we have seen and understood the concept of saving and deleting a single attribute, that is, customer's *name*, it will now be easier for us to learn and understand the concepts of saving, displaying, and deleting complete information of the customer that comprises of three attributes: name, emailid, and contactno.

Steps involved in this application are as follows:

1. Adding the ViewController class: AddCustomerController class.

2. Defining View for entering customer's information and connecting controls.

3. Coding in implementation file: AddCustomerController.m for accepting customer's information and invoking delegate methods.

4. Adding View Controller class: DisplayCustomerController for displaying customer's information.

5. Defining View and writing code in implementation file: DisplayCustomerController.m for displaying customer's information.

6. Implementing methods in the RootViewController class for storing customer's information.

The following sections will explain in detail how each of these steps are carried out. Let's begin with the task of enhancing our application with the first step, that is, by adding a ViewController class.

Adding the ViewController class

To enter information of the customer, we need to add a View Controller class that will display a navigation bar with two navigation bar items: *Save* and *Cancel*. This View Controller class will also display a View that prompts the user to enter the customer's *name, e-mail ID*, and *contact number*. The information of the customer will be then stored in the customersinfo.sqlite file. So, let us add a subclass of UIViewController to our application.

Before adding a new View Controller class, perform the following steps:

1. First delete the files `AddNameController.h`, `AddNameController.m`, and `AddNameController.xib` that we created in the earlier module (they were just for understanding the concept).

2. Right-click on the **Classes** group in the **Xcode Project** window, select the **Add | New File** option.

3. Select **Cocoa Touch Class** from under the **iPhone OS** heading in the left pane and select the **UIViewController subclass** as the template of the new file to choose from.

4. Select the checkbox **With XIB for user interface** (XIB file will be used for creating View for the View Controller that prompts user to enter name, e-mail ID, and contact number) followed by the **Next** button. We get a dialog box to specify the name of the View Controller.

5. Assign the name as: `AddCustomerController.m` and select the checkbox **Also create AddCustomerController.h** followed by the **Finish** button. Both the files: `AddCustomerController.h` and `AddCustomerController.m` will be created along with the `.xib` file and added to our project. The files will be placed at the default location: **Classes** group of our *Xcode Project window*.

6. Select the `AddCustomerViewController.xib` file in the **Classes** group and drag it to the **Resources** group, where the Interface Builder files are usually stored by default.

7. We can now define delegate, outlets, and action methods in the View Controller's header file. In the header file of the new View Controller class: `AddCustomerController.h`, we define the following:

   ° A delegate protocol with name: `AddCustomerControllerDelegate`.

   ° An instance variable with name: `delegate` (any name) of type: `id <AddCustomerControllerDelegate>`.

   ° The instance variable has property with the two attributes: *retain* and *nonatomic* for generating the accessor and mutators.

   ° The method of the `AddCustomerControllerDelegate` (between the @ `protocol` and @end directives).

   ° The method: `addcustomerController` that is, the class which will conform to this protocol will have to implement this method.

We write the following code in the header file of the newly added View controller class, `AddCustomerController.h`, as shown in the following code listing:

```
//  AddCustomerController.h
//  prob

#import <UIKit/UIKit.h>
#import "Customer.h"

@protocol AddCustomerControllerDelegate;

@interface AddCustomerController : UIViewController {
  Customer *cust;
  id <AddCustomerControllerDelegate> delegate;
  IBOutlet UIBarButtonItem *cancelbutton;
  IBOutlet UIBarButtonItem *savebutton;
  IBOutlet UITextField *newname;
  IBOutlet UITextField *newemailid;
  IBOutlet UITextField *newcontactno;
}

@property(nonatomic, retain) Customer *cust;
@property(nonatomic, retain) id <AddCustomerControllerDelegate>
delegate;
@property(nonatomic, retain) IBOutlet UIBarButtonItem *cancelbutton;
@property(nonatomic, retain) IBOutlet UIBarButtonItem *savebutton;
@property(nonatomic, retain) UITextField *newname;
@property(nonatomic, retain) UITextField *newemailid;
@property(nonatomic, retain) UITextField *newcontactno;

-(IBAction) cancel:(id) sender;
-(IBAction) save:(id)sender;

@end

@protocol AddCustomerControllerDelegate
-(void) addcustomerController:(AddCustomerController *)controller
  selectedsave:(BOOL) save;
@end
```

We define an object of the Customer class with the name: cust, which will store the customer's information temporarily before being stored in the persistent store. Also, three instance variables: newname, newemailid, and newcontactno of UITextField class are defined and marked as outlets (these outlets will be connected to the three *Text Field* controls that we will be dropping in the View for entering the name, e-mail ID, and contact number of the customer). Two instance variables of UIBarButtonItem class: cancelbutton and savebutton are defined and marked as outlets. These two outlets will be connected to the two Bar Button Items (that we will soon drag-and-drop onto the View) with the title: Save and Cancel (they will invoke the respective action methods to save or discard the customer's information). We can also see that the preceding file includes two action methods: cancel and save that will be connected to the two respective Bar Button Items: *Cancel* and *Save*. We can also see that the five instance variables (cancelbutton, savebutton, newname, newemailid, and newcontactno) along with the object cust (of *Customer* entity) are defined as properties with the two attributes: *retain* and *nonatomic* for generating their accessor and mutators. After adding the preceding code, we save the header file.

> The cust object of the Customer class will be used to handle the name, email address, and contact number entered by the user in the Text Field control in the View of the AddCustomerController class.

Defining a View for entering the customer's information and connecting controls

We have to design a View of the AddCustomerController class that displays three Text Field controls for the user to enter the name, e-mail ID, and contact number. Also, we have to add two Bar Button Item controls that invoke the action methods cancel and save to discard or to save the information entered (in Text Field controls) into the persistent store. Perform the following steps to design the view:

1. Open the AddCustomerController.xib file in Interface Builder and drag two Bar Button Item controls from the **Windows, Views & Bars** category of the **Library** window and drop them in the **Documents** window.

2. Select the two bar Button Item controls one after the other in the **Documents** window and with the help of **Attributes Inspector** set their **Title** to **Save** and **Cancel** respectively. Also drag-and-drop three **Label** and three **Text Field** controls on the View.

3. Double-click each **Label** control one by one and edit their text to **Name**, **Email Id**, and **Contact No** respectively, as shown in the following screenshot:

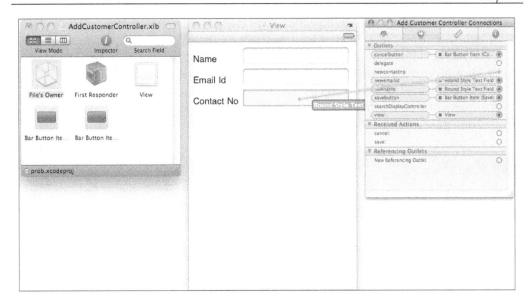

To connect the outlets: `newname`, `newemailid`, and `newcontactno` (instances of `UITextField` defined in header file) with the **Text Field** controls dropped in the View, perform the following steps:

1. Select the **File's Owner** icon in the **Documents** window and open the **Connections Inspector** window. The outlets and action methods that we defined in the header file will be visible in the **Connections Inspector** window under the headings: **Outlets** and **Received Actions**.

2. Select the circle to the right of each outlet one by one and keeping the mouse button pressed drag it to the respective Text Field control in the View.

Similarly, to connect the outlets of the Bar Button Items defined in the header file: `cancelbutton` and `savebutton` with the Bar Button Item controls dropped in the **Documents** window, select the circle to the right of the outlet: **savebutton** and drag it to the Bar Button Item control in the **Documents** window. Repeat the procedure to connect the **cancelbutton** outlet with the second Bar Button Item control.

To connect the `save` and `cancel` action methods (so that the action methods are invoked when the user selects the Bar Button Item control in the View) with the Bar Button Item controls, perform the following steps:

1. Select one **Bar Button Item** control (say with the title: **Save**) in the **Documents** window and open the **Connections Inspector** window.

2. In the **Connections Inspector** window, select the circle to the right of the selector (under the **Sent Actions** heading) and keeping the mouse button pressed, drag it to the **File's Owner** icon in the **Documents** window.

3. Two action methods will pop up, and we select the one that we want to connect to this Bar Button Item control. As the selected Bar Button Item control is the one with title **save**, we select the action method: **save** to connect it with the Bar Button Item control, as shown in the following screenshot. This means that when the user selects this Bar Button Item control in the View, the code (that we are going to write in the implementation file of the delegate class) in the save method will be executed.

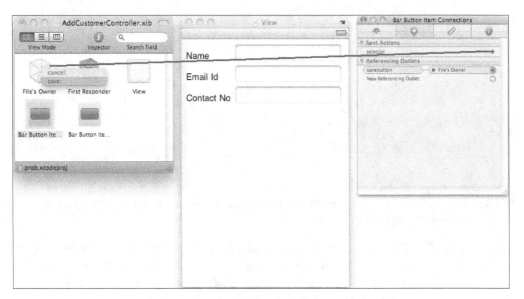

Repeat the procedure to connect the action method: **cancel** to the second Bar Button Item control.

Coding in the implementation file for accepting the customer's information and invoking delegate methods

We need to write the code in the implementation file of the View Controller class `AddCustomerController.m` to invoke the delegate methods for storing the customer's information when the respective Bar Button Item control is selected and we also write the code to place the Bar Button items on the left and right side of the navigation bar. The code that we write in the implementation file is as shown in the following code listing:

```
// AddCustomerController.m
// prob
#import "AddCustomerController.h"

@implementation AddCustomerController

@synthesize savebutton;
@synthesize cancelbutton;
@synthesize delegate;
@synthesize newname;
@synthesize newemailid;
@synthesize newcontactno;
@synthesize cust;

-(IBAction) cancel:(id) sender
{
  [delegate addcustomerController: self selectedsave:NO];
}

-(IBAction) save:(id)sender{
  cust.name=newname.text;
  cust.emailid=newemailid.text;
  cust.contactno=newcontactno.text;
  [delegate addcustomerController: self selectedsave:YES ];
}

// Implement viewDidLoad to do additional setup after loading the
view, typically from a nib.
- (void)viewDidLoad {
    [super viewDidLoad];
  self.title=@"New Customer";
  self.navigationItem.rightBarButtonItem=savebutton;
  self.navigationItem.leftBarButtonItem=cancelbutton;
}

- (void)dealloc {
  [savebutton release];
  [cancelbutton release];
  [newname release];
  [newemailid release];
  [newcontactno release];
  [cust release];
  [super dealloc];
}

@end
```

First of all, we synthesize the IBOutlets (savebutton, cancelbutton, delegate, newname, newemailid, newcontactno, and cust) for generating the accessor and mutator methods for them. In the action method: cancel, we write the code to invoke the addcustomerController method of the delegate class and set the value of the parameter selectedsave to NO. Similarly, in the action method: save, we invoke the addcustomerController method of the delegate and set the value of the parameter: selectedsave to YES. The value of the selectedsave parameter will decide whether to persist the information of the customer or not. In the save action method, we assign the information entered by the user in the three Text Fields to the name, emailid, and contactno attributes of the cust object (of Customer class).

In the viewDidLoad method, we set the Navigation Item's title to New Customer and its right Bar Button Item is set to savebutton—an instance variable of Bar Button Item with title: Save. Also, the left Bar Button Item of the navigation bar is set to cancelbutton—the instance variable of Bar Button Item with the title: Cancel. Finally, through the dealloc method, we release the memory reserved by different Outlets.

Adding the View Controller class for displaying the customer's information

To display information of the customer, we need to add one more View Controller class to our application. We will follow the given steps to do so:

1. Right-click on the **Classes** group in the **Xcode Project** window then select the **Add | New File** option.

2. Select **Cocoa Touch Class** from under the **iPhone OS** heading in the left pane and select the **UIViewController subclass** as the template of the new file to choose from. Also select the checkbox **With XIB for user interface** followed by the **Next** button. We get a dialog box to specify the name of the View Controller.

3. Assign the name as: DisplayCustomerController.m and select the checkbox **Also create AddCustomerController.h** followed by the **Finish** button.

Our application now has three View Controller classes: RootViewController, AddCustomerController, and DisplayCustomerController. We will define outlets in the View Controller's header file: DisplayCustomerController.h. The code that we will write in the header file is as shown in the following code listing:

```
// DisplayCustomerController.h
//   prob

#import <UIKit/UIKit.h>
```

```
#import "Customer.h"

@interface DisplayCustomerController : UIViewController {
    Customer *cust;
    IBOutlet UITextField *name;
    IBOutlet UITextField *emailid;
    IBOutlet UITextField *contactno;
}
@property(nonatomic, retain) Customer *cust;
@property(nonatomic, retain) UITextField *name;
@property(nonatomic, retain) UITextField *emailid;
@property(nonatomic, retain) UITextField *contactno;

@end
```

We define an object of Customer class by name: `cust` that will be used to temporarily store the customer's information retrieved from the `FetchedResultsController` and then display that information through Text Field controls placed in the View. Also, three instance variables: `name`, `emailid`, and `contactno` of `UITextField` class are defined and marked as outlets (these outlets will be connected to the three Text Field controls that we will be dropping in the View for displaying name, e-mail ID, and contact number of the customer). The three instance variables: `name`, `emailid`, and `contactno` along with the object `cust` (of `Customer` entity) are defined as properties with the two attributes: *retain* and *nonatomic* for generating their accessor and mutators. After adding the preceding code, we save the header file.

Defining the View and writing the code in the implementation file for displaying the customer's information

Let us design a View of the `DisplayCustomerController` class that displays three Text Field controls for displaying the name, e-mail ID, and contact number of the customer. The steps for designing the View are as follows:

1. Open the `DisplayCustomerController.xib` file in the Interface Builder and drag-and-drop three **Label** and three **Text Field** controls onto the View.

2. Double-click each **Label** control one by one and edit their text to **Name**, **Email Id**, and **Contact No** respectively.

3. To connect the outlets: **name**, **emailid**, and **contactno**, select the **File's Owner** icon in the **Documents** window and open the **Connections Inspector** window.

4. Under the heading: **Outlets**, select the circle to the right of each outlet one by one and keeping the mouse button pressed, drag it to the respective Text Field control in the View. The following screenshot demonstrates how the **contactno** outlet is connected to the **Text Field** control:

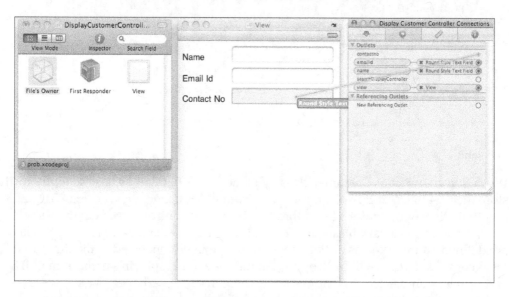

Now, we need to write code in DisplayCustomerController's implementation file: DisplayCustomer.m to display the customer's information in the Text Field controls of the View. We will write the code in the implementation file, as shown in the following code listing:

```
// DisplayCustomerController.m
//   prob

#import "DisplayCustomerController.h"

@implementation DisplayCustomerController
@synthesize name;
@synthesize emailid;
@synthesize contactno;
@synthesize cust;

// Implement viewDidLoad to do additional setup after loading the
view, typically from a nib.
- (void)viewDidLoad {
  [super viewDidLoad];
  self.title=@"Customer Information";
  name.text=cust.name;
```

```
    emailid.text=cust.emailid;
    contactno.text=cust.contactno;
    name.enabled=NO;
    emailid.enabled=NO;
    contactno.enabled=NO;
}

-  (void)dealloc {
    [name release];
    [emailid release];
    [contactno release];
    [cust release];
    [super dealloc];
}

@end
```

The IBOutlets (name, emailid, contactno, and cust) are synthesized for generating the accessor and mutator methods for them. In the viewDidLoad method, we set the Navigation Item's title to Customer Information, and assign the values in the name, emailid, and contactno attribute of the cust object to the three text Field controls placed in the View via their outlets. The cust object will be loaded with the customer's information (from the FetchedResultsController — we will write code for it in the implementation file of Root View Controller class, that is, RootViewController.m) selected by the user from the table view. We also set the *enabled* property of the three Text Field controls (via their outlets) to NO, so that a user can only view information and not edit them. The dealloc method releases the memory reserved by different Outlets.

Implementing the methods in the RootViewController class for storing the customer's information

We set the `RootViewController` class as a delegate of the `AddCustomerController` class as well of the `FetchedResultsController` class and so we need to implement the methods of both the classes. The header file of the `RootViewController` file may be modified to appear as shown in the following code listing. The code in bold is the modified code, and the rest of the code is the same as we saw in the *Declaring delegate and implementing methods for storing the name of the customers* section of *Chapter 5, Creating, Listing, and Deleting Names of Customers*:

```
// RootViewController.h
//  prob

#import <UIKit/UIKit.h>
#import <CoreData/CoreData.h>
#import "AddCustomerController.h"
#import "DisplayCustomerController.h"

@interface RootViewController : UITableViewController
<NSFetchedResultsControllerDelegate, AddCustomerControllerDelegate> {
@private
    NSFetchedResultsController *fetchedResultsController_;
    NSManagedObjectContext *managedObjectContext_;
}

@property (nonatomic, retain) NSFetchedResultsController
*fetchedResultsController;
@property (nonatomic, retain) NSManagedObjectContext
*managedObjectContext;

@end
```

The header file of the `RootViewController` class declares instance variables of `NSFetchedResultsController` and `NSManagedObjectModel` with the names: `fetchedResultsController` and `managedObjectContext`, respectively. Also, both the instance variables are defined as properties with the two attributes: *retain* and *nonatomic* for generating the accessors and mutators without any overhead code (when synthesized) and for keeping the objects retained to the mutators without being flushed from memory. Also, an action method is declared by name `addCustomer` that will be used to invoke the View of the `AddCustomerController` class (that prompts the user to enter name, e-mail ID, and contact number of the customer to be added).

The implementation file of `RootViewController` class may be modified to appear, as shown in the following code listing. Only the modified code has been listed next and the complete listing can be found in the code bundle for this chapter from the packtpub site:

```objc
// RootViewController.m
// prob
(....)
- (void)viewDidLoad {
  [super viewDidLoad];
  self.title=@"Customers List";
  // Set up the edit and add buttons.
  self.navigationItem.leftBarButtonItem = self.editButtonItem;
  UIBarButtonItem *addButton = [[UIBarButtonItem alloc] initWithB
arButtonSystemItem:UIBarButtonSystemItemAdd target:self action:@
selector(addCustomer)];
  self.navigationItem.rightBarButtonItem = addButton;
  [addButton release];
}
(....)


// Customize the appearance of table view cells.
- (UITableViewCell *)tableView:(UITableView *)tableView cellForRowAtIn
dexPath:(NSIndexPath *)indexPath {

  static NSString *CellIdentifier = @"Cell";

  UITableViewCell *cell = [tableView dequeueReusableCellWithIdentifier
:CellIdentifier];
  if (cell == nil) {
    cell = [[[UITableViewCell alloc] initWithStyle:UITableViewCellStyl
eDefault reuseIdentifier:CellIdentifier] autorelease];
    cell.accessoryType=UITableViewCellAccessoryDisclosureIndicator;
  }


(....)


- (IBAction)addCustomer
{
  AddCustomerController *addcustomerController=[[AddCustomerController
alloc] initWithNibName:@"AddCustomerController" bundle:nil];
  addcustomerController.delegate=self;
  addcustomerController.cust=(Customer *)[NSEntityDescription insertN
ewObjectForEntityForName:@"Customer" inManagedObjectContext:managedOb
jectContext_];
```

```
    UINavigationController *navController=[[UINavigationController
alloc] initWithRootViewController:addcustomerController];
    [self.navigationController   presentModalViewController:navController
animated:YES];
    [addcustomerController release];
    [navController release];

}


-(void) addcustomerController:(AddCustomerController *)controller
    selectedsave:(BOOL) save {
    if(!save)
    {
        [managedObjectContext_ deleteObject:controller.cust];
    }
    NSError *error;

    if(![managedObjectContext_ save:&error]){
        NSLog(@"Unresolved error %@ %@", error, [error userInfo]);
        exit(-1);
    }
    [self dismissModalViewControllerAnimated:YES];
}


- (void)tableView:(UITableView *)tableView didSelectRowAtIndexPath:(NS
IndexPath *)indexPath {

    DisplayCustomerController *displaycust =[[DisplayCustomerController
alloc] initWithNibName:@"DisplayCustomerController" bundle:nil];
    Customer *selectedcust=(Customer *) [fetchedResultsController_
objectAtIndexPath:indexPath];
    displaycust.cust=selectedcust;

    [self.navigationController pushViewController:displaycust
animated:YES];
    [displaycust release];
}

(....)

@end
```

The following sections provide explanations for the methods that are used in the preceding code.

viewDidLoad method

The `viewDidLoad` method sets the two Bar Button Item buttons to appear on the left and right side of the navigation bar respectively. The button displayed on left side is the *Edit* button and the one on the right side is the *Add* button. The *Edit* button will enable us to delete information of any customer and the *Add* button will take us to the View of the `AddCustomerClass` to enter information of the new customer. The *title* of the navigation item is set to display `Customers List`. After the creation and initialization of the left and right side bar button items of the navigation bar, the `performFetch:` message is invoked on an object returned by the `fetchedResultsController` method to display the result retrieved in the `fetchedResultsController` (that is, existing customer's list). Recall that the `fetchedResultsController` contains the entities specified by the fetch request, arranged on the attribute specified by the sort descriptor.

cell AtIndexPath method

As we want to display only the names of the customers in the table view, in the `cell AtIndexPath` method, we retrieve the *managed object* from the `fetchedResultsController` instance. The `NSFetchedResultsController` stores the set of entities from an `NSManagedObjectContext` (retrieved on the basis of `FetchRequest`). Then the value stored in the *name* attribute of the *managed object* is assigned to the table cell for display.

didSelectRowAtIndexPath method

The `didSelectRowAtIndexPath` method is for displaying the detailed information of the selected customer name from the table view. An instance of the `DisplayCustomerController` by the name: `displaycust` is initialized. The *managed object context* is retrieved from the `fetchedResultsController` (it is the object that is returned by calling the `objectAtIndexPath` on the *fetched results controller* and passing in the `indexPath` parameter to it) and is assigned to an instance: `selectedcust` of the `Customer` class. That is, the information of the customer whose name is selected from the table view is assigned to the `selectedcust` instance. The contents of the `selectedcust` are assigned to the `cust` object of `displaycust` (instance of the `DisplayCustomerController` class) as we want the information of the customer to be displayed via Text Field controls placed in the View of the `DisplayCustomerController` class. The view controller instance: `displaycust` is then pushed on the navigation stack (above the root view controller) causing the view of the `DisplayCustomerController` to be displayed and updates the navigation controls to reflect the changes. The `animated` attribute is set to `Yes` to display the view (associated with the `DisplayCustomerController)` with animation effect, that is, the view slides in from the left.

addCustomer method

The `addCustomer` method is invoked when the user selects the **plus** (**+**) button in the navigation bar. This method displays a View that prompts the user to enter the name, email id, and contact number of the customer. On selecting the **Save** button (after entering the name of the customer), a new managed object is created and inserted. We can see in the code that we create and initialize an instance of the `AddCustomerController` class by the name: `addcustomerController`. Also, we set the current View Controller file: `RootViewController.m` as the delegate of the `addcustomerController` instance. That is, this class will implement the delegate methods of the `AddCustomerController` class. Then we insert a new managed object into the managed context using the class method on `NSEntityDescription`. Also, we return the instance of class that represents the entity (`Customer`) and assign it to the `cust` object of `addcustomerController` (instance of `AddCustomerController` class)

To display a navigation bar in the View of `AddCustomerController`, we create and initialize an instance of the `UINavigationController` class by the name: `navController` and set its Root View controller to be the view of the `AddCustomerController` class. Then we display the View of the `AddCustomercontroller` modally using the `presentModalViewController:anima ted:` method, the view controller animates the appearance of the View and creates a parent-child relationship between the current View controller and the modal view controller.

addcustomerController method

The `addcustomerController` method is the implementation method for the delegate of the `AddCustomerController` class and is invoked by the `cancel` and `save` methods (defined in the implementation file of the `AddCustomerController` class). The `cancel` method calls the previous method and passes the `selectedsave` parameter set to value `NO` and the `save` method calls the method with the `selectedsave` parameter set to value `YES`. The value of the `selectedsave` parameter is assigned to the variable: `save`.

In this method, we check the value of the variable `save`. If the value of the `save` variable is `NO`, we delete the object (the `cust` object of the `Customer` entity class that we inserted in the preceding method) from the managed object context and save the context in the persistent store.

Finally, we dismiss the modal view of the `AddCustomerController` class and the View of the `RootViewController` appears to display the updated table view.

The delegate method: `controller:didChangeObject` of the `fetchedResultsController` class is implemented, which does the job of updating the table view contents.

Viewing the project

Now, we are ready to run the project. Let us select the *Build and Go* icon from the *Xcode Project window*. Initially, we get a blank table view (*image (a)*) with the **Edit** and **+ (plus)** buttons on the left and right side of the navigation bar, respectively. On selecting the **+** button, the View of the `AddCustomerController` class will appear that prompts the user to enter the name, email id, and contact number of the customer, as shown in the following *image (b)*. We can also see the two bar Button Item Controls with titles **Cancel** and **Save** respectively on the View of the `AddCustomerController` class. On selecting the **Save** button after entering the customer's information, the information will be stored in the persistent store and the table view will be refreshed (reloaded) to display the name of the new customer added, as shown in the following *image (c)*:

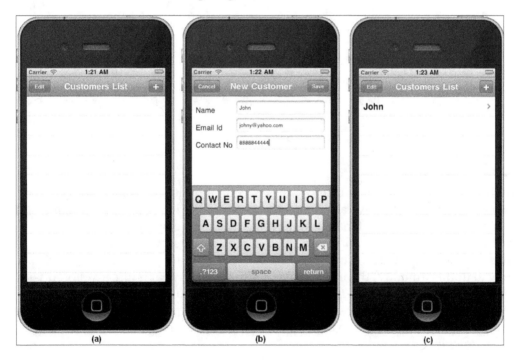

On selecting the customer's name from the table view, we will be navigated to the View of the `DisplayCustomerController` class that displays the information of the selected customer (shown in the following *image (a)*). We can select the **back** button with the text **Customers List** to go back to the table view.

On selecting the **Edit** Bar Button Item, our table will switch to edit mode displaying accessories for deletion of the table cell as shown in the following *image (b)*. On selecting one of the table cell's delete accessories, the accessory rotates 90 degrees and presents a **Delete** button, as shown in the following *image (c)*. On selecting the **Delete** button the row will be deleted.

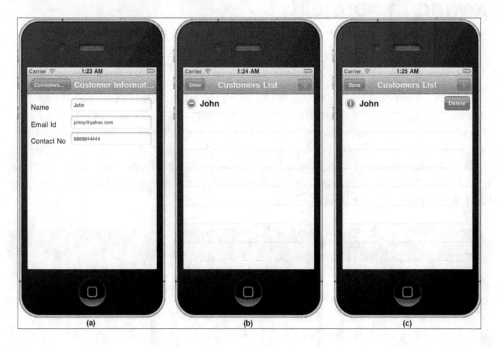

Summary

In this chapter, we saw how to apply the concept of multiple managed object context to our application. We have also seen how to merge the information in different managed object contexts. Finally, we have learnt the core of this chapter: how to maintain the customer's information, that is, we saw step-by-step how to save, display, and delete the information of the customer. In the next chapter, we will see how to update (modify) the information of the customer that is already stored with us. We will also be using KVO (Key Value Observing) to know what attribute of the object is updated. Besides this, we will also see the application of NSPredicate, a complex and powerful tool to apply a search facility to locate the desired customer name quickly.

7
Updating and Searching Records of Customers

In this chapter, we will see how to modify the information of the customer is unlike the Editing feature in *Chapter 6, Creating, Listing, Displaying, and Deleting Records of Customers*, which was limited to deletion of records. We will see how to Update (modify) the information of the customers that is already stored with us. In the last chapter, we saw that when any customer's name is selected from the table view, we are navigated to a View that displays detailed information of the customer, which includes the customer's name, e-mail ID, and contact number. This information is displayed via non-editable Text Fields so that the user can just look at the information without being able to modify it. In this chapter, we will learn about a procedure to add an *Edit* button at the top of the View that displays information of the selected customer. The *Edit* button when selected will make the Text Fields (through which a customer's information is displayed) editable allowing us to modify the information displayed in the Text Fields. We will also see how to save the modified information back to the persistent store.

We will also be using **KVO (Key Value Observing)** to know what attribute of the object is updated. Besides this, we will also see the application of NSPredicate to apply search facility to locate the desired customer name quickly.

Applying the update feature

Sometimes we need to update the information of our customers. This happens when the contact number or e-mail address of a customer is changed or some misspelling occurs while storing the customer's information. In these cases, we don't want to delete the customer's record but instead want to update or modify the information stored earlier. Let us apply the same feature to our application.

We will define a protocol by the name: DisplayCustomerControllerDelegate in the DisplayCustomerController class that will declare a method to save the modifications done in the customer's information to the persistent store. The RootViewController class will be declared as a *delegate* of the DisplayCustomerControllerDelegate protocol and hence, will implement the method of storing the modified customer's information to the persistent store. We will also add an *Edit* button to the View of the DisplayCustomerController class, which will invoke an action method, which will subsequently invoke the delegate's, that is, the RootViewController class's method to make the information of the customer editable.

There will be no changes in the probAppDelegate.h, probAppDelegate.m, AddCustomerController.h, AddCustomerController.m, Customer.h, and Customer.m files. Small modifications will be done in the following four files: DisplayCustomerController.h, DisplayCustomerController.m, RootViewController.h, and RootViewController.m.

The following are the steps for applying the update feature to the customer's information:

1. Defining protocol: DisplayCustomerControllerDelegate in the DisplayCustomerController class.

2. Adding the *Edit* button to enable modifications in the View of the DisplayCustomerController class.

3. Implementing the protocol's method in the RootViewController class for saving the modified customer information to the persistent store.

Defining a protocol in the DisplayCustomerController class

We need to define a protocol in the header file of the DisplayCustomerController class, DisplayCustomerController.h. The protocol is defined with the name: DisplayCustomerControllerDelegate and its instance variable with the name: delegate. The instance variable is defined as property with the two attributes: retain and nonatomic for generating the accessors and mutators. We also declare a method with the name: displaycust in the DisplayCustomerControllerDelegate protocol (between the @protocol and @end directives). The code of the header file: DisplayCustomerController.h is shown in the following code listing. You'll observe that most of the code is exactly the same as we saw in the *Adding the View Controller class for displaying the customer's information* section of *Chapter 6, Creating, Listing, Displaying, and Deleting Records of Customers*; only the highlighted statements are the ones that are newly added to it.

```
//   DisplayCustomerController.h
//   prob

#import <UIKit/UIKit.h>
#import "Customer.h"

@protocol DisplayCustomerControllerDelegate;

@interface DisplayCustomerController : UIViewController {
   Customer *cust;
   id <DisplayCustomerControllerDelegate> delegate;
   IBOutlet UITextField *name;
   IBOutlet UITextField *emailid;
   IBOutlet UITextField *contactno;
}

@property(nonatomic, retain) Customer *cust;
@property(nonatomic, retain) id <DisplayCustomerControllerDelegate>
delegate;
@property(nonatomic, retain) UITextField *name;
@property(nonatomic, retain) UITextField *emailid;
@property(nonatomic, retain) UITextField *contactno;
@end

@protocol DisplayCustomerControllerDelegate
-(void) displaycust:(DisplayCustomerController *)controller
    selecteddone:(BOOL) done;
@end
```

We will soon see how the main controller class of the application,
the RootViewController class, is declared as a delegate of the
DisplayCustomerControllerDelegate protocol. Consequently, the method:
displaycust that we declared in the preceding code will be implemented in it.
Recall that the class that conforms to a protocol has to implement its methods.

Adding Edit button to enable modifications in the View of DisplayCustomerController class

At the moment, the View of the DisplayCustomerController class doesn't contain the **Edit** button. Now, in the implementation file of the DisplayCustomerController class, DisplayCustomerController.m, we write the code to add an **Edit** button to the navigation bar and invoke the delegate methods to save the modifications applied to the customer's information. On implementing the following code, we would get an **Edit** button at the top of the View of the DisplayCustomerController class. The entire code of the implementation file of the DisplayCustomerController class appears as shown in the following code listing. Only the code which is highlighted is the new code, rest of the code is exactly the same as we saw in the *Defining the View and writing the code in the implementation file for displaying a customer's information* section of *Chapter 6, Creating, Listing, Displaying, and Deleting Records of Customers.*

```
// DisplayCustomerController.m
// prob

#import "DisplayCustomerController.h"

@implementation DisplayCustomerController

@synthesize name;
@synthesize emailid;
@synthesize contactno;
@synthesize cust;
@synthesize delegate;

// Implement viewDidLoad to do additional setup after loading the
view, typically from a nib.
- (void)viewDidLoad {
  [super viewDidLoad];
  self.title=@"Customer Information";
  name.text=cust.name;
  emailid.text=cust.emailid;
  contactno.text=cust.contactno;
  name.enabled=NO;
  emailid.enabled=NO;
  contactno.enabled=NO;
  self.navigationItem.rightBarButtonItem=self.editButtonItem;
}

-(void) setEditing:(BOOL) editing animated:(BOOL) animated {
```

```
    [super setEditing:editing animated:animated];
    name.enabled=YES;
    emailid.enabled=YES;
    contactno.enabled=YES;
    if(!editing)
    {
      cust.name=name.text;
      cust.emailid=emailid.text;
      cust.contactno=contactno.text;
      name.enabled=NO;
      emailid.enabled=NO;
      contactno.enabled=NO;
      [delegate displaycust: self selecteddone:YES ];
    }
}

- (void)dealloc {
    [name release];
    [emailid release];
    [contactno release];
    [cust release];
    [super dealloc];
}

@end
```

First of all, we synthesize the instance variable: `delegate` for generating the accessor and mutator methods. Next, we add an **Edit** button on the right of the navigation bar by using the property `editButtonItem` provided by the `UIViewController` class. As the `DisplayCustomerController` class inherits from the `UIViewController`, we can access that property using the dot notation and pass it to the mutator for `rightBarButtonItem`. The **Edit** button when selected will invoke the `setEditing` method and its *Title* will change to *Done* automatically.

In the `setEditing` method, we enable all the Text Field controls so that the user can change the contents of any field (`name`, `emailid`, or `contactno`). The moment the user selects the **Done** button in the View, the changes applied to the Text Field controls are assigned to the `name`, `emailid`, and `contactno` attributes of the `cust` instance (of the `Customer` class) and the Text Field controls are set to disabled mode. This means that the user can modify the information of the customer only when the **Edit** button is selected. Finally, the `displaycust` method of the delegate is invoked with the `selecteddone` parameter set to value `YES` to show that the user has selected the **Done** button in the navigation bar after applying all the modifications to the customer's information. The `RootViewController` class will implement this method to save the changes applied to the customer's information. In other words, if you run the code right now, you will see the changes but they are not permanent as they are not yet written to the persistence store.

Implementing the protocol's method for storing modified customer information

To declare the `RootViewController` class as a delegate of the `DisplayCustomerControllerDelegate` protocol, we need to add `DisplayCustomerControllerDelegate` in the angular brackets along with the other delegates: `NSFetchedResultsController` and `AddCustomerControllerDelegate`. The code in the implementation file of the `RootViewController` class is shown in the following code listing. Only the newly added code is shown; the rest of the code is exactly the same as we saw in the *Implementing the methods in the RootViewController class for storing information of the customer* section of *Chapter 6, Creating, Listing, Displaying, and Deleting Records of Customers*. Moreover, the code bundle of this chapter has complete code of the implementation file.

```
//    RootViewController.m
//    prob

#import "RootViewController.h"

@interface RootViewController ()
- (void)configureCell:(UITableViewCell *)cell atIndexPath:(NSIndexPath
*)indexPath;
@end

@implementation RootViewController

@synthesize fetchedResultsController, managedObjectContext;

#pragma mark -
```

```
#pragma mark View lifecycle

(....)

-(void) displaycust:(DisplayCustomerController *)controller
  selecteddone:(BOOL) done {
    if(done)
    {
      NSError *error;
      NSLog(@"in display cust saving");
      if(![managedObjectContext save:&error]){
        NSLog(@"Unresolved error %@ %@", error, [error userInfo]);
        exit(-1);
      }
    }
  }



(....)

@end
```

In the `displaycust` method, we check the value of the `done` parameter (that informs whether the **Done** button is selected or not, that is, whether the user is over with editing of the customer's information or not). If the value of the `done` parameter is YES meaning the user is over with the editing of information, then we just save the managed object context in the persistent store.

Let us run the project to see the updation facility that we have implemented:

- Select the *Build and Run* icon from the **Xcode Project** window. Assuming that the information of the two customers is already stored in our application, we get the names of two customers initially displayed in the table view (see the following *image (a)*).

- Select any customer's name from the table view (for example, John) to view his complete information. Note that in the navigation bar, an **Edit** button appears, as shown in the following *image (b)*. Also the Text Fields are currently in disabled mode, that is, we cannot edit any information at the moment.

- Select the **Edit** button to enable the Text Field controls. Click on any Text Field control to modify its contents. Note that the **Title** of the **Edit** button changes to **Done**, as shown in the following *image (c)*.

- Modify the name of the customer from **John** to **Annie** and also his contact number. On selecting the **Done** button, the modifications will be saved in the persistent store and the table view with modified contents will be displayed, as shown in the following *image (d)*:

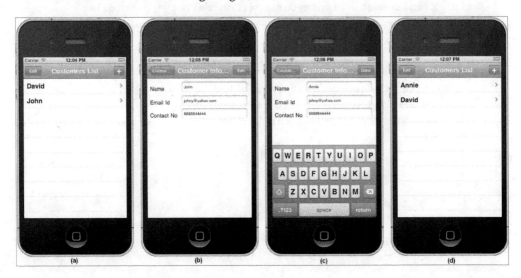

In order to know what contents are modified, we use the concept called Key Value Observing. So, let's have a look at it.

While updating information, we sometimes need to keep an eye on what attribute is updated and take necessary measures accordingly. In the next section, we will be learning about how KVO can be used to know what attribute is updated or modified by the user.

Using KVO to know what has been updated

Key Value Observing (KVO) is the sister API to KVC and is used to inform us if a particular attribute of an object is changed. Consequently, we can take necessary action on getting notification of the change(s) that took place on any attribute of the object. To get the notification, we have to register our controller class (referred to as self) as an observer of the object for the *keypath*, where *keypath* is the name of the attribute of the object that we want to observe.

To register the observer, we use `-addObserver:forKeyPath:options:context:` method and to remove the observers, we use `-removeObserver:forKeyPath:` method.

Let us have a look at the syntax of the method that registers an observer:

```
[object addObserver:self
forKeyPath:@"attribute"
options:0
context:NULL];
```

Here, `object` is the name of object whose keypath (attribute) we want to observe. In order to observe the `name` attribute of the `cust` object (of the `Customer` class), we may add an observer using the following statement:

```
[cust addObserver:self forKeyPath:@"name" options:(NSKeyValueObserving
OptionNew | NSKeyValueObservingOptionOld) context:NULL];
```

In the preceding code, we were adding *self* (our controller class) as an observer to the `cust` object and informing that when there is a change in the value of the `name` attribute, please notify *self* of that change and include both the old value of the attribute as well as its new value in that notification for further action.

The `options` argument allows us to request additional information about the change, such as the previous or new value of the changed attribute. Like in the preceding example, the option: `NSKeyValueObservingOptionNew` will display the new value of the attribute and the `NSKeyValueObservingOptionOldNSKey` option will display the old value of the attribute. If we don't want any new options, we pass the value `0` for the options argument. In the final argument, we specify the object name that we want to get passed along to the notification method. We specify `NULL` value here, if we don't have any object to be passed.

In order to see how the observer is registered and the notification is sent (when the attribute being observed is changed) and how the notification is set to execute a method to do the desired task, let us modify the preceding `DisplayCustomerController.m` file (see the *Adding Edit button to enable modifications in the View of DisplayCustomerController class* section). The View of the `DisplayCustomerController` class displays the information of the selected customer. The View contains an **Edit** button at the top in the navigation bar that allows to modify the information (name, e-mail ID, and contact number) of the customer.

We will modify the preceding `DisplayCustomerController.m` file, so that it will observe if the `name` attribute of the `cust` object (of the `Customer` class) is changed. The moment we change the name of the customer, a notification will be sent that will display the old as well as new name of the customer. The code of the implementation file, `DisplayCustomerController.m` is as shown in the following code listing. Only the statements which are highlighted are the newly added code; the rest of the code is the same as in the *Adding Edit button to enable modifications in the View of DisplayCustomerController class* section:

```objc
// DisplayCustomerController.m
// prob

#import "DisplayCustomerController.h"


@implementation DisplayCustomerController

@synthesize name, emailid, contactno, cust, delegate;


// Implement viewDidLoad to do additional setup after loading the
view, typically from a nib.
- (void)viewDidLoad {
[super viewDidLoad];
self.title=@"Customer Information";
name.text=cust.name;
emailid.text=cust.emailid;
contactno.text=cust.contactno;
name.enabled=NO;
emailid.enabled=NO;
contactno.enabled=NO;
self.navigationItem.rightBarButtonItem=self.editButtonItem;
[cust addObserver:self forKeyPath:@"name" options:(NSKeyValueObserving
OptionNew | NSKeyValueObservingOptionOld) context:NULL];
}


-(void) observeValueForKeyPath: (NSString *)keyPath ofObject:(id)
object
  change:(NSDictionary *) change context:(void*) context
  {
  NSLog(@"Attribute name is %@. Old name was %@. New name is %@",
keyPath, [change valueForKey:NSKeyValueChangeOldKey], [change valueFor
Key:NSKeyValueChangeNewKey]);
}


-(void) setEditing:(BOOL) editing animated:(BOOL) animated {
  [super setEditing:editing animated:animated];
  name.enabled=YES;
  emailid.enabled=YES;
  contactno.enabled=YES;
  if(!editing)
  {
    cust.name=name.text;
    cust.emailid=emailid.text;
```

```
        cust.contactno=contactno.text;
        name.enabled=NO;
        emailid.enabled=NO;
        contactno.enabled=NO;
        [delegate displaycust: self selecteddone:YES ];
    }
}

- (void)dealloc {
[name release];
[emailid release];
[contactno release];
[cust release];
[super dealloc];
}

@end
```

In the `viewDidLoad` method, we set `self` (`DisplayCustomerController` class) as an observer to observe if any changes are made to the `name` attribute of the `cust` object. When any changes are made to the `name` attribute, a notification is generated and the new and old values of the `name` attribute are passed to the notification. The notification will invoke the `observeValueForKeyPath` method where we display the keypath, that is, attribute: `name` and the new and old value of the `name` attribute by displaying the `NSKeyValueObservingOptionNew` and `NSKeyValueObservingOptionOld` options that are passed as arguments to the notification.

[The KVO makes the views automatically refresh themselves from the model when any attribute value is changed.]

Running the project

Let us run the project to see whether we get the old and new values entered for the name attribute (while modifying the information of the customer):

1. Select **Run | Console** option to open the console.

2. From the console's toolbar, select *Build and Run* icon from the **Xcode Project** window. We get the names of customers that are currently available in the persistent store in the table view (as shown in the following screenshot):

3. Select any customer's name from the table view to view his complete information. Such as, on selecting the customer: *John* his information will be displayed, as shown in the following screenshot. The Text Fields showing the customer's information are in the disabled mode, that is, we cannot edit any information at the moment.

4. Select the **Edit** button in the navigation bar to have all the Text Field controls enabled and we can click on any Text Field control to modify its contents. The **Title** of the **Edit** button changes to **Done** when the Text Fields are in the enabled mode.

5. Change the name of the customer from *John* to *Annie* and select the **Done** button. A notification will be generated because we have registered the observer on the `name` attribute of the `Customer` object and we get the following line in the console:

Attribute name is name. Old name was John. New name is Annie, as shown in the following screenshot:

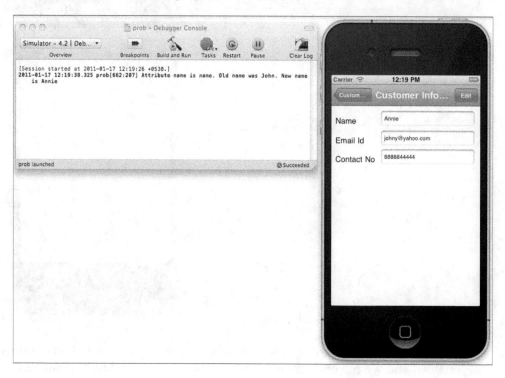

What if we want to search for a customer's name? Let us implement a search facility to our application.

Applying search facility

Let us add a *Search Bar* to our application that temporarily filters out the undesired rows and displays only those names of the customers that contain the characters typed in the Search Bar. A Search Bar displays a *TextField*, a *Cancel*, and a *Bookmark* button.

There will be no changes in the `probAppDelegate.h`, `probAppDelegate.m`, `AddCustomerController.h`, `AddCustomerController.m`, `Customer.h`, `Customer.m`, `DisplayCustomerController.h`, and `DisplayCustomerController.m` files. Only RootViewController's header and implementation files will be modified to implement the search facility.

Following are the steps to apply search facility to any customer's names:

- Defining outlet of UISearchBar class in the header file of the RootViewController class

- Placing the Search Bar control in the View of the RootViewController and specifying its delegate

- Implementing the delegate method in the RootViewController class to apply searching

Defining outlet of UISearchBar class in the header file of the RootViewController class

To read the text typed in the Search Bar control that is placed in the View, we need to access it through code and for that we have to connect the Search Bar control with an outlet in our class file. That is, for accessing the Search Bar control, which we will be placing in the View of the RootViewController class, we need to define an instance of UISearchBar class in the header file of the RootViewController class and will mark it as an outlet. The header file of RootViewController class: RootViewController.h may be modified to appear as shown in the following code listing. Only the highlighted statements are added to the RootViewController.h file that we saw in the *Implementing the methods in the RootViewController class for storing information of the customer* section of *Chapter 6, Creating, Listing, Displaying, and Deleting Records of Customers*:

```
//  RootViewController.h
//  prob

#import <UIKit/UIKit.h>
#import <CoreData/CoreData.h>
#import "AddCustomerController.h"
#import "DisplayCustomerController.h"

@interface RootViewController : UITableViewController
<NSFetchedResultsControllerDelegate, AddCustomerControllerDelegate,
DisplayCustomerControllerDelegate> {
  NSFetchedResultsController *fetchedResultsController;
  NSManagedObjectContext *managedObjectContext;
  IBOutlet UISearchBar *srchbar;
}

@property (nonatomic, retain) NSFetchedResultsController
*fetchedResultsController;
```

```
@property (nonatomic, retain) NSManagedObjectContext
*managedObjectContext;
@property(nonatomic, retain) UISearchBar *srchbar;

@end
```

We can see in the preceding code that an instance of the `UISearchBar` class is defined by the name `srchbar`. The instance variable, `srchbar`, is also defined as properties with the two attributes: `retain` and `nonatomic` for generating the accessors and mutators without any overhead code (when synthesized). After adding the preceding code, we save the preceding header file.

Placing the Search Bar control in the View of RootViewController and specifying its delegate

To place the Search Bar control on the top of the Table View, perform the following steps:

1. Open the `RootViewController.xib` in the Interface Builder.

2. Select a **Search Bar** control from the **Library** window and drop it at the header of the Table View control. We will see that a rounded blue rectangle appears at the top of the Table View.

3. We also need to specify a delegate for the Search Bar as we are going to implement its method for searching contents from the Table View. So, select the **Search Bar** control in the View and open the **Connections Inspector** window.

4. From the **Connections Inspector**, select the **delegate** connection (circle to the right of the **delegate** under the **Outlets** heading) and keeping the mouse button pressed drag it to the **File's Owner** icon (as shown in the following screenshot). This will declare the `RootViewController` class as the delegate of the Search Bar control.

5. Also, we need to connect the **srchbar** outlet that we defined in the header file (`RootViewController.h`) to the **Search Bar** control in the View. Select the **File's Owner** icon in the **Documents** window and open the **Connections Inspector** window.

6. Under the **Outlets** heading, we find the **srchbar** outlet. Select the circle to the right of the **srchbar** outlet and keeping the mouse button pressed, drag it to the **Search Bar** control in the View.

7. Save the `.xib` file and quit the Interface Builder.

Now we can implement methods of the Search Bar delegate protocol in our `RootViewController` class file.

Implementing delegate method in the RootViewController class to apply searching

In the implementation file: `RootViewController.m`, we will implement methods of the Search Bar delegate protocol to search the text typed in the Search Bar that we placed at the top of the Table View. There are a number of methods that a Search Bar control calls on its delegate. We will be discussing one Search Bar delegate method that we have implemented in our application: `textDidChange:`

The complete code of the implementation file, `RootViewController.m` is provided in the code bundle of this chapter. The following code listing shows the code that is added to the implementation file, rest of the code is exactly the same as we saw in the *Implementing protocol's method for storing modified customer information* section:

```
//   RootViewController.m
//   prob

#import "RootViewController.h"


@interface RootViewController ()
- (void)configureCell:(UITableViewCell *)cell atIndexPath:(NSIndexPath
*)indexPath;
@end
@implementation RootViewController
@synthesize fetchedResultsController, managedObjectContext;
```

```
@synthesize srchbar;


#pragma mark -
#pragma mark View lifecycle

(....)

-(void) searchBar:(UISearchBar *) searchBar textDidChange:(NSString *)
Tosearch{
  if([[searchBar text] length] >0)
  {
    NSPredicate *predicate=[NSPredicate predicateWithFormat:@"name
CONTAINS %@", [searchBar text]];
    [NSFetchedResultsController deleteCacheWithName:@"Root"];
    [fetchedResultsController.fetchRequest setPredicate:predicate];
  }
  else
  {
    [NSFetchedResultsController deleteCacheWithName:@"Root"];
    [fetchedResultsController.fetchRequest setPredicate:nil];
  }
  NSError *error = nil;
  if (![[self fetchedResultsController] performFetch:&error]) {
    // Handle error
    NSLog(@"Unresolved error %@, %@", error, [error userInfo]);
    exit(-1);   // Fail
  }
[self.tableView reloadData];
return;
}

(....)

- (void)dealloc {
  [fetchedResultsController release];
  [managedObjectContext release];
  [srchbar release];
  [super dealloc];
}

@end
```

The method: `textDidChange:` is invoked every time the text in the Search Bar's TextField is changed, so as to promptly update the table view contents on the basis of the text typed in the Search Bar's TextField. In this method, we check if the length of the text entered in the Search Bar's TextField is greater than zero. If it is, which means something is typed in the Search Bar's TextField, then we make use of the *NSPredicate* to write the following filter condition (predicate):

```
"name contains searchbar text"
```

The preceding *predicate* will retrieve only those names that contain the character(s) typed in the Search Bar's TextField.

Then the *predicate* is set to the *fetch request* to retrieve only those rows from the persistent store that agree with the *predicate* (filter condition) applied. If the Search Bar's TextField is blank, the *predicate* is set to `nil` declaring that there is no filter condition and hence it results in fetching all the rows from the persistent store.

The `performfetch` method is executed to retrieve the managed object context from the persistent store.

Let us explore the concept of NSPredicate in detail.

Understanding NSPredicate

NSPredicate is a complex and powerful tool used to filter out the undesired instances of an entity and to display only the desired instances. We can use it to construct a SQL-like query for retrieving the desired information.

We can build NSPredicate that accepts SQL-like NSString. It can accept any number of parameters after the NSString. We can see in the preceding `textDidChange` method that we have passed the text (entered in the text field of the Search Bar control) as an argument after the NSString. There are two useful methods of NSPredicate; let's have a look at them:

- `predicateWithFormat`: This method creates a new predicate from a formatted string. The following is the syntax for it:

  ```
  +(NSPredicate *) predicateWithFormatLNSString *) formatted string,
  argument list;
  ```

- `evaluateWithObject`: This method checks or evaluates a predicate with an object and returns a Boolean value YES – if the object matches with the Predicate (condition) – otherwise it returns a NO. The following is the syntax for it:

  ```
  -(BOOL) evaluateWithObject:(id) object
  ```

Here, the object is what the predicate has to be evaluated with.

The conclusion is that to get the filtered information, we first create a fetch request (as we usually do) to retrieve objects from Core Data. Also, we build an NSPredicate object (that takes an SQL-like query) and then associate it with the fetch request. Recall that while creating a fetch request, we set the entity to be retrieved and can optionally define NSPredicate to filter out the undesired objects and display only the desired ones.

> NSPredicate provides support for basic functions, correlated subqueries, and other advanced SQL. To combine two or more predicates using AND/OR statements, compound predicates can be built by using NSCompoundPredicate.

The preceding application will run well, that is, the desired customer names will appear at the top in the table view on typing initial characters of the customer name that we are looking for in the Search Bar control. But there is one problem: the keyboard still remains there even on selecting a customer name from the table view. Let's see how to remove the keyboard when we select a customer's name.

Removing the keyboard after selecting a customer's name

To remove the keyboard when any customer name is selected from the table view, we need to use the `tableView:willSelectRowAtIndexPath:` method. In this method, we inform the Search Bar to resign the first responder's status, which will cause the keyboard to go away and return the `indexPath`, as shown next:

```
-(NSIndexPath *)tableView:(UITableView *)tableView willSelectRowAtInde
xPath:(NSIndexPath *)indexPath{
  [srchbar resignFirstResponder];
  return indexPath;
}
```

We can also do the same by using `tableView:didSelectRowAtIndexPath:` method. On implementing the preceding method in the implementation file: `RootViewController.m`, we find that the keyboard goes away on selecting any customer's name from the table view.

Let us run the project to see the searching facility implemented by us. So, select the *Build and Run* icon from the **Xcode Project** window. Initially, the Search Bar is empty and hence the whole list of customer names will be displayed in the table view, as shown in the following *image (a)*). On typing any character in the Search Bar's text field, only the customer names having that character will be displayed (the rest of the customer names will be temporarily filtered out). On typing character 'c' in Search Bar's text field, we see that only the customer names that have character 'c' in them are left in table view, as shown in the following *image (b)*. Similarly, on typing the characters 'Ca', in the Search Bar's text field, the customer names having characters 'Ca' in them are left and displayed in table view, as shown in the following *image (c)*. On typing character 'Can' in the Search Bar's text field, the search becomes more precise and customer names having the character 'Can' are displayed in table view (only one customer name has characters 'Can') and rest of the customer names are temporarily filtered out, as shown in the following *image (d)*. When we select the filtered customer name, Candace, we find that the keyboard automatically gets hidden.

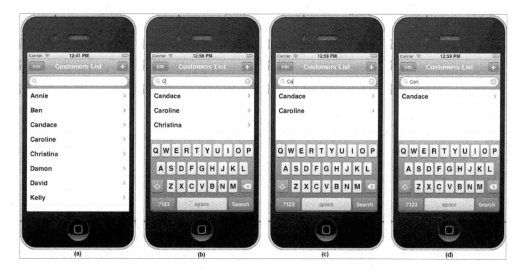

(a)   (b)   (c)   (d)

Using Predicate Builder for creating a search criterion

Xcode provides a visual tool: *Predicate Builder* that helps in creating predicates (queries for extracting rows from entities) for us. Let us try using the Predicate builder to display all customer names that contain characters 'Ca'.

So, let us open our Data Model by double-clicking the **prob.xcdatamodel** file in the **Resources** group in the **Xcode Project** window. Xcode's data modeling tool will open and we find our **Customer** entity in it. From the **Property** pane, select the **+ (plus)** button, a menu with several options such as: **Add Attribute**, **Add Fetched Property**, **Add Relationship**, and **Add Fetch Request** will popup. Out of these four options, **Add Fetched Property** and **Add Fetch Request** can be used for building predicates. Let us see them one by one.

Fetched properties

A fetched property is a type of attribute that associates a managed object with other managed objects based on the specified condition. That is, the predicate to define the objects that we want to be returned can be created by making use of the fetched properties. Remember that the fetched properties are *immutable* and their contents cannot be changed at runtime. Once we define the predicate using fetched properties, that is, once we define the criterion of the objects to be returned (through fetched properties), the desired objects can be retrieved by using the `valueForKey:` method. The execution of this method will return an array of objects that satisfies the specified condition/criterion. For example, look at the following statement:

```
NSArray *customers = [cust valueForKey:@"regularCustomers"];
```

Assuming that `regularCustomers` is the criterion name that specifies the characters we want to see in customer names, such as, if we want to see the customer names that have characters `Ca`, then the criterion `regularCustomers` will appear as shown next:

```
name LIKE[c] "Ca"
```

Here, `name` is the attribute of the `Customer` object and `c` in square brackets is an optional modifier for case insensitive comparison. In other words, the criterion with the name: `regularCustomers` will search all the customer names that contain characters `Ca` (in any case—lowercase or uppercase).

Fetch request templates

Again, fetch request is used to describe the criterion to retrieve the objects from a persistent store. We can define fetch request and store them in a managed object model as named templates. The fetch request will then retrieve the desired objects from the model when desired. If we want the objects to be retrieved on the basis of the condition that varies, that is, on the basis of the value specified by the user, we may also include variables in the fetch request template.

Let us build a fetch request in our Data Model that displays the names of the customers that have characters Ca. We will build two fetch requests: one *without variable* and the other *with variable*.

Building and accessing a fetch request without a variable

Follow these steps to build a fetch request without variable:

1. Open our Data Model by double-clicking the **prob.xcdatamodel** file in the **Resources** group in **Xcode Project** window. We can find our *Customer* entity in the data modeling tool that opens up.

2. To add a fetch request, select the **+ (plus)** button from the **Property pane**. A menu with several options such as: **Add Attributes, Add Fetched Property, Add Relationship**, and **Add Fetch Request** will pop up. Out of these four options, select the **Add Fetch Request** option. A fetch request is created and will be added to our **Customer** entity with a default name: **newFetchRequest**, as shown in the following screenshot:

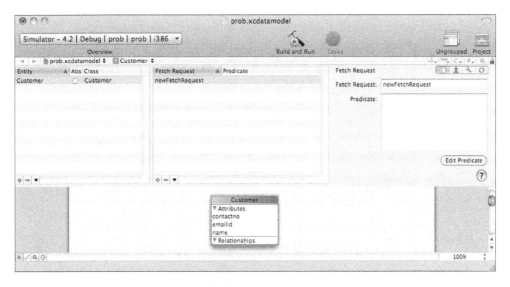

3. From the **Fetch Request:** textbox, select the default fetch request name: **newFetchRequest** and change it to **regularCustomers** (any string). We will find a button with the text: **Edit Predicate** at the bottom, which when selected opens the *Predicate Builder* to write criterion. The criterion that we will build using the Predicate Builder will appear in the text field above the **Edit Predicate** button.

4. In the Predicate Builder, the left-most popup menu is used to select the attribute of the selected data model (Customer entity) onto which we want to apply the search condition. The popup menu will display a few options such as: **Expression**, **Select Key Path**, **Attribute Names**, **Logical Connectors**, and so on, as shown in the following screenshot:

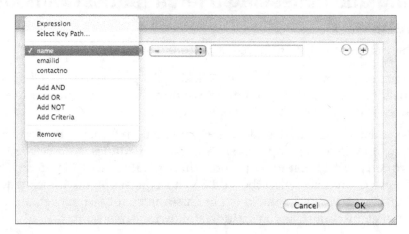

5. Let us have a brief idea of the options in the popup menu:
   - **Expression**: This option is used for entering a formatted string. We write such strings when we want to access an attribute using key value coding.
   - **Select Key**: This option opens a dialog to select an attribute. It is used for accessing attributes of other entities that are related to the current entity. This option is used for writing criterion that includes the attributes of the entity, which are in relationship with the current entity.
   - **Logical connectors**: The AND, OR, and NOT (including Add Criteria) are for adding another criterion (for building complex predicates).
   - **Remove**: This option is for removing the criterion.

6. Select the **name** attribute from the left-most popup as we want to write the predicate that displays the customer names that contain characters: Ca.

7. The middle popup menu displays the *Comparison operators*. The comparison operators change on the basis of the data type of the attribute selected from the left-most popup. As we want to display the names of the customers that contain the characters Ca, the comparison operator: **contains** appears to be the best choice for us. So, let us select it, as shown in the following screenshot:

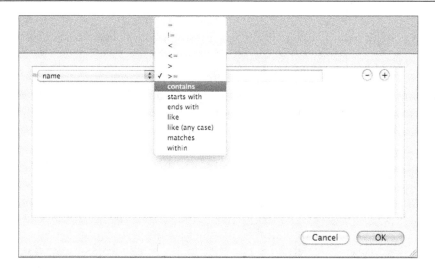

8. The last field is for writing the value or the variable with which we want to compare the attribute selected in the left-most popup. The value that we enter in the field is considered constant by default. In order to enter a variable, right-click on the empty space after the field and a popup menu will appear with several options in it, as shown in the following screenshot.

9. We can select the **Variable** option if we want the fetch request to work on the basis of the value supplied by the user. As the current example is on "*Fetch Request without variable*", we stick to the **Constant** option and enter Ca in the field, as we want to search the customer names that contain the characters 'Ca', as shown in the following screenshot:

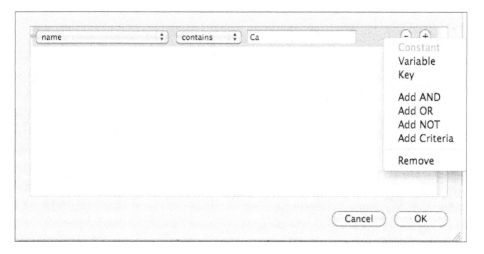

The menu shown in the preceding screenshot can be used to select the logical connectors (AND, OR, NOT) for creating complex queries.

On selecting the **OK** button, the Predicate Builder gets closed and we find the predicate created for us in the Text Field (above the **Edit Predicate** button). We can see our predicate created as:

```
name LIKE[c] "*Ca*"
```

Here, name is the attribute of the Customer object and C in square brackets is an optional modifier for case insensitive comparison and * is the wildcard character that refers to any number of character(s). In other words, the criterion with the name: regularCustomers will search all the customer names that contain characters Ca (in any case – lowercase or uppercase). The characters Ca may appear anywhere in the customer name, that is, there may be any number of characters before or after Ca.

We can see that the fetch request: **regularCustomers** appears in the Property Pane, as shown in the following screenshot:

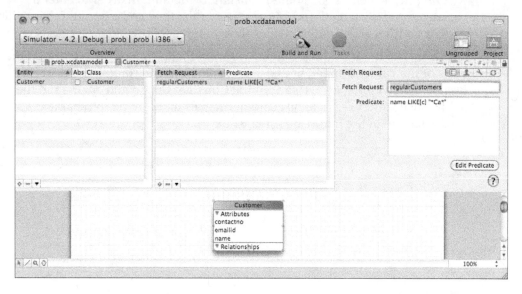

To access the fetch request template that we created with the name: regularCustomers, we need to write some code in the fetchedResultsController method in the implementation file: RootViewController.m. The highlighted code is added to the method (rest is the same as we saw in the *Implementing protocol's method for storing modified customer information* section):

```
- (NSFetchedResultsController *)fetchedResultsController {
```

```
  if (fetchedResultsController != nil) {
    return fetchedResultsController;
  }


  NSManagedObjectModel *model=[[self.managedObjectContext
persistentStoreCoordinator] managedObjectModel];
  NSFetchRequest *fetchRequest = [model fetchRequestTemplateForName:@"
regularCustomers"];
  // Set the batch size to a suitable number.
  [fetchRequest setFetchBatchSize:20];

  // Edit the sort key as appropriate.
  NSSortDescriptor *sortDescriptor = [[NSSortDescriptor alloc]
initWithKey:@"name" ascending:YES];
  NSArray *sortDescriptors = [[NSArray alloc]
initWithObjects:sortDescriptor, nil];

  [fetchRequest setSortDescriptors:sortDescriptors];

  // Edit the section name key path and cache name if appropriate.
  // nil for section name key path means "no sections".
  NSFetchedResultsController *aFetchedResultsController =
[[NSFetchedResultsController alloc] initWithFetchRequest:fetchReque
st managedObjectContext:managedObjectContext sectionNameKeyPath:nil
cacheName:@"Root"];
  aFetchedResultsController.delegate = self;
  self.fetchedResultsController = aFetchedResultsController;

  [aFetchedResultsController release];
  [fetchRequest release];
  [sortDescriptor release];
  [sortDescriptors release];

  return fetchedResultsController;
}
```

The fetch request is part of our Data Model and hence is accessed through the managed object model. So, in the preceding code, we first get the reference of our managed object model by making use of the persistent store coordinator and managed object context and then retrieve the fetch request by specifying its name: `regularCustomers` through the message: `fetchRequestTemplateForName` sent to the model.

Let us run the project to see all the names of the customers containing characters: Ca. So, select the *Build and Run* icon from the **Xcode Project** window. We find only the names of the customers that have characters: Ca that are displayed as shown in the following image:

Building and accessing a fetch request with a variable

We can specify a variable in our fetch request template so as to pass the value supplied by the user in order to filter the table view contents on the basis of the value supplied. Let us modify the fetch request to include a variable. Follow the given steps:

1. From the *Xcode's data model* editor, select the *fetch request: regularCustomers* from the *Property* pane and select the **Edit Predicate** button to modify the predicate we just created. The Predicate Builder will be opened.

2. Keep the **name** attribute selected in the left-most popup menu and the **contains** operator selected from the comparison operator menu.

3. Right-click on the empty space after the field so as to open a popup menu. Select the option **Variable** from the popup menu and enter the variable as **enteredName** in the field, as shown in in the following screenshot:

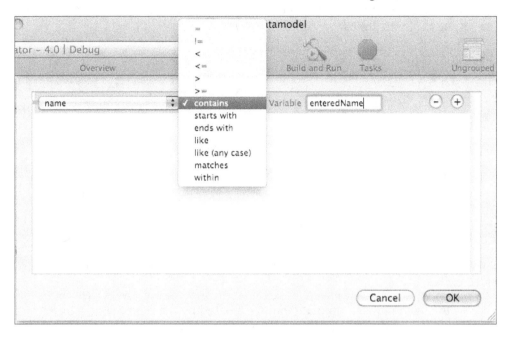

4. Select the **OK** button to come out of the predicate builder.

The preceding predicate will display only those customer names that contain the characters that we specify in the variable: **enteredName**. The criterion that we built using the Predicate Builder will appear in the text field above the **Edit Predicate** button. We can see that our predicate is created as shown next:

```
name LIKE[c] $enteredName
```

Here, name is the attribute of the Customer object, and C in square brackets is an optional modifier for *case insensitive comparison*, and $enteredName is a variable where we will supply the characters that the user wants to see in the customer names. We can see that the fetch request: **regularCustomers** appears in the **Property Pane**, as shown in the following screenshot:

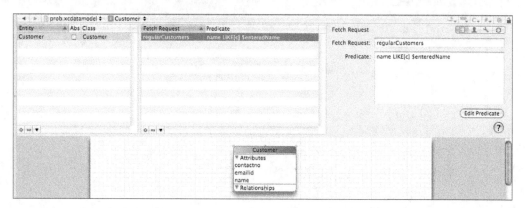

Let us write the code to supply the value to the variable **enteredName** created earlier.

To access the fetch request template that we created by the name: *regularCustomers,* we need to write some code in the fetchedResultsController method in the implementation file: RootViewController.m. Since this time we have to specify the value for the variable: **enteredName** used in the fetch request template, the code in the fetchedResultsController method may be written as shown next. The highlighted statements are modified (the rest of the code is the same as we saw in the *Implementing protocol's method for storing modified customer information* section):

```
- (NSFetchedResultsController *)fetchedResultsController {

  if (fetchedResultsController != nil) {
    return fetchedResultsController;
  }


  NSManagedObjectModel *model=[[self.managedObjectContext
persistentStoreCoordinator] managedObjectModel];
  NSString *toSearch=@"*Ca";
  NSDictionary *val=[NSDictionary dictionaryWithObject:toSearch
forKey:@"enteredName"];


  NSFetchRequest *fetchRequest = [model fetchRequestFromTemplateWithNa
me:@"regularCustomers" substitutionVariables: val];
  // Set the batch size to a suitable number.
```

```
[fetchRequest setFetchBatchSize:20];

    // Edit the sort key as appropriate.
    NSSortDescriptor *sortDescriptor = [[NSSortDescriptor alloc]
initWithKey:@"name" ascending:YES];
    NSArray *sortDescriptors = [[NSArray alloc]
initWithObjects:sortDescriptor, nil];

    [fetchRequest setSortDescriptors:sortDescriptors];

    // Edit the section name key path and cache name if appropriate.
    // nil for section name key path means "no sections".
        NSFetchedResultsController *aFetchedResultsController =
[[NSFetchedResultsController alloc] initWithFetchRequest:fetchReque
st managedObjectContext:managedObjectContext sectionNameKeyPath:nil
cacheName:@"Root"];
    aFetchedResultsController.delegate = self;
    self.fetchedResultsController = aFetchedResultsController;

    [aFetchedResultsController release];
    [fetchRequest release];
    [sortDescriptor release];
    [sortDescriptors release];

    return fetchedResultsController;
}
```

As said earlier, the fetch request being the part of our data model is accessed through managed object model. So, in the preceding code, we first get the reference of our managed object model by making use of the persistent store coordinator and the managed object context. We initialize a *NSString* variable toSearch to *Ca* (so as to get the customer names that contain characters Ca anywhere in the middle). After that we build a dictionary that contains the variable (enteredName) as the key value and the string (*Ca*) stored in the toSearch instance as a value. The dictionary: val containing the variable and its value is then used to retrieve the fetch request by specifying its name: regularCustomers through the message: fetchRequestFromTemplateWithName along with the dictionary: val containing the value to be substituted for the variable.

Let us run the project to see all the names of the customers containing characters Ca. So, select the *Build and Run* icon from the **Xcode Project** window. We get exactly the same output as we saw earlier, that is, only the names of the customers that have characters Ca will be displayed.

Summary

In this chapter, we saw how to apply updation and a searching facility to the customer's information. We saw the usage of NSPredicate in applying filtering conditions to the entity instances and hence displaying only the customer names that match with the characters typed in the Search Bar control.

In the next chapter, we will learn how to add one more entity: `Product` to our application that will be used for storing information to the different products sold to the customers. We will also learn how to set a relationship between the Customer and Product entities in that chapter.

8
Entering, Saving, Listing, and Deleting the Records of the Products Sold to the Customers

In the previous chapter, we saw how to apply the updation and searching facility to the customer's information. We also saw the usage of NSPredicate in applying the filtering condition to the entity instances. In this chapter, we will be:

- Adding one more entity with the name *Product* to our existing Data Model
- Establishing the relationship from the *Customer* entity to the *Product* entity along with the *Inverse relationship* from the *Product* entity to the *Customer* entity
- Entering, saving, listing, and deleting the information of the products sold to different customers

Adding the product entity to the Data Model

To store the information of different products sold to the customers, we have to add an entity with the name: *Product* to our application. Also, we need to define a relationship between the *Customer* and the *Product* entity. As a customer can purchase several products, there will be a *one to many* relationship between the *Customer* and the *Product* entity. Let us double-click the **prob.xcdatamodel** file from the **Resources** group to open the *Xcode's data modeling* tool. We find a Customer's entity (as shown in the following screenshot) already there that we created in *Chapter 4, Designing Data Model and Building Data Objects for Customers.*

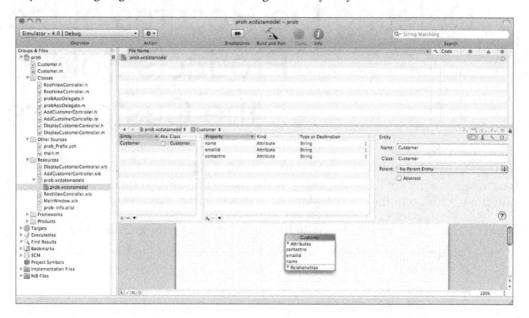

We can see that the *Customer* entity contains three attributes of the String data type: **name, emailid**, and **contactno** that will be used for storing the customer's information. To add the *Product* entity to our data model follow the given steps:

1. Select the **+** (plus) button at the bottom of the **Entity** pane or choose **Design | Data Model | Add Entity** from the menu bar. A blank entity (by default, **Name: Entity**) will be added to our data model, which we will rename to **Product**. Automatically, a subclass of **NSManagedObject** will be created for our **Product** entity.

2. To add attributes to our **Product** entity, we either choose **Design | Data Model | Add Attribute** from the menu bar or select the **+** button in the **Property** pane. When we select the **+** button (from the **Property** pane), a menu with several options such as: **Add Attributes, Add Fetched Property, Add Relationship**, and **Add Fetch Request** will popup.

3. We will select the **Add Attributes** option from the popup to add attributes to our **Product** entity. The attributes that we will add to our **Product** entity will be **itemname, quantity**, and **price** of data type: **String, Int 16**, and **Float** respectively.

The browser and the diagram view of the **Customer** and the **Product** entities along with their attributes will appear as shown in the following screenshot:

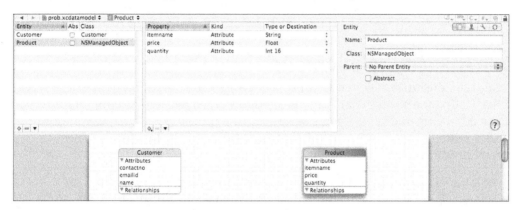

In order to maintain the information of the products sold to customers, we need to establish a relationship between the Customer and the Product entities. So, let's first have an idea of a relationship and its different types.

Relationship

Relationship is established between two or more entities to explain how they are mutually associated to each other. In fact, the relationships allow the managed object of a particular entity to maintain references to the managed objects of another entity (destinations). In Core Data, the relationships are defined in the same way as the attributes are defined. The relationships are assigned a name, that serves as the key value to set and retrieve the object(s) represented by the relationship.

 The relationships are added to the entities in the Xcode's data model editor in the same way attributes are added.

Types of relationships

The relationship can be of three types:

- One to one relationship
- One to many relationship
- Many to many relationship

One to one relationship

This relationship means a row in one entity will be associated with exactly one row in the destination entity. In other words, a managed object can contain a pointer to a single managed object of a specific entity. For example, the relationship from a child entity to a parent entity is a *one to one* relationship as a child can have only one parent.

One to many relationship

In this relationship, a row in one entity will be associated with more than one row in the destination entity. That is, a managed object will be associated with multiple managed objects in this case. For example, the relationship from the *Customer* to the *Product* entity is of a *one to many* relationship as a customer can purchase several products.

A *one to many* relationship is represented by instances of NSSet, which is an unordered, immutable collection that is not editable, or by NSMutableSet, an unordered collection that is editable.

Many to many relationship

In this relationship, a row in one entity will be associated with more than one row in the destination entity and vice versa is also true. That is, a row in the destination entity can be associated with more than one row in the source entity. For example, the relationship from an *Employee* to the *Project* entity is of *many to many* type as several employees can work on one project and an employee can work on several projects simultaneously.

 To define a *many to many* relationship, we have to use two *one to many* relationships. The first *one to many* relationship is set from the first entity to the second entity. The second *one to many* relationship is set from the second entity to the first entity.

Establishing a relationship between the Customer and the Product entities

In our Data Model, we have to establish relationships in two directions: one in the forward direction from the *Customer* to the *Product* entity and the other in the backward direction from the *Product* to the *Customer* entity.

Setting a relationship from the Customer entity to the Product entity

As a customer can purchase several products, the relationship from the *Customer* entity to the *Product* entity will be of the *one to many* type. To add the relationship, follow the given steps:

1. Select the **Customer** entity (in the Xcode's data model editor) in the **Entity** pane and from the **Attributes** pane select the **+** (plus button) to add an attribute (the relationship is stored in the form of an attribute in the Data Model).

2. From the menu that pops up, select the **Add Relationship** option. Specify the name of the relationship as `product`.

3. From the **Destination** drop-down list, select the **Product** entity (to declare that the relationship is from the *Customer* to the *Product* entity).

4. Leave the **Inverse** drop-down list at its default value: **No Inverse Relationship** as we will be setting inverse relationship later while establishing backward relationship, that is, from the **Product** to the **Customer** entity.

5. Select the **To-Many Relationship** checkbox, so that one managed object from the **Customer** entity can refer to several managed objects of the **Product** entity. In the diagram view of the Data Model Editor, we find that a line appears pointing from the **Customer** entity to the **Product** entity with two arrows (designating a *one to many* relationship), as shown in the following screenshot.

6. The **Delete Rule** is also left to display its default value: **Nullify**, so that the inverse relationship is updated when the customer object is deleted.

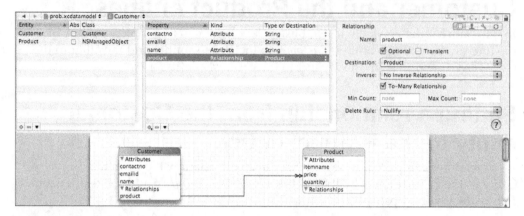

Delete rule

The delete rule decides the impact of deletion of a managed object of an entity onto the managed objects of the relationships. There are four possible delete rules:

- **Nullify**: This delete rule updates the inverse relationship when an object is deleted. If the inverse relationship is a to-one relationship, it is set to nil. If the inverse relationship is a to-many relationship, the deleted object will be removed from the inverse relationship.

- **No Action**: When an object is deleted, no modifications are applied to the other object in the relationship. This option is rarely used because the other object's inverse relationship will point to a non-existing object.

- **Cascade**: With this rule, if we delete a managed object, all the objects in the relationship are also removed.

- **Deny**: This rule will not allow deleting any object that is associated with some existing objects.

Setting a relationship from the Product entity to the Customer entity (inverse relationship)

Let us add a relationship from the *Product* entity to the *Customer* entity. The steps are as follows:

1. From the Xcode's data model editor, select the **Product** entity and from the **Attributes** pane select the + (plus button) and select the option **Add Relationship** to add a relationship (from the *Product* entity to the *Customer* entity).

2. Specify the name of the relationship as `customer`.

3. In the **Destination** drop-down list, select the **Customer** entity to declare that the relationship is from the *Product* entity to the *Customer* entity.

4. Set the *inverse relationship* by selecting **product** from the **Inverse** drop-down list (recall that the *product* is the name of the relationship set in the **Customer** entity). We find that in the diagram view of the relationship, an arrow (single) appears pointing to the **Customer** entity designating the relationship from the **Product** to the **Customer** entity, as shown in the following screenshot.

5. Leave the **To-Many Relationship** checkbox unchecked (as a product can have only one customer) and set the **Delete Rule** to **Cascade**, so that if the managed object of the **Customer** entity is deleted, all the product objects in the relationship must also be removed.

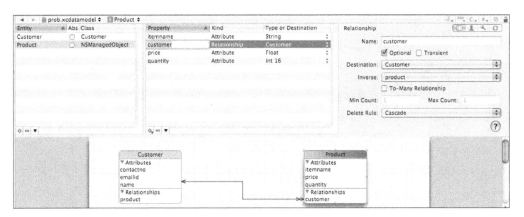

> In order to help Core Data in ensuring the data integrity, we should create inverse relationship.
>
> A relationship does not need to be the same kind as its inverse. That is, a to-many relationship can have an inverse relationship of type: to-one.

Building the data object for the Customer and the Product entities

To build the data objects (classes) associated with the entities and their relationships defined in the data model, we will follow the given steps:

1. Click an entity (*Customer* or *Product)* in the data model editor and then choose **File | New File** option. We get a dialog box to choose the template for the new file.

2. Select **Cocoa Touch Class** from under the **iPhone OS** heading in the left pane and select **Managed Object Class** template. We get a dialog box that prompts for the location of generating managed object class. Keeping the location as the default select the **Next** button.

3. Check the **Customer** and the **Product** entity in the dialog box that appears (as shown in the following screenshot). We find two checkboxes that are already checked: **Generate accessors** and **Generate Obj-C 2.0 Properties**. Keeping the two checkboxes checked, select the **Finish** button.

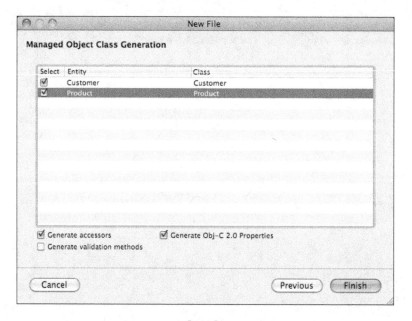

We will find four files: `Customer.h`, `Customer.m`, `Product.h`, and `Product.m`, which are automatically generated for us in the **Classes** group of the **Xcode Project** window (for the *Customer* and *Product* entities).

Understanding the role of the auto generated special methods of a relationship

The Xcode auto generates special methods for handling relationships. Let us look at the role of these methods. The contents of the header file `Customer.h` appears as shown next:

```
//   Customer.h
//   prob

#import <CoreData/CoreData.h>

@class Product;

@interface Customer :   NSManagedObject
{
}
@property (nonatomic, retain) NSString * emailid;
@property (nonatomic, retain) NSString * contactno;
@property (nonatomic, retain) NSString * name;
@property (nonatomic, retain) NSSet* product;

@end

@interface Customer (CoreDataGeneratedAccessors)
-  (void)addProductObject:(Product *)value;
-  (void)removeProductObject:(Product *)value;
-  (void)addProduct:(NSSet *)value;
-  (void)removeProduct:(NSSet *)value;

@end
```

In the preceding code, the `@class Product` statement is a *forward declaration* and is for informing the compiler that the class `Product` exists and it should not search for its header file. Also, we see that the properties are defined by names: `emailid`, `contactno`, and `name`. These properties are not declared in the header file as they will be created dynamically. Also as said earlier, the to-many relationship is represented by an instance of NSSet; we find that the to-many relationship of our data object: `product` is also defined as a property of the NSSet type.

Besides this, we also find four special methods generated for us. They are generated for each relationship and are used to add and delete managed objects from a to-many relationship. The meaning of each method is as follows:

- (void) addProductObject: (Product *) value: This adds a single-managed object of the *Product* entity to the *product* relationship (that we defined from the Customer to the Product entity).

- (void) removeProductObject: (Product *) value: This deletes a single-managed object of the *Product* entity from the *product* relationship.

- (void) addProduct: (NSSet *) value: This adds multiple objects to the *product* relationship. This method takes an instance of NSSet that contains the managed objects to be added to the relationship.

- (void) removeProduct: (NSSet *) value: This removes multiple managed objects from the *product* relationship.

The implementation file, Customer.m has the following code:

```
//  Customer.m
//  prob

#import "Customer.h"

#import "Product.h"

@implementation Customer

@dynamic emailid;
@dynamic contactno;
@dynamic name;
@dynamic product;

@end
```

In the implementation file, we find that the properties are marked as dynamic to inform the compiler not to generate accessors and mutators for the properties and will be provided (generated) by the superclass at runtime and hence not to display any warning message related to them.

The header file Product.h has the following code:

```
//  Product.h
//  prob

#import <CoreData/CoreData.h>

@class Customer;

@interface Product :  NSManagedObject
{
}
```

```
@property (nonatomic, retain) NSNumber * quantity;
@property (nonatomic, retain) NSNumber * price;
@property (nonatomic, retain) NSString * itemname;
@property (nonatomic, retain) Customer * customer;

@end
```

In the preceding code, again the `@class Customer` statement is for informing the compiler that the class `Customer` exists and it should not search for its header file. Also, we see that properties are defined by the name: `quantity`, `price`, and `itemname`. These properties are not declared in the header file as they will be created dynamically. Also, the to-one relationship (*customer*— that we defined from the *Product* to the *Customer* entity) is represented by an instance of the `Customer` class.

The implementation file, `Product.m` has the following code:

```
//   Product.m
//   prob
#import "Product.h"

#import "Customer.h"

@implementation Product

@dynamic quantity;
@dynamic price;
@dynamic itemname;
@dynamic customer;

@end
```

Again as said earlier, in the preceding implementation file, we find that the properties are marked as dynamic to inform the compiler that the accessors and mutators for the properties will be generated by the superclass at runtime and hence not to display any warning message related to them.

Entering the information of the products sold to the customers

To maintain the information of the product, we have to do three tasks:

1. Develop a View to enter the product's information.

2. Develop a Product's menu to add, edit, and display products sold to the selected customer.

3. Connect the Product's menu to the `DisplayCustomerController` class (the class that we created in *Chapter 6, Creating, Listing, Displaying, and Deleting Records of Customers*) that displays the information of the selected customer, so that the Product's menu can be invoked from there.

To execute the preceding tasks, we divide this chapter into three modules:

1. Module to develop the interface to enter the information of the *Product* sold to the selected customer.

2. Module to create menu for manipulating the *Product* information. That is, we create buttons that are connected to the methods to save, display, and delete the product information.

3. Module to connect the Product's menu to the rest of the project.

> The contents of the App Delegate files (`probAppDelegate.h` and `probAppDelegate.m`), code of the `AddCustomerController` class files (`AddCustomerController.h` and `AddCustomerController.m`), and `RootViewController` class files (`RootViewController.h` and `RootViewController.m`) will be exactly the same as we saw in the earlier chapters. So, we will not be discussing these files in this chapter.

Creating a module to develop an interface to enter the product information

In this module, we will learn how to add a View that allows us to enter the information of the product (that is sold to selected customers) and invoke the save action to save the information entered.

The steps involved in developing this module are as follows:

1. Adding the `ViewController` class: `AddProductController` class for entering information of the products sold to the customers.

2. Defining the protocol, outlets, and action methods in the header file: `AddProductController.h`.

3. Designing the View of the `AddProductController` class and connecting the controls.

4. Invoking the delegate methods from the implementation file: `AddProductController.m`.

Adding a ViewController class for entering the information of the products sold to the customers

We need to add a View Controller by the name `AddProductController` to the application. The View of the `AddProductController` class will display the UI controls to enter the information of the product, that is, user can enter the name of the product, its price, and the quantity sold to the customer. This View Controller will also display a navigation bar with two navigation bar items: *Save* and *Cancel*. On selecting the **Save** button, the information of the product will be stored in the selected customer's account. We have established a *to-many* relationship from the *Customer* entity to the *Product* entity (in the Data Model designed above in this chapter), which means a customer can purchase several products. Or the other way round; several products can be sold to a customer. So, all the products added through this View will be considered as the products sold to the selected customer. The information of the customer and the products will be stored in the `customersinfo.sqlite` file.

To add a View Controller class, follow the given steps:

1. Right-click on the **Classes** group in the **Xcode Project** window, select the **Add | New File** option. Select **Cocoa Touch Class** from under the **iPhone OS** heading in the left pane and select the **UIViewController** subclass as the template of the new file to choose from.

2. Select the checkbox **With XIB for user interface** (this will be used for creating the View for the View Controller to be used for entering the information of the product) followed by the **Next** button.

3. We get a dialog box to specify the name of the View Controller. Let us assign the name as: `AddProductController.m` and select the checkbox **Also create "AddProductController.h"** followed by the **Finish** button.

Both the files: `AddProductController.h` and `AddProductController.m` will be created along with the `.xib` file and added to our project. The files will be placed at the default location: **Classes** group of our **Xcode Project** window. We will shift (by click-and-drag method) the `AddProductController.xib` file from the **Classes** group to the **Resources** group, which is the default location for all XIB files.

Defining the protocol, outlets, and action methods in the header file

The code that we will write in the header file of the AddProductController class: AddProductController.h is as shown next:

```
// AddProductController.h
// prob

#import <UIKit/UIKit.h>
#import "Product.h"

@protocol AddProductControllerDelegate;

@interface AddProductController : UIViewController {
  id <AddProductControllerDelegate> delegate;
  IBOutlet UIBarButtonItem *cancelbutton;
  IBOutlet UIBarButtonItem *savebutton;
  IBOutlet UITextField *newitemname;
  IBOutlet UITextField *newquantity;
  IBOutlet UITextField *newprice;
  Product *prod;
}

@property(nonatomic, retain) Product *prod;
@property(nonatomic, retain) id <AddProductControllerDelegate>
delegate;
@property(nonatomic, retain)  UIBarButtonItem *cancelbutton;
@property(nonatomic, retain)  UIBarButtonItem *savebutton;
@property(nonatomic, retain) UITextField *newitemname;
@property(nonatomic, retain) UITextField *newquantity;
@property(nonatomic, retain) UITextField *newprice;

-(IBAction) cancel:(id) sender;
-(IBAction) save:(id)sender;

@end

@protocol AddProductControllerDelegate
-(void) addprodController:(AddProductController *)controller
  selectedsave:(BOOL) save;
@end
```

In the *AddProductController's* header file we define the protocol, outlets, and action methods. First of all, we define a protocol with the name: `AddProductControllerDelegate`. We define an instance variable with the name: `delegate` (any name) of type: `id <AddProductControllerDelegate>`. We also define an object of the `Product` class with the name: `prod` that will store the product's information (that is sold to the customer) temporarily before being stored in the persistent store. Also, three instance variables: `newitemname`, `newquantity`, and `newprice` of the `UITextField` class are defined and marked as outlets (these outlets will be connected to the three Text Field controls that we will be dropping in the View for entering item name, quantity, and price of the product). Two instance variables of the `UIBarButtonItem` class: `cancelbutton` and `savebutton` are defined and marked as outlets. These two outlets will be connected to the two Bar Button Items (that we will soon drag-and-drop on the View) with the titles: **Save** and **Cancel** (they will invoke the respective action methods to save or discard the product's information). The two action methods are also defined with the names: `cancel` and `save` that will be connected to the two respective Bar Button Items: *Cancel* and *Save*. All the five instance variables(`cancelbutton`, `savebutton`, `newitemname`, `newquantity`, and `newprice`) along with the object `prod` (of the `Product` class) are defined as properties with the two attributes: *retain* and *nonatomic* for generating their accessors and mutators. We also declare a method for the `AddProductControllerDelegate` protocol (between the `@protocol` and `@end` directives). The name of the method declared is: `addprodController`. We will be declaring a class: `ProductInfoController` (which we are going to create in the next module) as the delegate of the `AddProductControllerDelegate` and hence, it will implement the `addprodController` method. After adding the preceding code, we save the header file.

Designing the View of the AddProductController class and connecting the controls

The View of the `AddProductController` class will prompt the user to enter information of the product sold to the selected customer. That is, it will contain a few Text Field controls where information related to a product can be entered. Besides this, the View will also contain two Bar Button Item controls with the text: `Save` and `Cancel` respectively to perform the task of saving or discarding the information of the product entered. So, let us design the View by following the given steps:

1. Open the `AddProductController.xib` file in the Interface Builder and from the **Inputs & Values** category of the **Library** window, drag-and-drop three **Label** and three **Text Field** controls on the View.

2. Double-click the **Label** controls one by one and edit their text to **Product Name**, **Price**, and **Quantity** respectively.

3. From the **Windows, Views & Bars** category of the **Library** window drag a Bar Button Item control and drop it to the **Documents** window.

4. Repeat the procedure as we want the two Bar Button Item controls in the navigation bar (of the View of the AddProductController class) to represent the **Cancel** and **Save** buttons respectively.

5. From the **Attributes Inspector**, set the **Titles** of the two Bar Button Item controls to **Cancel** and **Save** respectively (the title of the Bar Button Item appears as button text in the View).

The next step is to connect the three outlets (newitemname, newprice, and newquantity defined in the header file: AddProductController.h) to the three Text Field controls dropped in the View. To do so, we will perform the following steps:

1. Select the **File's Owner** icon in the **Documents** window and open the **Connections Inspector**.

2. Select the circle to the right of each outlet (under the **Outlets** section in the **Connections Inspector**) and keeping the mouse button pressed, drag it to the respective Text Field control.

The following screenshot shows how the **newquantity** outlet is connected to the respective **Text Field** control:

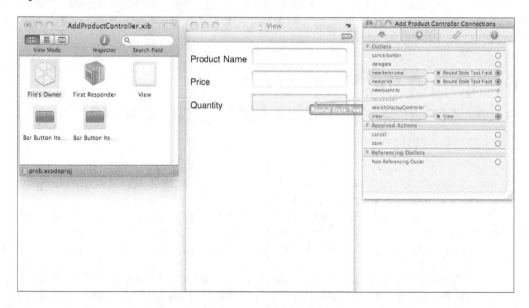

Also, we need to connect the outlets of the Bar Button Item controls: `cancelbutton` and `savebutton` to the two Bar Button Item controls dropped in the **Documents** window. The procedure is the same, select the circle to the right of the outlet in the **Connections Inspector** and keeping the mouse button pressed, drag it to the respective Bar Button Item control in the **Documents** window. The following screenshot shows the procedure of connecting **cancelbutton** outlet to the Bar Button Item control (the one with the **Title: Cancel**):

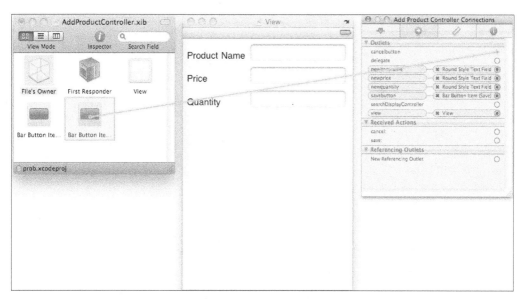

The next step is to connect the Bar Button Item controls to the action methods: `cancel` and `save` defined in the header file of the `AddProductController` class (`AddProductController.h`), so that when any Bar Button Item control is selected from the navigation bar, the code in the respective action method is executed to do the desired task. Perform the following steps for connecting the Bar Button Item controls:

1. Select the Bar Button Item control in the **Documents** window (the one whose **Title** is set as: **Save**) and open the **Connections Inspector**.

2. In the **Connections Inspector** under the heading **Sent Actions**, select the circle to the right of **selector** and keeping the mouse button pressed, drag it to the **File's Owner** icon in the **Documents** window and release the mouse button. On releasing the mouse button, two action methods defined in the header file will pop up: **cancel** and **save**.

3. Select the **save** (action method) to connect it to the selected Bar Button Item control, as shown in the following screenshot.

4. Repeat the procedure for connecting the second Bar Button item control (with the **Cancel** title) to **cancel** the action method.

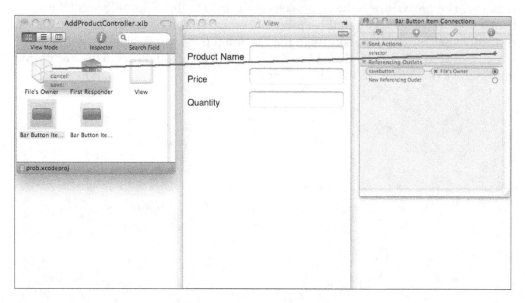

Invoking the delegate methods from the implementation file

In the implementation file of the AddProductController class (AddProductController.m), we need to write the code for displaying the Bar Button Item controls (to be displayed on the left and right sides of the navigation bar) and for the action methods: cancel and save (that will subsequently invoke the methods of the delegate class (to discard or save the product information in the persistent store) respectively. We will write the following code in the implementation file, AddProductController.m:

```
// AddProductController.m
// prob

#import "AddProductController.h"

@implementation AddProductController

@synthesize newitemname, newquantity, newprice;
@synthesize prod, delegate, cancelbutton, savebutton;

-(IBAction) cancel:(id) sender
{
```

```
        [delegate addprodController: self selectedsave:NO];
    }


    -(IBAction) save:(id)sender{
        prod.itemname=newitemname.text;
        prod.quantity=[NSNumber numberWithInt:(int)  [newquantity.text
    intValue]] ;
        prod.price=[NSNumber numberWithInt:(int) [newprice.text intValue] ];
        [delegate addprodController:self selectedsave: YES];
    }


    // Implement viewDidLoad to do additional setup after loading the
    view, typically from a nib.
    - (void)viewDidLoad {
      [super viewDidLoad];
      self.title=@"New Product";
      self.navigationItem.rightBarButtonItem=savebutton;
      self.navigationItem.leftBarButtonItem=cancelbutton;
    }


    - (void)dealloc {
      [newitemname release];
      [newquantity release];
      [newprice release];
      [savebutton release];
      [cancelbutton release];
      [prod release];
      [super dealloc];
    }


    @end
```

We can see in the preceding code that first of all, we synthesize the IBOutlets
(newitemname, newquantity, newprice, prod, delegate, cancelbutton, and
savebutton) for generating the accessor and mutator methods for them. In the
action method: cancel, we write code to invoke the addprodController method
of the delegate class (ProductInfoController class that we are going to create
in the following module) and set the value of the parameter selectedsave to NO.
Similarly, in the action method: save, we invoke the addprodController method of
the delegate and set the value of the parameter: selectedsave to YES. The value of
the selectedsave parameter will decide whether to persist the information of the
product or not. In the save action method, we assign the information of the product
entered by the user in the three Text Fields to the item name, quantity, and price
attributes of the prod object (of the Product class).

In the `viewDidLoad` method, we set the Navigation Item's title to **New Product** and its right Bar Button Item is set to `savebutton` (instance variable of Bar Button Item with the **Title: Save**). Also, the left Bar Button Item of the navigation bar is set to `cancelbutton` — the instance variable of the `UIBarButtonItem` class with **Title: Cancel**. Finally, through the `dealloc` method, we release the memory reserved by different outlets.

We cannot run this module until and unless we implement the methods of the `AddProductControllerDelegate` protocol in the `ProductInfoController` class, which we are going to create in the following module.

Developing a module to create a menu for manipulating the product information

In this module, we will learn how to create a Product's menu that contains several buttons, which can be invoked to see the information of the products sold to the selected customer, to add more products, and to delete existing products.

The steps involved in developing this module are as follows:

1. Adding the `ViewController` class: `ProductInfoController` class to display the Product's menu to manipulate the product's information.

2. Defining the outlets and action methods in the header file: `ProductInfoController.h`.

3. Designing the View of the `ProductInfoController` class and connecting the controls.

4. Coding in the implementation file: `ProductInfoController.m` to save, edit, and display the product's information.

Adding a ViewController class to display the Product's menu to manipulate the product's information

We will add a View Controller with the name `ProductInfoController` that displays the information of the products sold to the customers. This View Controller will contain a table view to display the list of products sold to the customers and will have a toolbar at the header of table view with three buttons: **Back**, **Edit**, and **Add**. The **Back** button will navigate us back to the View of the `DisplayCustomerController` from where this `ViewController` class will be invoked, the **Edit** button will display the **Delete** accessory to delete an entry of product, and the **Add** button will navigate us to the View of `AddProductController` (we have just created in the first module to enter the information of the products sold to the customer).

The steps for adding View Controller, `ProductInfoController` are as follows:

1. Right-click on the **Classes** group in the **Xcode Project** window, and select the **Add | New File** option.

2. Select **Cocoa Touch Class** from under the **iPhone OS** heading in the left pane and select the `UIViewController` subclass as the template of the new file to choose from.

3. Select the checkbox **With XIB for user interface** (which will be used for creating View for the View Controller to display the product information and a toolbar) followed by the **Next** button.

4. We get a dialog box to specify the name of the View Controller. Let us assign the name as: `ProductInfoController.m` and select the checkbox **Also create "ProductInfoController.h"**, followed by the **Finish** button. Both the files: `ProductInfoController.h` and `ProductInfoController.m` will be created along with the `.xib` file and added to our project. The files will be placed at the default location: `Classes` subfolder of our application folder.

5. Select the `ProductInfoController.xib` file in the `Classes` folder and drag it to the `Resources` folder, the default location of Interface Builder files.

Defining the outlets and action methods in the header file

In the header file: `ProductInfoController.h` we will declare the `ProductInfoController` class as a delegate of the `NSFetchedResultsControllerDelegate` as well as of the `AddProductControllerDelegate` protocols. It means that we will be implementing the methods declared in these two protocols in the implementation file of the `ProductInfoController` class (`ProductInfoController.m`). We also define objects of the `Customer` and `Product` class with names: `cust` and `product` respectively that will be used to store the information of the selected customer (whose product information we want to store) and the information of the product(s) sold to him, respectively. An instance variable of the `UITableView` class is created with the name: `tableView` and is defined as an outlet for connecting with the Table View control that we will be placing in the View (which will be used for displaying products sold to the customer). A Mutable array *products* is also defined that will hold the list of all the products sold to the customer for display in the Table View control. An instance variable of the `NSFetchedResultsController` class is declared by the name: `fetchedResultsController`. Three instance variables of the `UIButtonItem` class are created: `backbutton`, `editbutton`, and `addbutton`. These are defined as outlets (which will be used for connecting them to the three Bar Button Item controls that we will be placing in the View).

The code that we will write in the header file of the `ProductInfoController` class: `ProductInfoController.h`, is as shown next:

```
//  ProductInfoController.h
//  prob

#import <UIKit/UIKit.h>
#import "Customer.h"
#import "Product.h"
#import "AddProductController.h"

@interface ProductInfoController : UIViewController
<NSFetchedResultsControllerDelegate, AddProductControllerDelegate> {
   Customer *cust;
   Product *prod;
   UITableView *tableView;
NSMutableArray *products;
NSFetchedResultsController *fetchedResultsController;
   IBOutlet UIBarButtonItem *backbutton;
   IBOutlet UIBarButtonItem *editbutton;
   IBOutlet UIBarButtonItem *addbutton;
```

```
}
@property (nonatomic, retain) NSFetchedResultsController
*fetchedResultsController;
@property(nonatomic, retain) Customer *cust;
@property(nonatomic, retain) Product *prod;
@property(nonatomic, retain) NSMutableArray *products;
@property(nonatomic, retain)  UIBarButtonItem *backbutton;
@property(nonatomic, retain)  UIBarButtonItem *editbutton;
@property(nonatomic, retain)  UIBarButtonItem *addbutton;
@property(nonatomic, retain)  IBOutlet UITableView *tableView;

-(IBAction) back:(id) sender;
-(IBAction) addproduct:(id)sender;
-(IBAction) editproduct:(id)sender;

@end
```

All the instance variables are defined as properties with the two attributes: *retain* and *nonatomic* for generating the accessors and mutators without any overhead code (when synthesized) and for keeping the objects retained to the mutators without being flushed from the memory. Also three action methods are declared by the names: back, addproduct, and editproduct respectively. The action method back will take us back to the View of the DisplayCustomerController class (from where the current class: ProductInfoController will be invoked; in the following module, we will see how). The addproduct action method will invoke the View of the AddProductController class (to enter the information of the products sold to the customer) and the editproduct action method will be used to display the Deletion accessory to delete the entry of any product.

Designing the View of a ProductInfoController class and connecting the controls

The View of the ProductInfoController class will be used for displaying the list of the products sold to the selected customer (the customer that is selected from the View of the DisplayCustomerController class).

 The ProductInfoController class will be invoked from the View of the DisplayCustomerController class. In the following module, we will see how the DisplayCustomerController and the ProductInfoController classes are connected.

Besides displaying the list of products sold to the selected customer, this View will also display a Toolbar with three Bar Button Item controls. The three Bar Button Item controls will respectively do the following three tasks:

- Navigating back to the `DisplayCustomerController` class
- Navigating to the `AddProductController` class (to enter the information of the products sold to the customer)
- To edit (delete) any entry of the product

So, let us begin with the procedure of designing the view of the `ProductInfoController` class:

1. From the **Resources** group in the **Xcode Project** window, open the **ProductInfoController.xib** file in **Interface Builder** and drag-and-drop a **Toolbar** control at the top in the View. The **Toolbar** control comes with a default *Bar Button Item* control. We will drop two more *Bar Button Item* controls onto the **Toolbar** control.

2. Drag-and-drop the **Flexible Space Bar Button Item** controls at the beginning, at the end, and in between the Bar Button item controls to create uniform spacing among them.

3. Drag-and-drop a **Table View** control below the **Toolbar** control. The Bar Button Item controls in the **Toolbar** control have a default title as: `Item`. So, we take the help of the **Attributes Inspector** to set the **Titles** of the Bar Button Item controls to **Back**, **Edit**, and **Add** respectively.

The next step is to connect the `backbutton`, `editbutton`, and `addbutton` outlets (defined in the header file: `ProductInfoController.h`) to the three Bar Button Item controls in the toolbar, respectively. For connecting the outlets with the Bar Button Item controls, we will follow the given steps:

1. Select the **File's Owner** icon in the **Documents** window and open the **Connections Inspector**.

2. In the **Connections Inspector** under the **Outlets** heading, we get the list of outlets defined in the header file of the `ProductInfoController` class. Select the circle to the right of each outlet one by one and keeping the mouse button pressed, drag it to the respective Bar Button Item control.

3. Similarly, to connect the **tableView** outlet with the **TableView** control in the View, select the circle to the right of the **tableView** outlet and keeping the mouse button pressed, drag it to the **TableView** control in the View, as shown in the following screenshot:

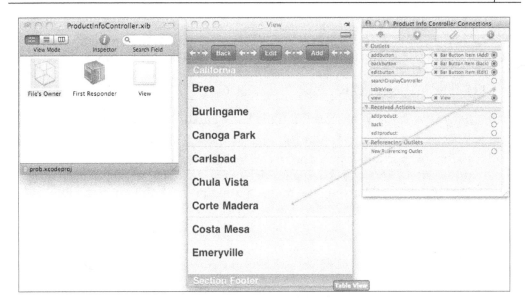

We will also connect the action methods: **back**, **editproduct**, and **addproduct** defined in the header file (`ProductInfoController.h`) to the three Bar Button item controls with Titles: **Back**, **Edit**, and **Add** respectively. Just select the circle to the right of each individual action method found under the heading **Reserved Actions** (in the **Connections Inspector**) and keeping the mouse button pressed, drag it to the respective Bar Button Item control in the **Toolbar** control. We can see the procedure of connecting **editproduct** action method with the **Edit** Bar Button Item control, as shown in the following screenshot:

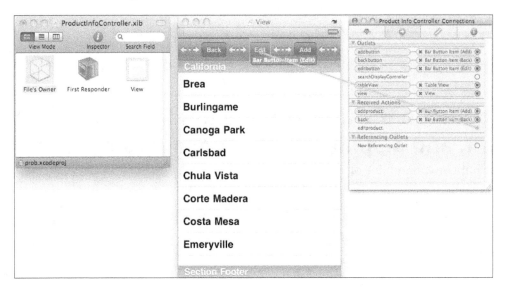

We also have to declare the ProductInfoController class as the *Data Source* and *Delegate* of the *TableView* control as it is this class that will provide the contents for the *TableView* (for display) and will also implement its delegate methods. To declare the ProductInfoController class as *Data Source* and *Delegate* of *TableView* control, we will follow the given steps:

1. Select the **Table View** control in the View and open the **Connections Inspector**.

2. In the **Connections Inspector**, under the **Outlets** section, we find the two outlets: **dataSource** and **delegate**. Select the circle to the right of each outlet (one by one) and keeping the mouse button pressed, drag it to the **File's Owner** icon in the **Documents** window (that represents the ViewController class of the NIB file that is open), as shown in the following screenshot:

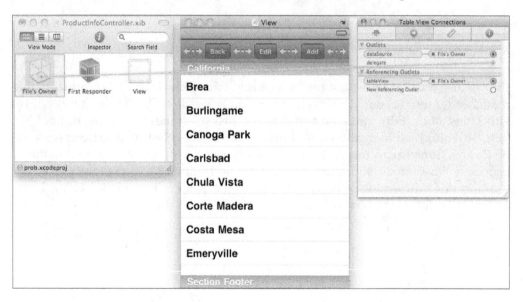

Coding in the implementation file to save, edit, and display the product's information

The implementation file of the ProductInfoController class (ProductInfoController.m) contains code to add and edit the information of different products sold to the selected customer. The complete code of the ProductInfoController.m file is provided in the code bundle of this chapter. The code that needs explanation is as shown next:

```
//   ProductInfoController.m
//   prob
```

```
#import "ProductInfoController.h"

@implementation ProductInfoController

@synthesize backbutton, editbutton, addbutton, tableView;
@synthesize cust, prod, products;
@synthesize fetchedResultsController;

-(IBAction) back:(id) sender
{
   [self dismissModalViewControllerAnimated:YES];
}
```

In the preceding implementation file of the ProductInfoController class, we see that all the IBOutlets (backbutton, editbutton, addbutton, tableView, cust, prod, products, and fetchedResultsController) are synthesized for generating the accessor and mutator methods for them. In the action method: back (which is invoked when Bar Button Item control with **Title: Back** is selected from the Toolbar), we dismiss the modal view of the ProductInfoController class (a view that helps in adding and editing the product's information) to display the View of the DisplayCustomerController class to display the information of the selected customer. Recall that the ProductInfoController class is invoked from the DisplayCustomerController class:

```
-(IBAction) addproduct:(id)sender
{
   AddProductController *addprodController=[[AddProductController
alloc] initWithNibName:@"AddProductController" bundle:nil];
   addprodController.delegate=self;
   UINavigationController *navigController=[[UINavigationController
alloc] initWithRootViewController:addprodController];
   [self    presentModalViewController:navigController animated:YES];
   NSManagedObjectContext *context = [cust managedObjectContext];

   prod = [NSEntityDescription insertNewObjectForEntityForName:@"Produ
ct" inManagedObjectContext:context];
   [cust addProductObject: prod];
   addprodController.prod=prod;
   [addprodController release];
   [navigController release];
}
```

In the action method: addproduct (that is invoked when Bar Button Item with **Title: Add** is selected from the Toolbar), the code is written to navigate to the View of the AddProductController class that prompts the user to enter information of the product sold to the customer. We create and initialize an instance of the AddProductController class by the name: addprodController. Also, we set the current View Controller file: ProductInfoController.m as the delegate of the addprodController instance. That is, this class will implement the delegate methods of the AddProductController class. To display a navigation bar in the View of the AddProductController, we create and initialize an instance of the UINavigationController class by the name: navigController and set its Root View controller to be the view of the AddProductController class. Then we display the View of the AddProductController class modally using the presentModalVie wController:animated: method, the View Controller animates the appearance of the view and creates a parent-child relationship between the current view controller and the modal view controller.

We retrieve a managed object context from the cust instance (of the Customer class) and assign it to the instance: context (of the NSManagedObjectContext class). Then we insert a new managed object (of the *Product* entity) into the managed context: context using the class method on NSEntityDescription. Also, we return the instance of class that represents the *Product* entity and assign it to the prod object (of the Product class), which in turn is assigned to the prod object of the addprodController (instance of the AddProductController class), which will be used to accept the information of the new product (sold to the customer). Also, the prod instance is added to the cust object using one of the auto generated methods (on defining relationship): addProductObject. Recall that addProductObject adds a single managed object of the *Product* entity to the product relationship:

```
-(IBAction) editproduct:(id)sender
{
  if([editbutton.title isEqualToString:@"Edit"])
  {
    editbutton.title=@"Done";
    [self.tableView setEditing:YES animated:YES];
  }
  else
  {
    editbutton.title=@"Edit";
    [self.tableView setEditing:NO animated:YES];
  }
}
```

The method `editproduct` is invoked when Bar Button Item control with title: `Edit` is selected. This method changes the title of the **Edit** button to **Done** and enables the table's editing feature (by setting the value of the `setEditing` message to `YES`. When the table's editing feature is set to `On`, a red deletion icon appears to the left of each table cell, which when selected prompts for confirmation of deletion of the selected cell. On selecting the **Done** button, the table's editing feature is switched `Off` (by setting the value of the `setEditing` message to `NO`):

```
-(void) addprodController:(AddProductController *)controller
selectedsave:(BOOL) save {
  NSManagedObjectContext *context = [cust managedObjectContext];
  if(!save)
  {
    [cust removeProductObject:prod];
  }
  NSError *error;

  if(![context save:&error]){
    NSLog(@"Unresolved error %@ %@", error, [error userInfo]);
    exit(-1);
  }
  [self dismissModalViewControllerAnimated:YES];
}
```

The `addprodController` method is the implementation method for the delegate of the `AddProductController` class and is invoked by the `cancel` and `save` methods (defined in the implementation file of the `AddProductController` class). The `cancel` method calls the previous method and passes the `selectedsave` parameter set to value `NO` whereas, the `save` method calls the method with the `selectedsave` parameter set to value `YES`. The value of the `selectedsave` parameter is assigned to the variable: `save`. In the method, we check that if the value of the variable save is `NO`, then we delete the `prod` instance from the `cust` object (a managed object of the *Product* entity was added to the product relationship in the `addproduct` method) and then save the context in the persistent store:

```
(.....)

//Customize the appearance of table view cells.
- (UITableViewCell *)tableView:(UITableView *)tableView cellForRowAtIndexPath:(NSIndexPath *)indexPath {
  static NSString *CellIdentifier = @"Cell";
  UITableViewCell *cell = [self.tableView dequeueReusableCellWithIdentifier:CellIdentifier];
  if (cell == nil) {
```

```
    cell = [[[UITableViewCell alloc] initWithStyle:UITableViewCellStyl
eDefault reuseIdentifier:CellIdentifier] autorelease];
    }
    Product *prd=[products objectAtIndex:indexPath.row];
    cell.textLabel.text=prd.itemname;
    return cell;
}
```

In the `cellForRowAtIndexPath` method, we fetch the instance of the *Product* instance from the product's array and the `itemname` attribute of the product instance is displayed as the table cell's text:

```
- (void)tableView:(UITableView *)tableView commitEditingStyle:(UITabl
eViewCellEditingStyle)editingStyle forRowAtIndexPath:(NSIndexPath *)
indexPath {
    if (editingStyle == UITableViewCellEditingStyleDelete) {

        NSManagedObjectContext *contxt = [fetchedResultsController
managedObjectContext];
        [contxt deleteObject:[fetchedResultsController
objectAtIndexPath:indexPath]];
        Product *prod = [products objectAtIndex:indexPath.row];
        [cust removeProductObject:prod];
        [products removeObject:prod];
        NSManagedObjectContext *context = prod.managedObjectContext;
        [context deleteObject:prod];

        [self.tableView deleteRowsAtIndexPaths:[NSArray
arrayWithObject:indexPath] withRowAnimation:UITableViewRowAnimationT
op];
    }
}
```

In the `commitEditingStyle` method that is executed when we select the `Delete` accessory on any table cell, we retrieve a managed object context from the `fetchedResultsController` instance and assign it to the instance: `contxt` (of the `NSManagedObjectContext` class) and delete the object from the `contxt` object table cell whose `Delete` accessory is selected. Besides this, we also delete the `prod` instance from the `cust` object (a managed object of *Product* entity that was added to the product relationship in the `addproduct` method). We also delete the `prod` instance from the product's table (that represents all the products sold to the selected customer). We also retrieve the managed object context from the prod instance (of the Product's entity) and assign it to the instance: `context` and delete the `prod` instance from the context too.

We cannot execute this module until and unless it is connected with the rest of the project via the `DisplayCustomerController` class (we will learn this connection procedure in the following module).

Creating a module to connect the Product's menu to the rest of the project

In this module, we will see how to connect the Product's menu (View of the `ProductInfoController` class) to the `DisplayCustomerController` class (the class that displays information of the selected customer) so that the product's menu can be invoked from there allowing us to enter/edit information of the products sold to the customer.

The steps involved in developing this module are as follows:

1. Defining the outlets and action methods in the header file: `DisplayCustomerController.h`.

2. Adding the Toolbar control to the View of the `DisplayCustomerController` class.

3. Coding in the implementation file: `DisplayCustomerController.m` to invoke the View of the `ProductInfoController` class.

Defining the outlets and action methods in the header file

The `ProductInfoController` class has to be invoked from the View of the `DisplayCustomerController` class (that displays the information of the selected customer). So, we need to add a Toolbar in the View of the `DisplayCustomerController` class that contains a Bar Button Item controller, which when selected navigates us to the View of `ProductInfoController` class. We declare an action method by the name: `showproduct` in the header file of the `DisplayCustomerController` class (which will be invoked when the Bar Button Item control in the Toolbar control is selected). Also, we need to import the header file of the `ProductInfoController` class in the `DisplayCustomerController` class, so that we can create its instance for navigating it. The header file of the `DisplayCustomerController` class (`DisplayCustomerController.h`) may be modified to appear as shown next:

```
//   DisplayCustomerController.h
//   prob
#import <UIKit/UIKit.h>
```

```
#import "Customer.h"
#import "ProductInfoController.h"

@protocol DisplayCustomerControllerDelegate;

@interface DisplayCustomerController : UIViewController {
   Customer *cust;
   id <DisplayCustomerControllerDelegate> delegate;
   IBOutlet UITextField *name;
   IBOutlet UITextField *emailid;
   IBOutlet UITextField *contactno;
}

@property(nonatomic, retain) Customer *cust;
@property(nonatomic, retain) id <DisplayCustomerControllerDelegate>
delegate;
@property(nonatomic, retain) UITextField *name;
@property(nonatomic, retain) UITextField *emailid;
@property(nonatomic, retain) UITextField *contactno;
-(IBAction) showproduct:(id)sender;

@end

@protocol DisplayCustomerControllerDelegate
-(void) displaycust:(DisplayCustomerController *)controller
   selecteddone:(BOOL) done;
@end
```

Adding a Toolbar control to the View of the DisplayCustomerController class

After defining the action method in the header file, the next step is to place a *Toolbar* control in the View of the DisplayCustomerController class. Follow the given steps to do so:

1. Open the DisplayCustomerController.xib file in the **Interface Builder** and drag a Toolbar control from the **Windows, Views & Bars** category of the **Library** window and drop it at the bottom of the View. The *Toolbar* control contains a *Bar Button Item* control by default (with **Title**: Item).

2. Drag the two **Flexible Space Bar Button Item** from the **Windows, Views & Bars** category and drop it on either side of the Bar Button Item control (of the toolbar) to shift it at the center of the Toolbar control.

3. From the **Attributes Inspector**, change the **Title** of the Bar Button Item control to **Product Information**.

To invoke the action method: showproduct (that we defined in the header file: DisplayCustomerController.h) when the *Bar Button Item* control is selected in the View, we need to connect the Bar Button Item control with the action method. Follow the given steps to do so:

1. Select the **File's Owner** icon in the **Documents** window and open the **Connections Inspector** window.

2. Under the **Received Actions** heading, we find the action method: **showproduct** (that we defined in the header file). Select the circle to the right of the action method: **showproduct** and keeping the mouse button pressed, drag it to the Bar Button Item control in the Toolbar control, as shown in the following screenshot.

3. Quit the Interface Builder by selecting **Interface Builder | Quit Interface Builder**. We will be prompted whether to save the .xib file; select the **Save** button to save the file.

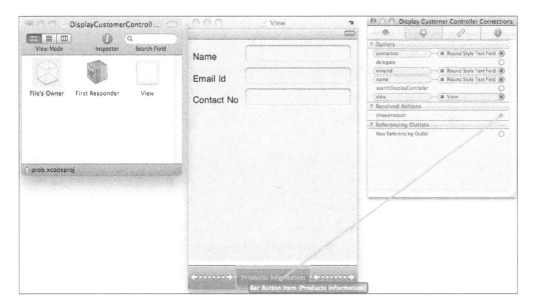

Coding in the implementation file to invoke the View of the ProductInfoController class

We need to write code for the action method: showproduct in the implementation file of the DisplayCustomerController class that will navigate us to the View of ProductInfoController class. Only the statements in bold are added to the implementation file: DisplayCustomerController.h (rest of the code is the same as we saw in *Chapter 7, Updating and Searching Records of Customers*).

```
//  DisplayCustomerController.m
//  prob

#import "DisplayCustomerController.h"

@implementation DisplayCustomerController

@synthesize name;
@synthesize emailid;
@synthesize contactno;
@synthesize cust;
@synthesize delegate;

// Implement viewDidLoad to do additional setup after loading the
view, typically from a nib.
- (void)viewDidLoad {
    [super viewDidLoad];
  self.title=@"Customer Information";
  name.text=cust.name;
  emailid.text=cust.emailid;
  contactno.text=cust.contactno;
  name.enabled=NO;
  emailid.enabled=NO;
  contactno.enabled=NO;
  self.navigationItem.rightBarButtonItem=self.editButtonItem;
}

-(void) setEditing:(BOOL) editing animated:(BOOL) animated {
  [super setEditing:editing animated:animated];
  name.enabled=YES;
  emailid.enabled=YES;
  contactno.enabled=YES;
  if(!editing)
  {
    cust.name=name.text;
```

```
        cust.emailid=emailid.text;
        cust.contactno=contactno.text;
        name.enabled=NO;
        emailid.enabled=NO;
        contactno.enabled=NO;
        [delegate displaycust: self selecteddone:YES ];
    }
}


-(IBAction) showproduct:(id)sender
{
    ProductInfoController *prodinfo =[[ProductInfoController alloc] init
WithNibName:@"ProductInfoController" bundle:nil];
    prodinfo.cust=cust;
    [self    presentModalViewController:prodinfo animated:YES];
    [prodinfo release];
}

-  (void)dealloc {
    [name release];
    [emailid release];
    [contactno release];
    [cust release];
        [super dealloc];
}


@end
```

An instance of the `ProductInfoController` class with the name: `prodinfo` is created and initialized. The `alloc` method is used to create the view controller object and is initialized with the help of the `initWithNibName:@"ProductInfoController"` `bundle:nil`. The `init` method specifies the name of the NIB file that has to be loaded by the controller followed by the bundle where the NIB file is expected to be found. The bundle parameter is set to nil as we want the method to look for the NIB file in the main bundle. The information of the selected customer (from the table view of `DisplayCustomerController` class) is then assigned to the `cust` instance: of the `ProductInfoController` class (`prodinfo`) as we will be using the information of the selected customer in the `ProductInfoController` class. Then we display the View of the `ProductInfoController` modally using the `presentModalViewController:an` `imated:` method; the view controller animates the appearance of the view and creates a parent-child relationship between the current view controller and the modal view controller. Finally, the memory allocated to the `prodinfo` instance is released.

Running the project

As all the three modules are complete, we can now run the project. Let us select the *Build and Go* icon from the **Xcode Project** window. Initially, we get a table view with existing list of customers (*image (a)*) with the **Edit** and the **+** (plus) button on the left and right sides of the navigation bar. We can add or delete the customers if desired. On selecting a customer from the table cell, his detailed information comprising his name, e-mail ID, and contact number will be displayed, as shown in the following *image (b)*. We can edit the customer's information by selecting the **Edit** button in the navigation bar and also can select the **Product Information** button in the toolbar at the bottom of the View to enter or edit the information of the products sold to the selected customer. On selecting the **Products Information** button, we get a View, as shown in the following *image (c)*:

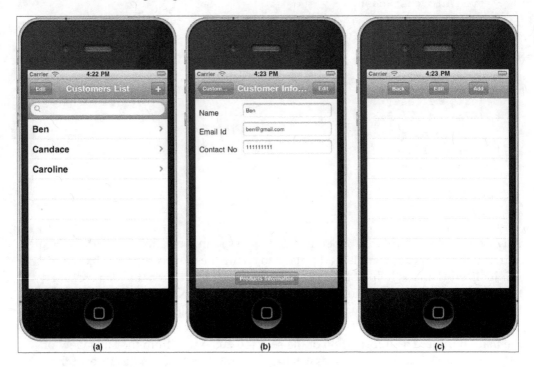

On selecting the **Add** button from the toolbar, we get a View to enter the information of the product (item name, price, and quantity) sold to the selected customer, as shown in the following *image (a)*. The added product will appear in the table view on selecting the **Save** button (after entering the product's information), as shown in the following *image (b)*. The list of all products sold to the selected customer appears, as shown in the following *image (c)*:

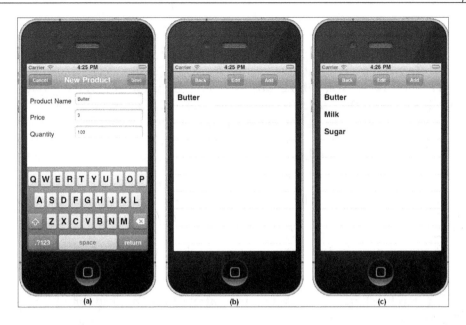

On selecting the **Edit** button from the toolbar, the deletion accessory (icons in red) appears on the left of each table cell (*image (a)*). The **Delete** button appears (asking for confirmation) when the deletion accessory of any table cell is selected (*image (b)*). On selecting the **Delete** button, the table cell is deleted and table view is updated, as shown in the following *image (c)*:

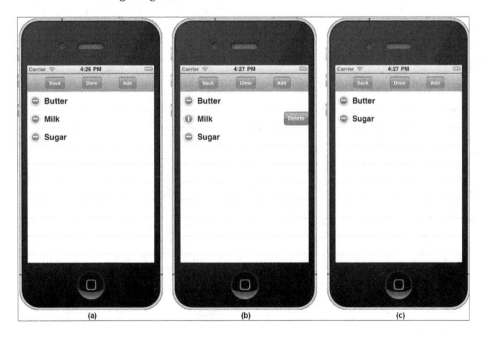

Summary

In this chapter, we saw how a *Product* Entity is added to our existing Data Model. We saw different types of relationships and learned to establish relationship in both forward as well as backward directions between the Customer and the Product entities. We also saw the usage of Inverse relationship. We also saw different options of Delete Rules and how do they effect another managed object when one managed object is deleted. We also developed Data Model (classes) associated with both the entities. We also saw the role of the special methods that are auto generated for the relationship that we established from the *Customer* to the *Product* entity.

In this chapter, we also learnt how to enter and maintain the information of the product(s) sold to the selected customer. The task being a bit large, it was divided into three modules. We first developed a module that created a View to enter the information of the product(s) that is sold to the selected customer. Then, to allow the user to add, save, and edit the information of the products entered, we have learned about the creation of a second module that explained the creation of the product's menu in a step-by-step manner (containing buttons to be invoked for adding, saving, and editing the product's information). The third and final module explained how to connect the product's menu to the `DisplayCustomerController` class (that displays the information of the selected customer), so that information of the product(s) sold to the selected customer can be entered. In the next chapter, we will learn to create a *MasterProduct* entity that will be used for storing the information of products that the vendor is dealing with, that is, stock. Also, we will learn how the transformable data type can be used for creating custom data types for storing images of the products. We will also be learning how Image Picker works and is used in selecting images. Besides this, we will be learning how Value Transformer is created that is used for converting a custom object into an NSData instance for saving in the persistent store.

9
Entering, Displaying, and Deleting the Stock

In the previous chapter, we learnt now to add a *Product* entity to our existing Data Model and also how to enter and maintain the information of the product(s) sold to the selected customer. In this chapter, we will learn:

- To create a *MasterProduct* entity that will be used for storing the information of products that the vendor is dealing with, that is, stock.

- The concept of the data type: *transformable* that is used for creating custom data types for storing the image of the product. Also, we will be learning how Image Picker works and is used in selecting images. Besides this, we will be learning about some methods that will be used to make the image to appear within the specified *size*.

- How a *Value Transformer* is created that is used for converting custom object into an NSData instance for saving in persistent store.

- How to enter, save, display, delete, and modify the information of the master products that our vendor deals with.

The information of the products entered in the *MasterProduct* entity is very different from the information of the product entered in the *Product* entity. In the *Product* entity, we store the information of the products that are sold to the customers (that is, it keeps the record of *Sales*), whereas the information of the products entered in the *MasterProduct* entity refers to the products that are available for sale (that is, it keeps the record of available *Stock*).

Adding the MasterProduct entity to the Data Model

We need an extra entity to store the information of different products that a vendor is supposed to sell through this application. The information of master product includes product name, price, quantity in hand, and product image, so the entity that we are going to create will consist of four attributes: *itemname*, *price*, *quantity*, and *image*. The steps for adding the *MasterProduct* entity are as follows:

1. Let us open the Xcode's Data Modeling tool by double-clicking the **prob. xcdatamodel** file from the **Resources** group in **Xcode Project** window.

2. To add a new entity to our data model, select the **+** (plus) button at the bottom of the **Entity** pane or choose **Design | Data Model | Add Entity** from the menu bar. A blank entity (by default **name**: **Entity**) will be added to our data model, which we will rename to `MasterProduct`. Automatically, a subclass of **NSManagedObject** will be created for our **MasterProduct** entity.

3. To add attributes to our **MasterProduct** entity, we either choose **Design | Data Model | Add Attribute** from the menu bar or select the **+** (plus) button in the **Property** pane. When we select the **+** button (from the **Property** pane), a menu with several options such as: **Add Attributes**, **Add Fetched Property**, **Add Relationship**, and **Add Fetch Request** will popup.

4. Select the **Add Attributes** option from the popup to add attributes to our **MasterProduct** entity. The attributes that we will add to our **MasterProduct** entity will be **itemname, quantity, price**, and **image** of data types: **String, Integer 16, Float**, and **Transformable** respectively. The **MasterProduct** entity with its attributes may appear, as shown in the following screenshot.

As the **MasterProduct** table is not related to any of the existing entities (neither with **Customer** nor with **Product** entity), in the diagram view of the following screenshot, we see that the **MasterProduct** entity appears as isolated:

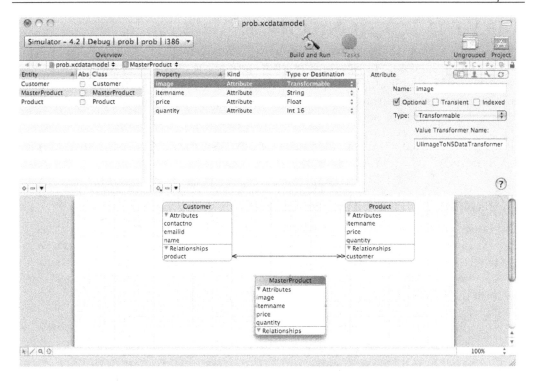

Storing the image of the MasterProduct

For storing the image of the master product, we will be assigning a special data type to the image attribute of the **MasterProduct** entity. That special data type is **Transformable** data type. So, let us have an idea of that data type before we move further.

Transformable data type

The *Transformable* data type is a special data type that allows us to create attributes based on an Objective-C class (custom objects). This data type is heavily used for storing instances of *UIImage, UIColor*, and so on. As the information stored in the persistent store has to be in the form of *NSData* instance, while using Transformable data type, we need to create *Value Transformers* to convert the custom object (information in attribute of Transformable data type) into an instance of NSData (before storing in the persistent store) and to convert the instance of NSData back to custom object while retrieving from the persistent store.

The Value Transformer Name: field

In this field, we specify the name of the Value Transformer class that will be used for converting a custom object (information store in the attribute of the *Transformable* data type) into an NSData instance for saving in the persistent store, and vice versa. Let us name our value transformer class as: `UIImageToNSDataTransformer` as shown in the preceding screenshot.

Let us create our value transformer class for our Transformable (image attribute) data type.

Creating a value transformer

The value transformers are used for converting objects of image type, color type, and so on into NSData object for storing in the persistent store, and vice versa, that is, take the NSData object from the persistent store and convert it into their custom object type (older format—color, image, and so on). To create the Value transformer, perform the following steps:

1. Right-click on the **Classes** folder in the **Xcode Project** window and select **Add | New File** option.

2. Select the **Objective-C class** option (for the template of our new file) as shown in the following screenshot.

3. Leave the subclass of the drop-down to be **NSObject**. Select the **Next** button.

4. We will be asked to specify the name of the new **NSObject** subclass. Assign the name as: `UIImageToNSDataTransformer.h` and select the **Finish** button.

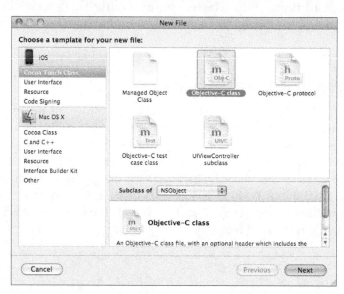

The header and implementation files of our value transformer class:
UIImageToNSDataTransformer will be created. Write the following code in the file
UIImageToNSDataTransformer.h:

```
//   UIImageToNSDataTransformer.h
//   prob

#import <UIKit/UIKit.h>

@interface UIImageToNSDataTransformer : NSValueTransformer {
}

@end
```

As we can see in the preceding code, for creating a value transformer, we need to
subclass the NSValueTransformer class.

Write the following code in the UIImagetoNSDataTransformer.m file:

```
//   UIImageToNSDataTransformer.m
//   prob

#import "UIImageToNSDataTransformer.h"

@implementation UIImageToNSDataTransformer
+(Class)transformedValueClass{
  return [NSData class];
}

+(BOOL) allowsReverseTransformation{
  return YES;
}

-(id)transformedValue:(id) value
{
return UIImagePNGRepresentation(value);
}

-(id)reverseTransformedValue:(id) value{

  return [[[UIImage alloc] initWithData:value] autorelease];
}

@end
```

As we can see in the preceding code, we need to override the `transformedValueClass` method that returns the class of the converted object. This method will return an instance of the `NSData` class as the image will be stored in this format only in the persistent store. Recall that we want our Value Transformer to transform an instance of *UIImage* (data in an image attribute) to an instance of the `NSData` class (for storing in the persistent store) and vice versa, for retrieving the data in the form of an instance of NSData (from the persistent store) and transforming it back to the instance of the `UIImage` class. The `allowsReverseTransformation` method is overridden for allowing reverse transformation procedure (converting the instance of NSData to the instance of UIImage). We set this method to return *YES* to make the reverse transformation possible.

The `transformedValue` method is overridden to accept the instance of the `UIImage` class and return the instance of the transformed class (the `NSData` class). Similarly, the `reverseTransformedValue` method is overridden to accept the instance of the transformed class (the `NSData` class) and transform back to the instance of the original class (the `UIImage` class).

Building the data object for the MasterProduct entity

To build the data objects (classes) for the *MasterProduct* entity defined in the data model, follow the given steps:

1. Click any entity in the data model editor and then choose the **File | New File** option. We get a dialog box to choose the template for the new file.

2. Select **Cocoa Touch Classes** from under the **iPhone OS** heading in the left-pane and select the **Managed Object Class** template. We get a dialog box that prompts for the location of generating the managed object class. Keeping the values as default select the **Next** button.

3. Check the **MasterProduct** entity in the dialog box that appears (there is no need for selecting the checkbox for Customer and Product's entity as their managed object classes are already created). We find two checkboxes that are already checked: **Generate accessors** and **Generate Obj-C 2.0 Properties**. Keeping the two checkboxes checked, select the **Finish** button.

We find two files: `MasterProduct.h` and `MasterProduct.m` (`Customer.h`, `Customer.m`, `Product.h`, and `Product.m` were already there) generated in the **Classes** folder of the **Xcode Project** window with the following contents:

```
//  MasterProduct.h
//  prob
```

```
#import <CoreData/CoreData.h>

@interface MasterProduct : NSManagedObject
{
}

@property (nonatomic, retain) NSNumber * price;
@property (nonatomic, retain) NSNumber * quantity;
@property (nonatomic, retain) id image;
@property (nonatomic, retain) NSString * itemname;


@end
```

In the preceding code, we see that the properties are defined with the names: `price`, `quantity`, `image`, and `itemname`. These properties are not declared in the header file as they will be created dynamically.

The implementation file, `MasterProduct.m` will have the following code by default:

```
//   MasterProduct.m
//   prob

#import "MasterProduct.h"

@implementation MasterProduct

@dynamic price;
@dynamic quantity;
@dynamic image;
@dynamic itemname;

@end
```

In the implementation file, we find that the properties are marked as dynamic to inform the compiler not to generate accessors and mutators for the properties and will be generated by the super class at runtime and hence not to display any warning message related to them.

Maintaining the MasterProduct information

To maintain information of the MasterProduct, we have to do four tasks:

- Develop a View to enter the MasterProduct's information
- Develop a MasterProduct's menu to add, delete, and display information of master products
- Connect the MasterProduct's menu to the `RootViewController` class (the class that displays the first View when application is launched) so that MasterProduct's menu can be invoked from there
- Develop a View to display and modify the selected MasterProduct's information

To execute these preceding tasks, we need to create four modules:

- Module to develop an interface to enter information of the MasterProduct that the vendor deals with
- Module to create a menu for manipulating the MasterProduct information. That is, we create buttons that are connected to methods to save, display, and delete MasterProduct's information
- Module to connect the MasterProduct's menu to the rest of the project
- Module to modify the information of the MasterProduct

For the sake of convenience, we will be learning to create only first and second module in this chapter. We will learn about the third and fourth modules in the next chapter.

There is an important concept that we need to understand before we begin with the creation of the first module. As we wish to store the image of the MasterProduct too, we need to understand two things:

- Image Picker — used in selecting images
- How to make an image appear within the specified size (for display)

So, before we look at the creation of the preceding modules, let us see what an Image Picker is and how an image can be confined within a particular size.

Image Picker

Image Picker is used for displaying images allowing the user to choose or pick any image. There are three sources from where the Image Picker can pick the images to display:

- Photo library
- Camera
- Saved photos

We can define the source of the image picker by setting its `sourceType` property.

The syntax is as follows:

```
imagePicker.sourceType =value
```

Where `imagePicker` is an instance of the `UIImagePickerController` class and the `sourceType` property can have any of the following three values:

- `UIImagePickerControllerSourceTypePhotoLibrary` for setting source to Photo Library (a built-in library provided by iPhone SDK)
- `UIImagePickerControllerSourceTypeCamera` for setting source to Camera (images taken with our camera)
- `UIImagePickerControllerSourceTypeSavedPhotosAlbum` for setting source to the photos saved on the phone

We can set the `sourceType` property of the `imagePicker` instance, as shown in the following example:

```
imagePicker.sourceType=UIImagePickerControllerSourceTypePhotoLibrary;
```

> The default source type is
> `UIImagePickerControllerSourceTypePhotoLibrary`.

Adding custom images to the Image Picker

To add our own photos to the Photo Library, we follow the given steps:

1. In iPhone Simulator, click **Home**, then click the **Photos** icon (refer to the following *image (a)*).
2. We get the **Albums** page, as shown in the following *image (b)*. As we have not created any photo album yet, the image displays the message, No Photos.

3. Drag the image from your Mac onto the simulator screen. Tap on the image and hold down the mouse on the image until the popover comes up, as shown in the following *image (c)*. Choose the **Save Image** button to save the image.

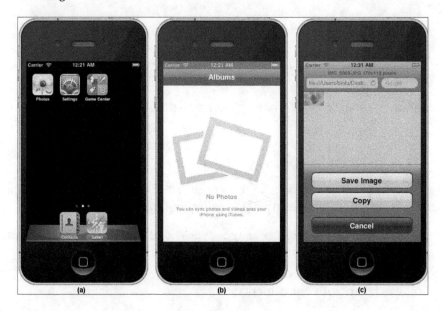

4. Repeat the procedure for other images. Assuming we have saved four images, the simulator will display the images, as shown in the following *image (a)*.

5. On clicking back to **Photos**, we find that an album **Saved Photos** appears with one of the images considered as the icon of the photo album (*image (b)*). The number **(4)** in parenthesis represents that there are four images in this photo album.

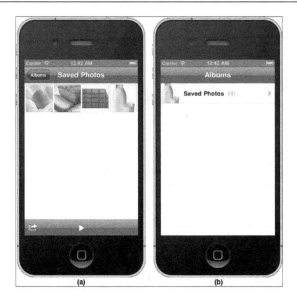

(a)　　　　(b)

Making an image appear within a given size

We will be making use of the following structures and functions to assign a specified size to an image. Let us get an idea of what is the usage of these structures and functions.

`CGSize structure`: The CGSize structure represents the size of a rectangle and is used for storing information related to the width and height of the object.

Examples:

```
CGSize size=pimage.size;
```

The width and height of the image in `pimage` instance (of the `UIImage` class) is assigned to size instance of the CGSize.

```
CGSize size=CGSizeMake(100.0, 150.0);
```

The width of 100 pixels and height of 150 pixels is assigned to *size* instance of the CGSize.

`CGSizeMake function`: CGSizeMake function is used for defining the width and height of an element. Only coordinates to specify width and height of the object are provided (and not of the origin).

Example:

```
CGSize size = CGRectMake(x1,y1);
```

Where x1 and y1 are the coordinates that define the width and height of an object. An instance size of CGSize structure is defined with the width and height defined by x1 and y1 coordinates.

CGRect: The CGRect structure is used for defining the frame of a window on the screen. It includes four floating point values:

- The first two floating point values represent the origin (upper-left corner of the window): horizontal and vertical coordinates
- The third and fourth float point values represent the width and height of the window

Example:

```
CGRect rect = CGRectMake(x1,y1,x2,y2);
```

Where x1, y1 are the coordinates for the upper-left corner of the window and x2, y2 are the coordinates that represent the width and height of the window.

In the preceding example, the instance rect of CGRect is created with the help of CGRectMake function, that is, the frame of a window for the *rect* instance is defined with the help of CGRectMake function.

CGRectMake function: CGRectMake function is used for defining the frame of a window of an object. With the help of this function, we specify the coordinates of the origin as well as the width and height of the frame.

Example:

```
CGRect rect = CGRectMake(x1,y1,x2,y2);
```

We define an instance *rect* of CGRect structure.

UIGraphicsBeginImageContext(): This creates bitmap based graphics context (drawing environment).

UIGraphicsEndImageContext(): This removes the graphics context (from the top of the context stack).

UIGraphicsGetImageFromCurrentimageContext(): After the graphics context is created, we use this function to retrieve the image based on the contents of the current context.

Example:

Assuming we have an image in the instance pimage (of the UIImage class) that we want to confine within the defined size of the frame (of width and height of 50 and 70 pixels, respectively) and want to display it in a table cell, the code for doing so is as follows:

```
CGRect rect = CGRectMake(0.0, 0.0, 50.0, 70.0);
UIGraphicsBeginImageContext(rect.size);
[pimage drawInRect:rect];
cell.imageView.image=UIGraphicsGetImageFromCurrentImageContext();
UIGraphicsEndImageContext();
```

We create an instance rect for defining a frame of a window of width and height 50 and 70 pixels respectively. Then, we configure the drawing environment, that is, we create a bitmap based graphics context using the UIGraphicsBeginImageContext(). In this function, we specify the size of the graphics context (equal to the size of the *rect* instance). After that, we make the image in *pimage* instance to display (render) within the display region specified in the *rect* instance using the drawInRect method. Once the context is created, we retrieve the image based on the contents of the current context using the UIGraphicsGetImageFromCurrentimageContext() and assign it to the *imageView* of the table cell for display. When our job is over, we clean up the bitmap drawing environment (that we created with UIGraphicsBeginImageContext()) and remove the graphics context (from the top of the context stack) using the UIGraphicsEndImageContext().

Module to develop interface to enter the information of the MasterProduct

In this module, we will learn how to add a View that allows us to enter information of the master products. Master Products are the products that we assume that our Vendor deals with, that is, these are the products that are available for sale.

Steps involved in developing this module are as follows:

1. Adding the ViewController class: the AddMasterProductController class for entering information of the master products available for sale.

2. Defining protocol, outlets, and action methods in the header file: AddMasterProductController.h.

3. Designing View of the MasterProductController class and connecting controls.

4. Invoking the *delegate* and the *ImagePicker* methods from the implementation file: AddMasterProductController.m.

Adding the ViewController class for entering information of the master products

The View Controller that we are going to add to the application is the
`AddMasterProductController` class that will provide us a view to add a new
Master Product. The steps for adding the view controller are as follows:

1. Right-click on the **Classes** folder and select the **Add | New File** option.

2. Select the template as: **UIViewController subclass** option.

3. Don't forget to select the checkbox: **With XIB for user interface** followed by
   the **Next** button.

4. Specify the name of the new UIViewController subclass with XIB as
   `AddMasterProductController.m`.

5. Keep the checkbox: **Also create AddMasterProductController.h** checked
   followed by the **Finish** button. Three files, `AddMasterProductController.h`,
   `AddMasterProductController.m`, and `AddMasterProductController.xib`
   will be created in the `Class` folder.

6. Drag the **AddMasterProductController.xib** from the **Classes** to the
   Resources folder — the usual location for the XIB files.

Defining protocol, outlets, and action methods in the header file

In the AddMasterProductController's header file we will define protocol,
outlets, and action methods. First of all, we define a protocol with the name:
`AddMasterProductControllerDelegate`. We define an instance variable by the
name: delegate (any name) of type `id <AddMasterProductControllerDelegate>`.
We also define an object of the `MasterProduct` class with the name: `mastprod` that
will hold the master product's information (that is entered by the user). Also, three
instance variables: `itemname`, `quantity`, and `price` of the `UITextField` class and
an instance variable: `prodimage` of the `UIImageView` class are defined and marked
as outlets (these outlets will be connected to the three Text Field controls and the
UIImageView control that we will be dropping in the View for entering item name,
quantity, price, and image of the master product).

We will write the code as shown in the following header file of the
`AddMasterProductController` class: `AddMasterProductController.h`:

```
// AddMasterProductController.h
// prob

#import <UIKit/UIKit.h>
```

```objc
#import "MasterProduct.h"

@protocol AddMasterProductControllerDelegate;

@interface AddMasterProductController : UIViewController
<UINavigationControllerDelegate, UIImagePickerControllerDelegate>{
  id <AddMasterProductControllerDelegate> delegate;
  MasterProduct *mastprod;
  IBOutlet UIBarButtonItem *cancelbutton;
  IBOutlet UIBarButtonItem *savebutton;
  IBOutlet UITextField *itemname;
  IBOutlet UITextField *quantity;
  IBOutlet UITextField *price;
  IBOutlet UIImageView *prodimage;
}

@property(nonatomic, retain) MasterProduct *mastprod;
@property(nonatomic, retain) id <AddMasterProductControllerDelegate>
delegate;
@property(nonatomic, retain) IBOutlet UIBarButtonItem *cancelbutton;
@property(nonatomic, retain) IBOutlet UIBarButtonItem *savebutton;
@property(nonatomic, retain) UITextField *itemname;
@property(nonatomic, retain) UITextField *quantity;
@property(nonatomic, retain) UITextField *price;
@property(nonatomic, retain) UIImageView *prodimage;

-(IBAction) cancel:(id) sender;
-(IBAction) save:(id)sender;
-(IBAction) selectimagebutton:(id)sender;

@end

@protocol AddMasterProductControllerDelegate
-(void) addmastprodController:(AddMasterProductController *)controller
  selectedsave:(BOOL) save;
@end
```

We can see in the preceding code that two instance variables of the UIBarButtonItem class: cancelbutton and savebutton are defined and marked as outlets. These two outlets will be connected to the two Bar Button Items (that we will soon drag-and-drop on the View) with the titles: Save and Cancel (they will invoke the respective action methods to save or discard the Master Product's information). Three action methods are also defined by the name: cancel, save, and selectimagebutton that will be connected to the two Bar Button Items: Cancel and *Save* and to the *Round Rect button* control respectively. All the instance variables are defined as properties with the two attributes: *retain* and *nonatomic* for generating their accessors and mutators. We also define the method of the AddMasterProductControllerDelegate (between the @protocol and @end directives). We define the method: addmastprodController, that is, the class which will conform to this protocol will have to implement this method. After adding the preceding code, we save the header file.

Designing the View of the MasterProductController class and connecting controls

The View of the AddMasterProductController class will be used to enter information for the new master products.

> The AddMasterProductController class will be invoked from the View of the MasterProductInfoController class. This is the class we will be creating in the second module and will display Master Product's menu to invoke the methods to save, delete, and so on the information of the master products.

The View will consist of three Labels, three Text Fields, a Round Rect button and a UIImageView control. The three Text Fields will be used to enter the name, price, and quantity in hand of the Master Product. The Round Rect button control will invoke the ImagePicker control to select the image of the Master Product. Let us start with the designing of the View by following the given steps:

1. From the **Resources** group in the **Xcode Project** window, open the **AddMasterProductController.xib** file in the Interface Builder and drag-and-drop three **Labels**, three **Text Fields**, a **Round Rect button** control, and a **UIImageView** control in the View.

2. Double-click the **Label** and **Round Rect button** control to edit their text to appear as shown in following screenshot. Besides this, the View also contains two **Bar Button Item** controls with the text: **Save** and **Cancel** respectively to perform the task of either saving or discarding the information of the Master Product entered. So, from the **Windows, Views & Bars** category of the **Library** window drag the **Bar Button Item** control and drop it in the **Documents** window.

3. Repeat the procedure as we want two Bar Button Item controls in the navigation bar (in the View of the AddMasterProductController class) to represent the **Cancel** and **Save** button respectively.

4. From the **Attributes Inspector**, set the title of the Bar Button item controls as **Cancel** and **Save** respectively (the title of the **Bar Button Item** appears as button text in the View).

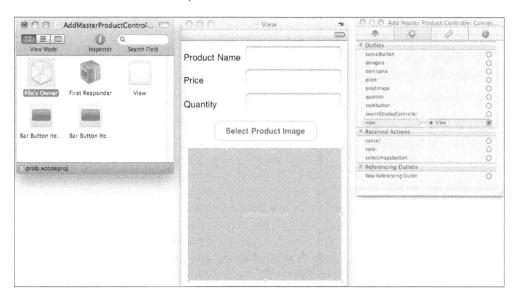

Next step is to connect the four outlets (itemname, price, quantity, and prodimage defined in the header file: AddMasterProductController.h) to the three Text Field controls and the Image View control in the View. Let's do that through the following steps:

1. Select the **File's Owner** icon in the **Documents** window and open the **Connections Inspector**.

2. Select the circle to the right of each outlet (under the Outlets section in **Connections Inspector**) and keeping the mouse button pressed drag it to the respective **Text Field** or **ImageView** control.

Also, we need to connect the outlets of the **Bar Button Item** controls: **cancelbutton** and **savebutton** to the two Bar Button Item controls dropped in the **Documents** window. The procedure is the same; select the circle to the right of the outlet in **Connections Inspector** and keeping the mouse button pressed drag it to the respective Bar Button Item control in the **Documents** window. The following screenshot shows the procedure of connecting the **savebutton** outlet to the **Bar Button Item** control (the one with the title **Save**):

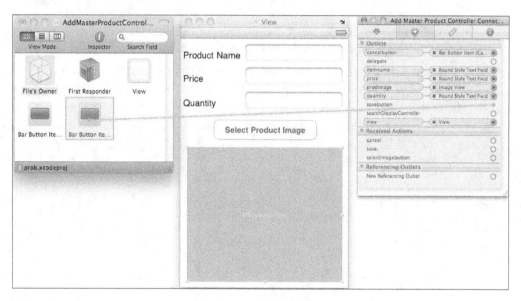

The next step is to connect the *Bar Button Item* controls and the *Round Rect button* control to the action methods: `cancel`, `save`, and `selectimagebutton` defined in the header file of the `AddMasterProductController` class (`AddMasterProductController.h`), so that when any Bar Button Item control (from the navigation bar) or the Round Rect button control from the View is selected, the code in the respective action method is executed to do the desired task. To connect the Action method: `selectimagebutton` to the Round Rect button control, we follow the given steps:

1. Select the circle to the right of the action method: **selectimagebutton** and keeping the mouse button pressed drag it to the **Round Rect button** control and release the mouse button. A menu pops up to select the option that decides when to fire the action method.

2. Select the option: **Touch Up Inside** from the popped up menu (as shown in the following screenshot) so as to invoke the action method: **selectimagebutton** when the user touches the button and lifts the finger without dragging it.

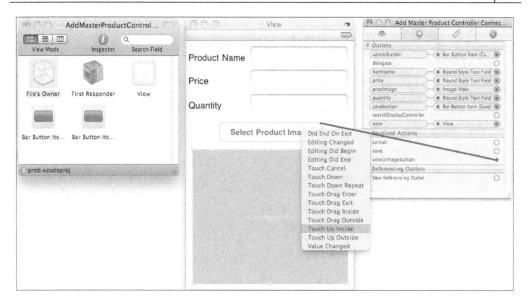

To connect the action methods to the **Bar Button Item** controls, we perform the
following steps:

1. Select the **Bar Button Item** control in the **Documents** window (the one whose
   Title is set as: **Cancel**) and open the **Connections Inspector**.

2. In the **Connections Inspector** under the heading **Sent Actions**, select the
   circle to the right of **selector** and keeping the mouse button pressed drag it
   to the **File's Owner** icon in the **Documents** window and release the mouse
   button.

3. On releasing the mouse button, three action methods defined in the header
   file pop up: **cancel**, **save**, and **selectimagebutton**. We select the **cancel** (action
   method) to connect it to the selected **Bar Button Item** control, as shown in the
   following screenshot.

4. Repeat the procedure for connecting the **Bar Button Item** control with **Save** title to the **save** action method.

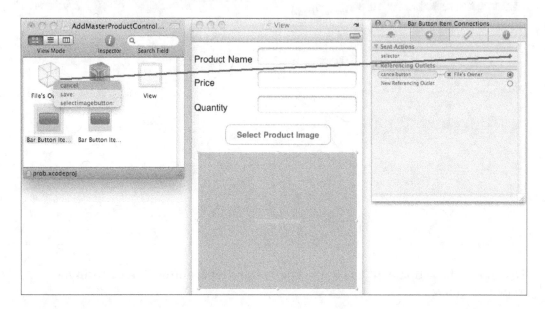

 To make the images selected for the master product to be confined within the boundary of the Image View control dropped in the View, select the Image View control in the View and open the Attributes Inspector. Just check the two checkboxes: **Clip Subviews** and **Autoresize Subviews** are checked (they are already selected by default) to resize them as per the region of the Image View control and clip the region of the image that falls outside the boundary of the Image View control.

Invoking the delegate and ImagePicker methods from the implementation file

In the implementation file of the AddMasterProductController class (AddMasterProductController.m), we need to write the code to display the Bar Button Item controls (to be displayed on the left and right sides of the navigation bar) and for the action methods: cancel and save to invoke the methods of the delegate class (to discard or save the product information in the persistent store) respectively. Also, we need to invoke the ImagePicker control to select the image of the Master Product. The code that we will write in the implementation file will be as follows:

```
//   AddMasterProductController.m
//   prob
```

```objc
#import "AddMasterProductController.h"

@implementation AddMasterProductController

@synthesize savebutton;
@synthesize cancelbutton;
@synthesize delegate;
@synthesize itemname;
@synthesize quantity;
@synthesize price;
@synthesize prodimage;
@synthesize mastprod;

-(IBAction) cancel:(id) sender
{
   [delegate addmastprodController: self selectedsave:NO];
}

-(IBAction) save:(id)sender{
  mastprod.itemname=itemname.text;
  mastprod.quantity=[NSNumber numberWithInt: [quantity.text
intValue]];
  mastprod.price=[NSNumber numberWithFloat: [price.text floatValue]];
  [delegate addmastprodController: self selectedsave:YES ];
}

-(IBAction) selectimagebutton:(id)sender{
  UIImagePickerController *imagePicker = [[UIImagePickerController
alloc] init];
  imagePicker.delegate = self;
  [self presentModalViewController:imagePicker animated:YES];
  [imagePicker release];
}

- (void)imagePickerController:(UIImagePickerControll
er *)picker didFinishPickingImage:(UIImage *)selectedImage
editingInfo:(NSDictionary *)editingInfo {
  prodimage.image=selectedImage;
  mastprod.image=selectedImage;
[self dismissModalViewControllerAnimated:YES];
}

- (void)imagePickerControllerDidCancel:(UIImagePickerController *)
picker {
  [self dismissModalViewControllerAnimated:YES];
```

```objc
}
-(BOOL) textFieldShouldReturn:(UITextField *) textField
{
   if(textField==quantity)
   {
      [quantity resignFirstResponder];
   }
   return YES;
}
// Implement viewDidLoad to do additional setup after loading the
view, typically from a nib.
- (void)viewDidLoad {
   [super viewDidLoad];
   self.title=@"Add Product";
   self.navigationItem.rightBarButtonItem=savebutton;
   self.navigationItem.leftBarButtonItem=cancelbutton;
quantity.delegate=self;
}
- (void)dealloc {
   [savebutton release];
   [cancelbutton release];
   [itemname release];
   [quantity release];
   [price release];
   [prodimage release];
   [mastprod release];
   [super dealloc];
}
@end
```

In the preceding code, first of all, we synthesize the IBOutlets: savebutton,
cancelbutton, delegate, itemname, quantity, price, prodimage, and mastprod)
for generating the accessor and mutator methods for them. In the action method:
cancel, we write the code to invoke the delegate's (MasterProductInfoController
class's) addmastprodController method and set the value of the parameter:
selectedsave to *NO*. Whereas, in the action method: save, we invoke the
addmastprodController method of the delegate with the parameter: selectedsave
set to *YES*. The value of the selectedsave parameter will decide whether to persist
the information of the master product or not (the information of the master product
will be stored in the persistent store if the value of the parameter: selectedsave is
YES). Also, we assign the information entered by the user in the three Text Fields
to the itemname, quantity, and price attributes of the mastprod object (of the
MasterProduct class).

The MasterProductInfoController class will be declared as a delegate of the AddMastProductController class.

The action method: selectimagebutton that is invoked by the Round Rect button control with the text: Select Product Image, defines imagePicker as an instance of the UIImagePickerController class that is used as an image selector.

In the selectimagebutton method, we see that the delegate of the image picker is set to self meaning the same class (the View Controller class: AddMasterProductController) will implement the methods (didFinishPickingImage and imagePickerControllerDidCancel) of the UIImagePicker delegate protocol. The method: didFinishPickingImage is invoked when the user selects an image and the method imagePickerControllerDidCancel is invoked when the user cancels the image selection.

In the didFinishPickingImage method, we assign the selected image (from the image picker) to the prodimage (Image View control placed in the View) for display and to the image attribute of the mastprod object (of the MasterProduct class) and finally, we dismiss the image picker control. In the imagePickerControllerDidCancel method, we simply dismiss the image picker control.

The textFieldShouldReturn method returns a Boolean value informing whether the user has pressed the return key or not (in the keyboard that pops up while the user clicks on any text field control). In this method, we are checking that if the return key of the keyboard is pressed after the user has entered the value in the Text Field: quantity, then we invoke the resignFirstResponder to dismiss the keyboard. The reason for dismissing the keyboard is that the Round Rect button control with text: Select Product Image becomes invisible with the presence of the keyboard (which pops up when the user enters the information of the new master product). This makes it difficult for us to select the image of the Master Product. So, when the user presses the *return* key on the quantity text field, the keyboard is dismissed making the Select Product Image visible, which can then be selected to invoke the image picker.

In the viewDidLoad method, we set the Navigation Item's title to Add product and its right Bar Button Item is set to savebutton (instance variable of Bar Button Item with the title: **Save**). Also, the left Bar Button Item of the navigation bar is set to cancelbutton (the instance variable of UIBarButtonItem class with the title: **Cancel**). Finally, through the dealloc method, we release the memory reserved by different outlets.

Module to create a menu for manipulating the MasterProduct information

In this module, we will learn how to create a MasterProduct's menu that contains several buttons, which can be invoked to see the information of the master products (that are available for sale), to add more master products, and to delete existing master products.

The steps involved in developing this module are as follows:

1. Adding a View Controller class: `MasterProductInfoController` to display the menu for adding, editing, and displaying MasterProducts.

2. Defining outlets and action methods in the header file: `MasterProductInfoController.h`.

3. Designing the View of the `MasterProductInfoController` class and connecting controls.

4. Coding in the implementation file: `MasterProductInfoController.m` to save, edit, and display master product's information.

Adding the View Controller class to display a menu for adding, editing, and displaying the MasterProducts

The View Controller that we are going to add to the application is the `MasterProductInfoController` class that will provide us a view, as shown in the following screenshot, to add and edit the information of the MasterProduct. It will consist of a toolbar with three Bar Button Item controls with text: `Customers List`, `Edit`, and `Add` respectively. The **Customers List** button will navigate us back to the main view (first view) of the application: **Customers List** and the **Edit** and **Add** button will provide us views to edit and add master products respectively. Follow these steps to add the View Controller class:

1. Right-click on the **Classes** folder and select the **Add | New File** option.

2. Select the template as: **UIViewController subclass** option. Don't forget to select the checkbox: **With XIB for user interface** followed by the **Next** button.

3. Specify the name of the **New UIViewController subclass with XIB** as `MasterProductInfoController.m`.

4. Keep the checkbox: **Also create MasterProductInfoController.h** selected followed by the **Finish** button. Three files MasterProductInfoController.h, MasterProductInfoController.m, and MasterProductInfoController.xib will be created in the **Classes** folder.

5. Drag the MasterProductInfoController.xib from the **Classes** to the **Resources** folder.

Defining the outlets and action methods in the header file

The code that we will write in the header file of the MasterProductInfoController class: MasterProductInfoController.h will be as follows:

```
// MasterProductInfoController.h
// prob

#import <UIKit/UIKit.h>
#import "MasterProduct.h"
#import "AddMasterProductController.h"

@interface MasterProductInfoController : UIViewController
<NSFetchedResultsControllerDelegate,
AddMasterProductControllerDelegate> {
  MasterProduct *mastprod;
  NSMutableArray *mastproducts;
  NSFetchedResultsController *fetchedResultsController;
  IBOutlet UIBarButtonItem *custlistbutton;
  IBOutlet UIBarButtonItem *editmastbutton;
  IBOutlet UIBarButtonItem *addmastbutton;
  UITableView *tableView;
}

@property (nonatomic, retain) NSFetchedResultsController
*fetchedResultsController;
@property(nonatomic, retain) MasterProduct *mastprod;
@property(nonatomic, retain) NSMutableArray *mastproducts;
@property(nonatomic, retain)  UIBarButtonItem *custlistbutton;
@property(nonatomic, retain)  UIBarButtonItem *editmastbutton;
@property(nonatomic, retain)  UIBarButtonItem *addmastbutton;
@property(nonatomic, retain)  IBOutlet UITableView *tableView;

-(IBAction) custlist:(id) sender;
-(IBAction) addmastproduct:(id)sender;
```

```
-(IBAction) editmastproduct:(id)sender;

@end
```

In the preceding header file we set the `MasterProductInfoController` class as a delegate of the `FetchedResultsController` as well as of the `AddMasterProductController` class, that is, we will be implementing the methods defined in the delegate protocols of these classes. We also define the object of the `MasterProduct` class with the name: `mastprod` that will be used to store the information of the new master product added to the application. An instance variable of the `NSFetchedResultsController` class is declared by the name: `fetchedResultsController`. Three instance variables of the `UIButtonItem` class are created: `custlistbutton`, `editmastbutton`, and `addmastbutton` and are defined as outlets (will be used for connecting them to the three Bar Button Item controls that we will be placing in the View). An instance variable of the `UITableView` class is created and is defined as an outlet (for connecting with the table view that we will be placing in the View).

All the instance variables are defined as properties with the two attributes: *retain* and *nonatomic* for generating the accessors and mutators without any overhead code (when synthesized) and for keeping the objects retained to the mutators without being flushed from memory. Also three action methods are declared by the name `custlist`, `addmastproduct`, and `editmastproduct` respectively. The action method `custlist` will take us back to the main view of the application: `Customers List` view (`RootViewController` class). The `addmastproduct` action method will invoke the View of the `AddMasterProductController` class (that we will be soon adding to the project to enter the information of the master products dealt by the vendor) and `editmastproduct` action method will be used to display *Deletion* accessory to delete the entry of any master product.

Designing the View of the MasterProductInfoController class and connecting controls

The View of the `MasterProductInfoController` class will be used as the main menu of the Master Products that will not only display the existing master products but will also provide buttons to add, edit, and modify their contents.

 The `MasterProductInfoController` class will be invoked from the View of the `RootViewController` class.

Besides displaying the list of master products, this View will also display a Toolbar with three Bar Button Item controls that will help in navigating back to the RootViewController class, to the AddMasterProductController class (to enter information of the new master products), and also to edit (delete) any entry of the master product. So, let us begin with the procedure of dropping controls such as Table View, a toolbar, and Bar Button Item controls onto the View of the MasterProductInfoController class. The steps for doing so are as follows:

1. From the **Resources** group in the **Xcode Project** window, open the **MasterProductInfoController.xib** file in the Interface Builder and drag-and-drop a Toolbar control at the top in the View. The toolbar control comes with a default Bar Button Item control.

2. We will drop two more Bar Button Item controls onto the toolbar.

3. Drag-and-drop a table View control below the Toolbar control.

4. The Bar Button Item controls in the toolbar have a default title: **Item**. So, we take the help of the **Attributes Inspector** to set the **Titles** of the Bar Button Item controls to Customers List, Edit, and Add respectively.

The next step is to connect the custlistbutton, editmastbutton, and addmastbutton outlets (defined in the header file: MasterProductInfoController.h) to the three Bar Button Item controls in the toolbar, respectively. Let's do it by following these steps:

1. Select the **File's Owner** icon in the **Documents** window and open the **Connections Inspector**.

2. In the **Connections Inspector** under the **Outlets** heading, we get the list of outlets that we defined in the header file of the MasterProductInfoController class. Select the circle to the right of each outlet one by one and keeping the mouse button pressed drag them to the respective Bar Button Item controls.

The following screenshot demonstrates the connection procedure of the **addmastbutton** outlet with the Bar Button Item control with the text: **Add**:

Similarly, to connect the **tableView** outlet (defined in the header file) with the **TableView** control in the View, select the circle to the right of the **tableView** outlet and keeping the mouse button pressed drag it to the **TableView** control in the View, as shown in the following screenshot:

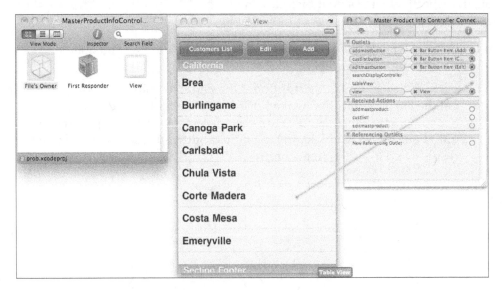

Next, we need to connect the Bar Button Item controls with the action methods defined in the header file. Again, the procedure is the same that we used for the outlets, that is, select the circle to the right of each action method (defined under the heading **Received Actions** in **Connections Inspector**) one by one and keeping the mouse pressed drag them to the respective **Bar Button Item** controls (the ones that we want to fire the action method). The following screenshot displays the procedure of connecting the **custlist** action method with the **Bar Button Item** control with the text: **Customers List**:

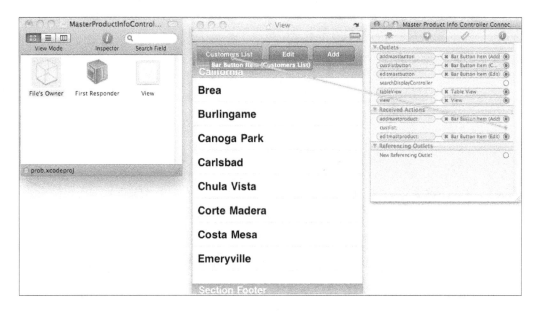

As we want the class `MasterProductInfoController.m` to implement the methods of the tableView (that we dropped in the View), we need to declare the `MasterProductInfoController` class as the delegate and dataSource of the table view. The steps for doing so are as follows:

1. Select the **TableView** control in the View and open the Connections Inspector. We find two outlets: **dataSource** and **delegate**.

2. Select the circle to each of the outlets one by one and keeping the mouse pressed, drag them to the **File's Owner** icon in the **Documents** window, as shown in the following screenshot.

Recall the File's Owner icon represents the View Controller class (MasterProductInfoController class), so this connection procedure will declare the MasterProductInfoController class as the delegate and dataSource of the **TableView** control.

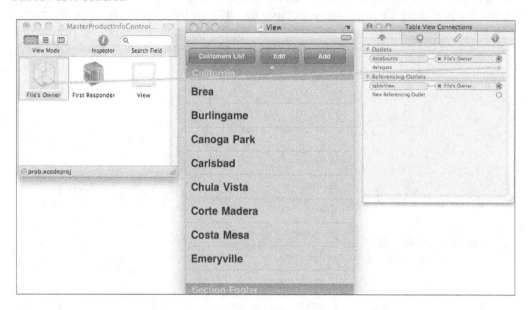

Coding in the implementation file to save, edit, and display the master product's information

The implementation file of the MasterProductInfoController class (MasterProductInfoController.m) will contain code to add and edit the information of the master products that the vendor deals with. The complete code of the implementation file, MasterProductInfoController.m is provided in the code bundle of this chapter. The code that needs explanation is provided as follows:

```
//   MasterProductInfoController.m
//   prob

#import "MasterProductInfoController.h"

@implementation MasterProductInfoController

@synthesize custlistbutton, editmastbutton, addmastbutton, tableView,
mastprod,  mastproducts, fetchedResultsController;

-(IBAction) custlist:(id) sender
{
    [self dismissModalViewControllerAnimated:YES];
}
```

We see that all the IBOutlets (`custlistbutton`, `editmastbutton`, `addmastbutton`, `tableView`, `mastprod`, and `fetchedResultsController`) are synthesized for generating the accessor and mutator methods for them. In the action method: `custlist` (which is invoked when the Bar Button Item control with **Title: Customers List** is selected from the toolbar), we dismiss the modal view of `MasterProductInfoController` class (View that displays master products along with bar buttons to add or edit them) to display the main view of the application: `Customers List` (displayed via the `RootViewController` class). The `MasterProductInfoController` class is invoked from the `RootViewController` class:

```
-(IBAction) addmastproduct:(id)sender
{
    NSManagedObjectContext *context = [self.fetchedResultsController
managedObjectContext];
    AddMasterProductController *addmastController=[[AddMasterProduc
tController alloc] initWithNibName:@"AddMasterProductController"
bundle:nil];
    addmastController.delegate=self;
    addmastController.mastprod = [NSEntityDescription insertNewObjectFo
rEntityForName:@"MasterProduct" inManagedObjectContext:context];
    UINavigationController *navigatController=[[UINavigationController
alloc] initWithRootViewController:addmastController];
    [self    presentModalViewController:navigatController animated:YES];
    [addmastController release];
    [navigatController release];
}
```

In the action method: `addmastproduct` (that is invoked when the Bar Button Item with **Title: Add** is selected from the toolbar), we write code to navigate to the View of the `AddMasterProductController` class that prompts the user to enter information of the master product. We create and initialize an instance of the `AddMasterProductController` class by the name: `addmastController`. Also, we set the current View Controller file: `MasterProductInfoController.m` as the delegate of the `addmastController` instance. That is, this class will implement the delegate methods of the `AddMasterProductController` class. To display a navigation bar in the View of the `AddMasterProductController`, we create and initialize an instance of the `UINavigationController` class with the name: `navigatController` and set its Root View controller to be the view of the `AddMasterProductController` class (via its instance: `addmastController`). Then we display the View of the `AddMasterProductController` class modally using the `presentModalViewContro ller:animated:` method. The view controller animates the appearance of the view and creates a parent-child relationship between the current view controller and the modal view controller.

In this method, we also retrieve a managed object context from the `fetchedResultsController` and assign it to the instance: `context` (of the `NSManagedObjectContext` class). Then we insert a new managed object (of the `MasterProduct` entity) into the managed context: `context` using the class method on `NSEntityDescription`. Also, we return the instance of class that represents the `MasterProduct` entity and assign it to the `mastprod` object (of the `MasterProduct` class), which in turn is assigned to the `mastprod` object of the `addmastController` (instance of `AddMasterProductController` class), which will be used to accept the information of the new master product entered by the user:

```
-(IBAction) editmastproduct:(id)sender
{
  if([editmastbutton.title isEqualToString:@"Edit"])
  {
    editmastbutton.title=@"Done";
    [self.tableView setEditing:YES animated:YES];
  }
  else
  {
    editmastbutton.title=@"Edit";
    [self.tableView setEditing:NO animated:YES];
  }
}
```

The method `editmastproduct` is invoked when the Bar Button Item control with **Title: Edit** is selected. This method changes the title of the **Edit** button to **Done** and enables the table's editing feature (by setting the value of `setEditing` message to *YES*. When the table's editing feature is set to On, a red deletion icon appears to the left of each table cell (each table cell displays a master product), which when selected prompts for confirmation of deletion of the selected cell (master product). On selecting the **Done** button the table's editing feature is switched Off (by setting the value of the `setEditing` message to *NO*):

```
-(void) addmastprodController:(AddMasterProductController *)controller
selectedsave:(BOOL) save {
  NSManagedObjectContext *context = [self.fetchedResultsController
managedObjectContext];
  if(!save)
  {
    [context deleteObject:controller.mastprod];
  }
  NSError *error;
  if(![context save:&error]){
    NSLog(@"Unresolved error %@ %@", error, [error userInfo]);
    exit(-1);
```

```
     }
     [self dismissModalViewControllerAnimated:YES];
   }
```

The addmastprodController method is the implementation method for the delegate of the AddMasterProductController class and is invoked by the cancel and save methods (defined in the implementation file of the AddMasterProductController class). The cancel method calls the previous method and passes the selectedsave parameter set to value NO whereas the save method calls the method with the selectedsave parameter set to value YES. The value of the selectedsave parameter is assigned to the variable: save. In the method, we check that if the value of the variable save is NO, then we delete the mastprod instance from the context (a managed object of MasterProduct entity was added in the addmastproduct method) and then save the context in the persistent store:

```
// Customize the appearance of table view cells.
- (UITableViewCell *)tableView:(UITableView *)tableView cellForRowAtIn
dexPath:(NSIndexPath *)indexPath {
  static NSString *CellIdentifier = @"Cell";
  UITableViewCell *cell = [self.tableView dequeueReusableCellWithIdent
ifier:CellIdentifier];
  if (cell == nil) {
    cell = [[[UITableViewCell alloc] initWithStyle:UITableViewCellStyl
eDefault reuseIdentifier:CellIdentifier] autorelease];
  }

  // Configure the cell.
  NSManagedObject *managedObject = [fetchedResultsController
objectAtIndexPath:indexPath];
  cell.textLabel.text = [[managedObject valueForKey:@"itemname"]
description];
  UIImage *pimage=[managedObject valueForKey:@"image"];
  CGSize size=pimage.size;
  CGFloat ratio = 0;
  if (size.width > size.height) {
    ratio = 44.0 / size.width;
  }
  else {
    ratio = 44.0 / size.height;
  }
  CGRect rect = CGRectMake(0.0, 0.0, ratio * size.width, ratio * size.
height);
  UIGraphicsBeginImageContext(rect.size);
  [pimage drawInRect:rect];
  cell.imageView.image=UIGraphicsGetImageFromCurrentImageContext();
```

```
    UIGraphicsEndImageContext();
    return cell;
}
```

In the `cellForRowAtIndexPath` method, we retrieve the *Managed Object* from the *Fetched Results Controller* by just calling the `objectAtIndexPath:` on the fetched results controller and pass in the `indexPath` parameter. The `fetchedResultsController` will return the desired objects for each table cell. To display the text (master product name) in the table cell, we use `valueForKey` (the key value method used for retrieving attribute values) to retrieve the contents in the `itemname` attribute of the managed object.

As we want to display the master product image (also) to the left of the master product name in the table view cell, we retrieve the image from the image attribute of the managed object and temporarily assign it to an `UIImage` instance: `pimage`. The image in `pimage` instance has to be scaled down to accommodate it in the table cell.

Besides the fetched results controller, we can also retrieve the managed object context from the application delegate.

We define an instance: size of the CGSize structure. The CGSize structure represents a rectangle and is used for storing information related to width and height of the object. So, the width and height of the image in the *pimage* instance (retrieved from the image attribute of the managed object) is assigned to the *size* instance of the CGSize. Assuming the table row's height is 44 pixels, we find out the ratio by which the height and width of the image has to be scaled down.

We define an instance *rect* of CGRect structure. The CGRect structure is used for defining the frame of a window on the screen. It includes four floating point values as discussed in the CGRect structure at the beginning of the chapter.

The instance rect of CGRect is created with the help of the `CGRectMake` function. The frame of a window for the rect instance is defined with the help of the `CGRectMake` function through which we specify the coordinates of the origin as well as width and height of the frame.

To make the image in instance pimage to get displayed within the defined size of the frame (of a window), we configure the drawing environment, that is, we create a bitmap based graphics context using the `UIGraphicsBeginImageContext()`. In this function, we specify the size of the frame equal to the size of the `rect` instance (we use size property of the `rect` object (CGRect structure) to assign the size to the graphics context.

We make the image in pimage instance to display (render) within the display region specified in *rect* (instance of CGRect structure - having the frame size equal to the size accommodated by a table cell) using the `drawInRect` method.

Once the context is created, we retrieve the image based on the contents of the current context using the `UIGraphicsGetImageFromCurrentimageContext()` and assign it to the imageView of the table cell for display. When our job is over, we clean up the bitmap drawing environment (that we created with `UIGraphicsBeginImageContext()`) and remove the graphics context (from top of the context stack) using the `UIGraphicsEndImageContext()`:

`CGFloat` is a `typedef` for either float or double.

```
- (void)tableView:(UITableView *)tableView commitEditingStyle:(UITabl
eViewCellEditingStyle)editingStyle forRowAtIndexPath:(NSIndexPath *)
indexPath {
  if (editingStyle == UITableViewCellEditingStyleDelete) {
  // Delete the managed object for the given index path
    NSManagedObjectContext *context = [self.fetchedResultsController
managedObjectContext];
    [context deleteObject:[[self fetchedResultsController]
objectAtIndexPath:indexPath]];
    NSError *error;
    if (![context save:&error]) {
      // Handle the error...
    }
  }
}
```

In the `commitEditingStyle` method that is executed when we select Delete accessory on any table cell, we retrieve a managed object context from the `fetchedResultsController` instance and assign it to the instance: `contxt`.(of the `NSManagedObjectContext` class) and delete the object from the `contxt` object (table cell) whose *Delete* accessory is selected. Besides this, we also delete the prod instance from the cust object (a managed object of the *Product* entity that was added to the *product* relationship in the `addproduct` method). We also delete the prod instance from the products table (that represents all the products sold to the selected customer). We also retrieve the managed object context from the prod instance (of products entity) and assign it to the instance: `context`. and delete the prod instance from the context too.

Summary

In this chapter, we saw how a *MasterProduct* entity is added to our existing Data Model. We also saw creation of image attribute (for storing image of master product) of Transformable data type and created a *Value Transformer* to be used for converting an instance of UIImage into an NSData instance (while storing image to the persistent store) and for converting the NSData instance back to the UIImage instance while retrieving it from the persistent store for display. We also developed a Data Model (classes) associated with the *MasterProduct* entity. Also, we focused on entering and maintaining the information of the master product that our vendor deals with. The maintenance of the master product's information includes displaying, adding, deleting, and modifying the information and hence, the task is divided into four modules. We first developed a module that created a View to enter information of the master product that is available for sale. Then, to allow the user to add, save, and edit the information of the master products entered, we have learnt about the creation of the second module that step-by-step explained the creation of master product's menu (containing buttons to be invoked for adding, saving, and editing master product's information).

In the next chapter, we will learn to create the third module that will connect the master product's menu to the *RootViewController* class (that displays the first View when the application is launched) so that the information of the master product(s) available for sale can be entered. We will also learn to create the fourth and final module that will display the information of the selected master product and will also allow for modifying its information, such as its name, quantity, price, and its image.

10

Editing the Stock Information

In the previous chapter, we learned how to add a MasterProduct Entity to our existing Data Model for storing information of the products (master product) that the vendor deals with. We learned that for maintaining the information of the master product, that is, for displaying, adding, deleting, and modifying the master product's information, four modules were required. Out of these four modules, we learned how to develop the first two modules:

- Developing the View to enter the master product's information
- Developing the MasterProduct's menu to add, delete, and display the information of master products

In this chapter, we will learn how to develop the third and fourth modules required for maintaining the master product's information. The two modules are:

- Module to connect the MasterProduct's menu to the rest of the project
- Module to modify the information of the master product

Let us proceed to create the third and the fourth modules.

Module to connect the MasterProduct's menu to the rest of the project

In this module, we will learn how to invoke the MasterProduct's menu from the View of the `RootViewController` class (the first View that appears on launching the application). We will see how a *Toolbar* control is placed on the View and how it invokes an action method that subsequently displays the View of the MasterProduct's menu.

The following are the steps involved in developing this module:

1. Defining the outlets and action methods in the header file: `RootViewController.h`.

2. Adding a Toolbar and Bar Button Item in the `RootViewController` class.

3. Coding in the implementation file: `RootViewController.m` to invoke the View of the `MasterProductinfoController` class.

4. Making the Toolbar to appear at the bottom of the View.

For controlling the controls that we will be placing in the View through the code, we need to define the outlets and action methods for them. So, let's start with that.

Defining outlets and action methods in the header file

To invoke the view of the `MasterProductInfoController` from the `RootViewController`, we modify the header file of the `RootViewController` to appear as shown next. Only the statements that are highlighted are added; the rest of the statements are the same as we saw in *Chapter 7, Updating and Searching Records of Customers*:

```
//  RootViewController.h
//  prob

#import "AddCustomerController.h"
#import "DisplayCustomerController.h"
#import "MasterProductInfoController.h"

@interface RootViewController : UITableViewController
<NSFetchedResultsControllerDelegate, AddCustomerControllerDelegate,
DisplayCustomerControllerDelegate> {
  NSFetchedResultsController *fetchedResultsController;
  NSManagedObjectContext *managedObjectContext;
  IBOutlet UISearchBar *srchbar;
IBOutlet UIToolbar *toolbr;
}
@property (nonatomic, retain) NSFetchedResultsController
*fetchedResultsController;
@property (nonatomic, retain) NSManagedObjectContext
*managedObjectContext;
@property(nonatomic, retain) UISearchBar *srchbar;
@property(nonatomic, retain) IBOutlet UIToolbar *toolbr;
- (IBAction)addCustomer;
- (IBAction)showmasterinfo;
@end
```

In the preceding header file, we import the `MasterProductInfoController` class. Then an instance variable of the `UIToolbar` class is created: `toolbr` and is defined as outlets (which will be used for connecting to the *Toolbar* control that we will be placing in the View). The instance variable is defined as properties with the two attributes: `retain` and `nonatomic` for generating the accessors and mutators without any overhead code (when synthesized) and for keeping the objects retained to the mutators without being flushed from memory. Also, an action method is declared with the name `showmasterinfo`, which will take us to the view of the `MasterProductInfoController`.

Adding a Toolbar and a Bar Button Item in the RootViewController class

We need to add a toolbar to the RootView controller and set its Bar Button Item control to invoke the action method: `showmasterinfo` that is supposed to display the view of the `MasterProductInfoController`.

So, from the **Resources** group in the Xcode Project window, open the `RootViewController.xib` file in the Interface Builder. We know that the View of the `RootViewController` already has a *Navigation* bar at the top. Now, we need a Toolbar control in the same View at the bottom. Having both the **Navigation bar** and **Toolbar** controls in one view results in a problem. What is it? Let us see.

 When we have both the controls: **Navigation bar** and **Toolbar** in the same View, we have overlapping problems, that is, the two controls overlap each other and we need to take some steps to adjust the Toolbar control at the bottom of the View as explained in the *Making the Toolbar to appear at the bottom of the View* section of this chapter.

Let us continue with our step of adding the Toolbar and Bar Button Item in the `RootViewController` class.

Open the `RootViewController.xib` file in the Interface Builder and drag a Toolbar control from the **Library** window and drop it in the **Documents** window. The Toolbar control comes with a default Bar Button Item control with the title: **Item**. Then, we connect the `toolbr` outlet (defined in the header file: `RootViewController.h`) to the Toolbar control (dropped in the **Documents** window).

To establish a connection between the `toolbr` outlet with the Toolbar control, select the **File's Owner** in the **Documents** window and open the **Connections Inspector**. Under the heading: **Outlets**, we find an outlet: **toolbr**. Select the circle to the right of the outlet: **toolbr** and keeping the mouse button pressed, drag it to the Toolbar control dropped in the **Documents** window, as shown in the following screenshot:

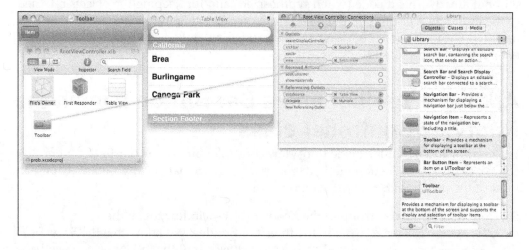

We change the title of the Bar Button Item control in the toolbar by selecting it in the Toolbar control and setting its **Title** to `Master Product Information` from the **Attributes Inspector**. Also, drag-and-drop the **Flexible Space Bar Button Item** from the **Windows, Views & Bars** category of the **Library** window on both sides of the Bar Button Item control in the toolbar to align it at the center of the Toolbar, as shown in the following screenshot:

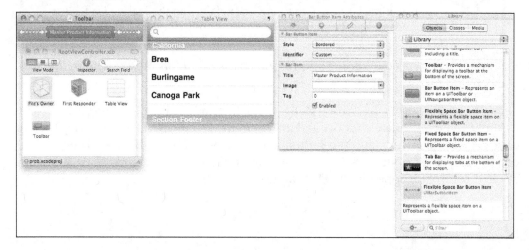

The next step is to connect the action method: **showmasterinfo** with the Bar Button Item control. Select the circle to the right of **showmasterinfo** in the **Connection Inspector** under the heading: **Received Actions** and keeping the mouse button pressed, drag it to the Bar Button Item control in the Toolbar, as shown in the following screenshot:

Coding in the implementation file to invoke the View of the MasterProductinfoController class

To make the View of the `MasterProductInfoController` to appear when the Bar Button Item control with title: **Master Product Information** is selected, we need to write the code for the action method: **showmasterinfo** in the implementation file of the `RootViewController` class (`RootViewController.m`). The complete file is provided in the code bundle of this chapter. Most of the code in the file is the same as we saw in *Chapter 7, Updating and Searching Records of Customers*. The code that is added to the file is as follows:

```
//   RootViewController.m
//   prob

#import "RootViewController.h"

@implementation RootViewController

@synthesize fetchedResultsController, managedObjectContext;
@synthesize srchbar;
@synthesize toolbr;

-(IBAction)showmasterinfo
{
```

```objc
    MasterProductInfoController *masterinfo
=[[MasterProductInfoController alloc] initWithNibName:@"MasterProductI
nfoController" bundle:nil];
 [self    presentModalViewController:masterinfo animated:YES];
  [masterinfo release];
}
- (void)viewWillAppear:(BOOL)animated {
  [super viewWillAppear:animated];
  CGFloat tbarHeight = [toolbr frame].size.height;
  CGRect rootbounds = self.parentViewController.view.bounds;
  CGFloat rootViewHeight = CGRectGetHeight(rootbounds);
  CGFloat rootViewWidth = CGRectGetWidth(rootbounds);
  CGRect rectframe = CGRectMake(0, rootViewHeight - tbarHeight,
rootViewWidth, tbarHeight);
  [toolbr setFrame:rectframe];
  [self.navigationController.view addSubview:toolbr];
  toolbr.hidden=FALSE;
}
(....)
- (void)tableView:(UITableView *)tableView didSelectRowAtIndexPath:(NS
IndexPath *)indexPath {
  toolbr.hidden=TRUE;
  DisplayCustomerController *displaycust =[[DisplayCustomerController
alloc] initWithNibName:@"DisplayCustomerController" bundle:nil];
  Customer *selectedcust=(Customer *) [fetchedResultsController
objectAtIndexPath:indexPath];
  displaycust.cust=selectedcust;
  [self.navigationController pushViewController:displaycust
animated:YES];
  [displaycust release];
}
(....)
- (void)dealloc {
  [fetchedResultsController release];
  [srchbar release];
  [managedObjectContext release];
  [toolbr release];
  [super dealloc];
}
@end
```

In the `showmasterinfo` method, we create and initialize an instance of the `MasterProductInfoController` class with the name: `masterinfo`. We make use of `alloc` to create the view controller object and initialize it. The `init` method specifies the name of the NIB file that has to be loaded by the controller (`MasterProductInfoController`) followed by the bundle where the NIB file is expected to be found. The bundle parameter is set to `nil` as we want the method to look for the NIB file in the main bundle. Finally, the `masterinfo` (the view associated with the `MasterProductInfoController`) is displayed with an animation effect. By default, the toolbar appears above the navigation bar (overlapped, as shown in the following *image (a)*):

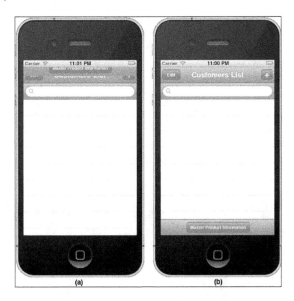

(a)   (b)

Making the Toolbar to appear at the bottom of the View

To make the Toolbar appear at the bottom, we have written the code in the `viewWillAppear` method (in the `RootViewController.h` file shown previously). In the method, we find out the height of the toolbar and the height and width of the Root View Controller. Then we define a frame in the form of an instance: `rectframe` (of the CGRect structure) and assign it the origin (upper-left corner) to begin at the bottom of the View and the size equal to the height and width of the toolbar. The Toolbar is assigned to appear within the frame defined in the instance: `rectframe`. We find that the Toolbar appears at the bottom of the View, as shown in preceding *image (b)*:

Running the application

Let us execute the application by selecting *Build and Run*. We get a view of the RootViewController, as shown in the following *image (a)* with the list of existing customers. We select the Bar Button Item with the title: **Master Product Information** in the toolbar at the bottom as we are interested in entering the information of the master products. We get a view as shown in the following *image (b)*. The view contains a toolbar with three Bar Button Item controls with the text: **Customers List**, **Edit**, and **Add** respectively.

The function of the three Bar Button Item controls is as follows:

- **Customers List**: This will take us back to the Main View of the application, as shown in the following *image (a)* from where we can add or edit the customer's information.

- **Edit**: This will allow us to delete the information of any master product. It will work when few master products are added to the list for sale.

- **Add**: This will allow us to add the new master products to the list. It displays the view as shown in the following *image (c)*. We get three text fields to enter the product name, price, and quantity.

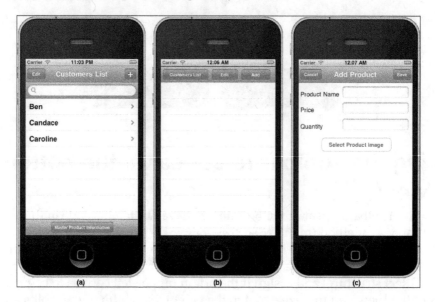

Let us select the **Add** button to add information of the master product. We get a view as shown in the preceding *image (c)* to enter name of the master product, its price, and the quantity in hand. The moment, we click on any text field, a keyboard appears to type in the information (following *image (a)*). When we have finished entering the information in the respective text fields, we can make the keyboard invisible by selecting the *return* key from the keyboard.

Selecting the image of the master product

On selecting the **Select Product Image** button, the Image Picker View will display the **Photo Album**, as shown in the following *image (b)*. The **Photo Album** displays the category **Saved Photos** created by us to contain the photos of the Master Products sold by the vendor. We have already seen how to create our own category of photos in the **Photo Album** in the *Adding custom images to the Image Picker* section of *Chapter 9, Entering, Displaying, and Deleting the Stock*. On selecting the category: **Saved Photos**, we will be shown all the images that we have saved in this category. Let us select the image that represents our product, as shown in the following *image (c)*. After selecting the product image, we can save the product information by selecting the **Save** button in the navigation bar. The **Cancel** button at the top is for canceling the addition operation of the master product.

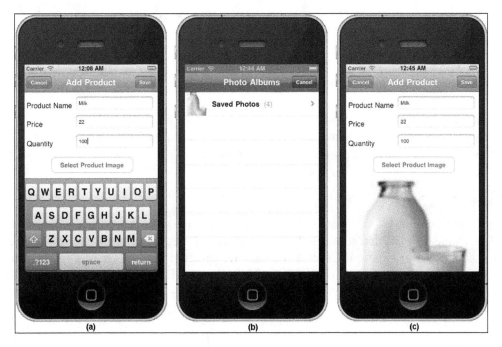

(a)   (b)   (c)

On selecting the **Save** button, we will be navigated back to the **Master Product List** view that displays the list of master products saved up till now. We will find the product `Milk` in the table view as shown in the following *image (a)*. Let us select the **Add** button (thrice) to add three more products: **Chocolate**, **Eggs** (refer to the following *image (b)*), and **Bread** (refer to the following *image (c)*). Let us keep the initial stock of all master products as **100** (just for ease of understanding).

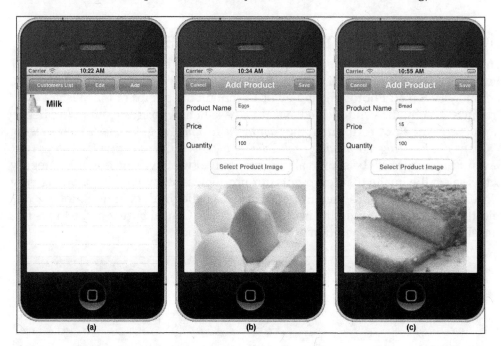

After adding four master products, our table view may appear, as shown in the following *image (a)*. The master products will be automatically sorted in the alphabetical order and displayed in the table view.

Deleting the master product

The **Edit** button in the navigation bar (in the following *image (a)*) is for deleting any existing master product from the list. On selecting the **Edit** button, we find a *Deletion* accessory that appears to the left of each master product in the form of a red deletion icon, as shown in the following *image (b)*. Note that the **Edit** button's text changes to the **Done** button, which we will use when we have finished the editing job.

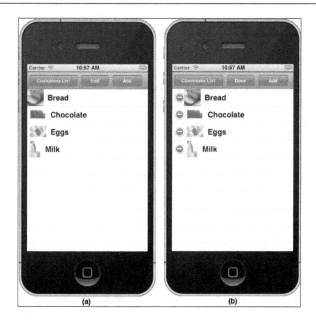

Selecting the deletion icon on any master product will display a **Delete** button that confirms whether we really want to delete the product. Suppose we want to remove the product named **Chocolate** from the list. On selecting its deletion icon, we get a **Delete** button as shown in the following *image (a)*, which when selected will delete the product from the table view as shown in the following *image (b)*. The deletion icon will disappear on selecting the **Done** button.

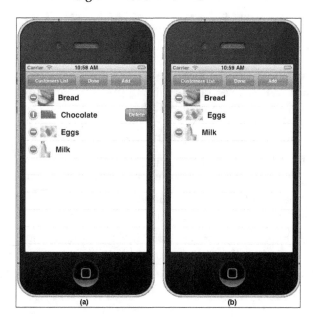

Module to modify the information of the master product

This module will display the information of the selected master product and will allow us to modify its contents (product name, quantity, price, and its image).

The following are the steps involved in developing this module:

1. Adding the `View Controller` class: `EditMasterProductController` to display the view to modify the selected master product.

2. Defining the outlets and action methods in the header file: `EditMasterProductController.h`.

3. Designing the View of the `EditMasterProductController` class.

4. Coding in the implementation file: `EditMasterProductController.m` to modify the master product's information.

5. Importing the delegate and the `View Controller` class, `EditMasterProductController` in the MasterProductInfoController's header file.

6. Coding in the implementation file, `MasterProductInfoController.m` to invoke the View of the `EditMasterProductController` class.

Adding the View Controller class to display the view to modify the selected master product

The View Controller that we are going to add to the application is the `EditMasterProductController` class that will provide us a view to modify the selected Master Product. The steps are as follows:

1. Right-click on the **Classes** folder and select the **Add | New File** option.

2. Select the template as: **UIViewController subclass** option. Don't forget to select the checkbox: **With XIB for user interface** followed by the **Next** button.

3. Specify the name of the **New UIViewController subclass with XIB** as `EditMasterProductController.m`.

4. Keep the checkbox: **Also create EditMasterProductController.h** selected followed by the **Finish** button. Three files, `EditMasterProductController.h`, `EditMasterProductController.m`, and `EditMasterProductController.xib` will be created in the **Classes** folder.

5. Drag the `EditMasterProductController.xib` from the **Classes** to the
   Resources folder.

Defining the outlets and action methods in the header file

The code that we will write in the header file of the `EditMasterProductController`
class: `EditMasterProductController.h` is as follows:

```
//   EditMasterProductController.h
//   prob

#import <UIKit/UIKit.h>
#import "MasterProduct.h"

@interface EditMasterProductController : UIViewController {
  MasterProduct *mastprod;
  IBOutlet UITextField *itemname;
  IBOutlet UITextField *quantity;
  IBOutlet UITextField *price;
  IBOutlet UIImageView *prodimage;
  IBOutlet UIBarButtonItem *backbutton;
}
@property(nonatomic, retain) MasterProduct *mastprod;
@property(nonatomic, retain) UITextField *itemname;
@property(nonatomic, retain) UITextField *quantity;
@property(nonatomic, retain) UITextField *price;
@property(nonatomic, retain) UIImageView *prodimage;
@property(nonatomic, retain) IBOutlet UIBarButtonItem *backbutton;
-(IBAction) changeimage:(id) sender;
-(IBAction) back:(id) sender;

@end
```

In the EditMasterProductController's header file, we defined an object of the
`MasterProduct` class with the name: `mastprod` that will hold the master product's
information (that is selected by the user for editing purposes). Also, three instance
variables: `itemname`, `quantity`, and `price` of the `UITextField` class and an instance
variable: `prodimage` of the `UIImageView` class are defined and marked as outlets
(these outlets will be connected to the three **Text Field** controls and an **UIImageView**
control that we will be dropping in the View for displaying the existing information:
item name, quantity, price, and image of the selected master product).

An instance variable of the UIBarButtonItem class: backbutton is defined and marked as outlets. This outlet will be connected to the Bar Button Items (that we will soon drag-and-drop on the View) with the title: **Cancel** (it will invoke the respective action method to discard the changes made in the master product's information). Two action methods are also defined with the names: changeimage and back that will contain the code to change the image of the selected master product and cancel the process of modification respectively. All the instance variables are defined as properties with the two attributes: retain and nonatomic for generating their accessors and mutators. After adding the preceding code, we save the header file.

Designing the View of EditMasterProductController class

Let us open the EditProductController.xib file in Interface Builder to design the view required for editing the master product. The steps are as follows:

1. Drag-and-drop three Label controls, three TextField controls, a Round Rect Button control, and an UIImage View control in the View.

2. Double-click the **Label** controls one by one and edit their text to **Product Name**, **Price**, and **Quantity** respectively. Also, double-click the **Round Rect Button** control to edit its text to **Change Product Image**.

3. From the **Windows, Views & Bars** category of the **Library** window, drag a Bar Button Item control and drop it into the **Documents** window.

4. From the **Attributes Inspector**, set the title of the Bar Button Item control as **Back**. The title of the Bar Button Item will appear as button text in the View.

5. Connect the three outlets (itemname, price, and quantity defined in the header file: EditMasterProductController.h) to the three Text Field controls in the View. Select the **File's Owner** icon in the **Documents** window and open the **Connections Inspector**. Select the circle to the right of each outlet (under the **Outlets** section in the **Connections Inspector**) and keeping the mouse button pressed, drag it to the respective Text Field control. Similarly, connect the outlet: **prodimage** with the **Image View** control dropped in the View.

6. Also, connect the outlet of the Bar Button Item control: **backbutton** to the Bar Button Item control dropped in the **Documents** window by selecting the circle to the right of the outlet in the **Connections Inspector** and keeping the mouse button pressed, drag it to the Bar Button item control in the **Documents** window.

7. Connect the Bar Button Item control to the action method: back defined in the header file of the EditMasterProductController class (EditMasterProductController.h), so that when any Bar Button Item control is selected from the navigation bar, the code in the action method: back is executed to do the desired task. Select the Bar Button Item control in the **Documents** window (the one whose title is set as: **Back**) and open the **Connections Inspector**. In the **Connections Inspector**, under the heading **Sent Actions**, select the circle to the right of **selector** and keeping the mouse button pressed, drag it to the **File's Owner** icon in the **Documents** window and release the mouse button. On releasing the mouse button, an action method **back** defined in the header file pops up. We select the **back** (action method) to connect it to the Bar Button Item control.

8. As we want an action: **changeimage** to be invoked when the user selects the Round Rect Button control with the text: **Change Product Image**, we need to connect them. From the **Received Actions** heading (from the **Connections Inspector** window), select the circle to the right of the action: **changeimage** and keeping the mouse button pressed, drag it to the **Round Rect Button** (**Change Product Image**) in the **View** window and select the **Touch Up Inside** option from the menu that appears. We have selected the **Touch Up Inside** option so as to invoke the **changeimage** method when the user presses and releases his/her finger after touching inside the button.

After connecting all the objects of the **View** window with the instance variables of the header file, the **Connections Inspector** window may appear as shown in the following screenshot:

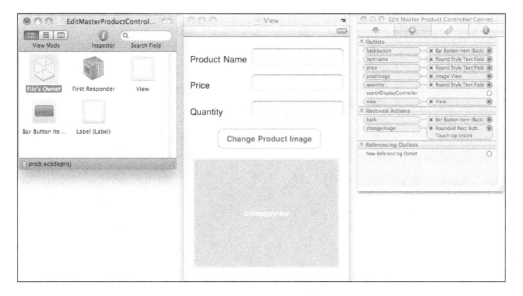

Coding in the implementation file to modify the master product's information

In the implementation file of the EditMasterProductController class (EditMast erProductController.m), we need to write the code that allows us to modify the information (item name, price, quantity, or image) of the selected master product. For changing the image of the master product, we will be invoking the *ImagePicker* control. The code that we will write in the implementation file is as follows:

```
//  EditMasterProductController.m
//  prob

#import "EditMasterProductController.h"

@implementation EditMasterProductController

@synthesize itemname,quantity, price, prodimage, backbutton;
@synthesize mastprod;
-(IBAction) back:(id) sender
{
    [self dismissModalViewControllerAnimated:YES];
}
```

In the preceding code, first of all, we synthesize the IBOutlets: itemname, quantity, price, prodimage, backbutton, and mastprod for generating the accessor and mutator methods for them. In the action method: back(which is invoked when the Bar Button Item control with the title: **Back** is selected from the toolbar), we dismiss the modal view of the EditMasterProductController class (the View that allows us to modify the information of the master product) to display the view of the MasterProductInfoController class, which displays the view to add/edit the master products that the vendor deals with.

The EditMasterProductController class is invoked from the MasterProductInfoController class.

```
-(IBAction) changeimage:(id) sender{
    UIImagePickerController *imagePicker = [[UIImagePickerController
alloc] init];
    imagePicker.delegate = self;
    [self presentModalViewController:imagePicker animated:YES];
    [imagePicker release];
}
```

The action method: changeimage is invoked by the Round Rect Button control with the text: Change Product Image defining the imagePicker as an instance of the UIImagePickerController class that is used as an image selector. We assume that our own photos (custom photos) are added to the Photo Library. In this method, we see that the delegate of the image picker is set to self meaning the same class (the View Controller class: EditMasterProductController) will implement the methods (didFinishPickingImage and imagePickerControllerDidCancel) of the UIImagePicker delegate protocol. Recall that the method: didFinishPickingImage is invoked when a user selects an image and the method imagePickerControllerDidCancel is invoked when the user cancels the image selection.

```
- (void)imagePickerController:(UIImagePickerControll
er *)picker didFinishPickingImage:(UIImage *)selectedImage
editingInfo:(NSDictionary *)editingInfo {
   prodimage.image=selectedImage;
   mastprod.image=selectedImage;
   [self dismissModalViewControllerAnimated:YES];
}

- (void)imagePickerControllerDidCancel:(UIImagePickerController *)
picker {
   [self dismissModalViewControllerAnimated:YES];
}
```

In the didFinishPickingImage method, we assign the selected image (from the image picker) to the prodimage (the Image View control placed in the View) for displaying the modified image and to the image attribute of the mastprod object (of the MasterProduct class) for persistence and finally, we dismiss the image picker control. In the imagePickerControllerDidCancel method, we simply dismiss the image picker control.

```
// Implement viewDidLoad to do additional setup after loading the
view, typically from a nib.
- (void)viewDidLoad {
   [super viewDidLoad];
   self.title=@"Master Product";
   itemname.text=mastprod.itemname;
   NSString *str=[NSString stringWithFormat:@"%d", [mastprod.quantity
intValue]];
   quantity.text=str;
   str=[NSString stringWithFormat:@"%f", [mastprod.price floatValue]];
   price.text=str;
   prodimage.image=mastprod.image;
   itemname.enabled=NO;
```

```
     quantity.enabled=NO;
     price.enabled=NO;
     self.navigationItem.leftBarButtonItem=backbutton;
     self.navigationItem.rightBarButtonItem=self.editButtonItem;
}
```

In the `viewDidLoad` method, we set the Navigation Item's title to `Master Product` and the contents in the `itemname`, `quantity`, and `price` attributes of the `mastprod` object (existing information) are displayed in the three Text Field controls placed in the View. Also, the image of the master product stored in the image attribute of the `mastprod` object is displayed via the *ImageView* control (connected to outlet: `prodimage`) placed in the View. The `enabled` property of the three Text Field controls displaying the master product information is set to `NO` to keep them in the disabled mode (no user will be able to modify the information). We want the user to be able to modify the master product's information when he selects the **Edit** button from the toolbar. Also, the left Bar Button Item of the navigation bar is set to **backbutton**—the instance variable of the `UIBarButtonItem` class with the title: **Back**. Next, we add an **Edit** button on the right of the navigation bar by using the property `editButtonItem` provided by the `UIViewController` class. As the `EditMasterProductController` inherits from `UIViewController`, we can access that property using the dot notation and pass it to the mutator for the `rightBarButtonItem`. The **Edit** button when selected, invokes the `setEditing` method and its title changes to **Done** automatically.

```
-(void) setEditing:(BOOL) editing animated:(BOOL) animated {
  [super setEditing:editing animated:animated];
  itemname.enabled=YES;
  quantity.enabled=YES;
  price.enabled=YES;
  if(!editing)
  {
    mastprod.itemname=itemname.text;
    mastprod.quantity=[NSNumber numberWithInt: [quantity.text
intValue]];
    mastprod.price=[NSNumber numberWithFloat: [price.text
floatValue]];
    itemname.enabled=NO;
    quantity.enabled=NO;
    price.enabled=NO;
    NSError *error;
    NSManagedObjectContext *context = [mastprod
managedObjectContext];
    if(![context save:&error]){
      NSLog(@"Unresolved error %@ %@", error, [error userInfo]);
    }
  }
}
```

In the setEditing method, we enable all the Text Field controls so that the user can change the contents of any field (itemname, quantity, or price). The moment the user selects the **Done** button, the changes applied to the Text Field controls are assigned to the itemname, quantity, and price attribute of the mastprod instance (of the MasterProduct class) and the Text Field controls are set to the disabled mode (as the user can modify the contents only when the **Edit** button is selected). Finally, we save the modifications to the persistent store by saving the context.

```
- (void)dealloc {
    [itemname release];
    [quantity release];
    [price release];
    [prodimage release];
    [mastprod release];
    [backbutton release];
    [super dealloc];
}

@end
```

The last method releases the memory reserved by the outlets.

Importing the delegate and the View Controller class in the header file

Recall that the MasterProductInfoController class file is the one that displays all the master products in a table (refer to the following *image (a)*). As we want the class file, EditMasterProductController that is meant for modifying the information of the master product to be invoked when the user selects any master product from the table, we need to import the application delegate and the view controller class, EditMasterProductController in the MasterProductInfoController's header file. The complete code is provided in the code bundle of this chapter; only the newly added code, which is highlighted, is shown next:

```
//  MasterProductInfoController.h
//  prob

#import <UIKit/UIKit.h>
#import "MasterProduct.h"
#import "AddMasterProductController.h"
#import "probAppDelegate.h"
#import "EditMasterProductController.h"
```

Coding in the implementation file to invoke the View of the EditMasterProductController class

In the implementation file, MasterProductInfoController.m, we need to write the code to display the **>** (greater than sign) in every table row displaying the master products (refer to the following *image (a)*), so that the user knows that the table rows are selectable and will result into navigation. We also need to write the code to invoke the class file, EditMasterProductController when the user selects any master product from the table. The class file, EditMasterProductController is the one that we just created and that will help in modifying the information of the selected master product. The complete code of the implementation file, MasterProductInfoController.m is provided in the code bundle of this chapter; just the newly added code is as follows:

```
// MasterProductInfoController.m
// prob

#import "MasterProductInfoController.h"

@implementation MasterProductInfoController
   (....)
// Customize the appearance of table view cells.
- (UITableViewCell *)tableView:(UITableView *)tableView cellForRowAtIndexPath:(NSIndexPath *)indexPath {

   static NSString *CellIdentifier = @"Cell";

   UITableViewCell *cell = [self.tableView dequeueReusableCellWithIdentifier:CellIdentifier];
   if (cell == nil) {
      cell = [[[UITableViewCell alloc] initWithStyle:UITableViewCellStyleDefault reuseIdentifier:CellIdentifier] autorelease];
      cell.accessoryType=UITableViewCellAccessoryDisclosureIndicator;
   }

   // Configure the cell.
   NSManagedObject *managedObject = [fetchedResultsController objectAtIndexPath:indexPath];
   cell.textLabel.text = [[managedObject valueForKey:@"itemname"] description];
   UIImage *pimage=[managedObject valueForKey:@"image"];
   CGSize size=pimage.size;
   CGFloat ratio = 0;
   if (size.width > size.height) {
      ratio = 44.0 / size.width;
```

```
  }
  else {
    ratio = 44.0 / size.height;
  }
  CGRect rect = CGRectMake(0.0, 0.0, ratio * size.width, ratio * size.
height);
  UIGraphicsBeginImageContext(rect.size);
  [pimage drawInRect:rect];
  cell.imageView.image=UIGraphicsGetImageFromCurrentImageContext();
  UIGraphicsEndImageContext();
  return cell;
}
- (void)tableView:(UITableView *)tableView didSelectRowAtIndexPath:(NS
IndexPath *)indexPath {
  EditMasterProductController *editmastprodController
=[[EditMasterProductController alloc] initWithNibName:@"EditMasterProd
uctController" bundle:nil];
  MasterProduct *selectedmastprod=(MasterProduct *)
[fetchedResultsController objectAtIndexPath:indexPath];
  editmastprodController.mastprod=selectedmastprod;
  UINavigationController *naviggController=[[UINavigationController
alloc] initWithRootViewController:editmastprodController];
  [self    presentModalViewController:naviggController animated:YES];
}

(....)
@end
```

When any master product is selected from the table view (following *image (a)*), the didSelectRowAtIndexPath method is invoked and we will be navigated to the view of the EditMasterProductController. That is, an instance of the EditMasterProductController is created with the name: editmastprodController and the selected master product (from the table View) is assigned to the mastprod instance of the editmastprodController (so as to display the initial original content of the master product and allow the user to modify them). The initial content of the selected master product may appear as shown in the following *image (b)*.

The information being displayed is in the non editable form. To modify the information of the master product, we will have to select the **Edit** button from the navigation bar. The **Edit** button on selection changes to the **Done** button. After modifying the information of the master product, we will have to select the **Done** button to inform that the editing is completed.

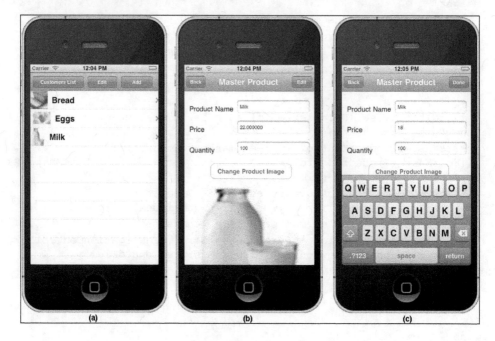

We can also change the image of the master product besides its name, price, and quantity. To change the image of the master product, we will select the **Change Product Image** button (preceding *image (b)*). The **Photo Albums** view will get opened showing the **Saved Photos** album (the one that we saw while inserting the information of the new master products). On selecting the **Saved Photos** album, we get all the images that exists in it and we can choose any of them as the new image of the master product.

Summary

This chapter was focused on maintaining the information of the master product that our vendor deals with. The maintenance of the master product's information includes displaying, adding, deleting, and modifying the information and hence, the task was divided into four modules. We developed the first two modules in the previous chapter. We learned how to develop the third and the fourth modules in this chapter. The third module explained how to connect the master product's menu to the `RootViewController` class (that displays the first View when an application is launched), so that the information of the master product(s) available for sale can be entered. The fourth and the final module displayed the information of the selected master product and allowed us to modify its information including its name, quantity, price, and image.

In the next chapter, which is the last chapter of our book, we will learn how to apply the *Search Facility* to the Products and will learn how to update the stock. That is, we will learn how to apply the search bar while displaying the products for sale to the customers, so that he/she can quickly search the products that they are looking for. Also, when a product is sold, we will learn how to update the stock, that is, we will reduce the quantity of the master product by the quantity that is sold.

11
Displaying the Products for Sale and Updating the Stock

Our data-driven application is almost complete. Just two more features need to be added. They are as follows:

- Auto displaying of products available for sale – In *Chapter 8, Entering, Saving, Listing, and Deleting the Records of the Products Sold to the Customers*, we entered the information of the product sold to the customer manually, that is, we entered the product name, price, and quantity sold to the customer manually; we need to remember the list of products that are available for sale and their price. What we want now, is to automatically display the list of products available for sale from the MasterProduct entity and we just need to click the product that is sold to the customer. Also we would want the product name, its image, and price to appear automatically on selecting the product, so that we just have to enter the quantity sold to the customer.

- The second thing is to update the stock, that is, we want the quantity of the master product to be reduced by the quantity that is sold to the customers.

Refer to the images in *Chapter 8, Entering, Saving, Listing, and Deleting the Records of the Products Sold to the Customers*, where we saw that on selecting any customer's name from the main view, we navigate to the view that displays the information of the selected customer (*DisplayCustomerController*). The view also displays a *Product's Information* button at the bottom, which when selected will display a product menu (*ProductInfoController*) containing buttons, such as **Edit** and **Add** to be used to add, list, and delete the information of the products sold to the selected customer. On selecting the **Add** button from the product menu, we used to get a view, where we were supposed to enter the name of the product sold to the customer along with its price and quantity (*AddProductController*), that is, the navigation between the views of the classes that we saw in *Chapter 8, Entering, Saving, Listing, and Deleting the Records of the Products Sold to the Customers*, was **DisplayCustomerController | ProductInfoController | AddProductController**.

Now, on selecting the **Add** button from the product menu, we want all the products stored in the *MasterProduct* entity to be automatically displayed along with a *Search Bar* at the top. That is, instead of manually entering the name of the products and their prices, we should get the list of all the products that are available for sale and we just need to click on the products that are sold to the customer. Also, we want that when a user selects any product, its price and image be displayed and we should be asked to enter only the quantity of the product that is sold.

In other words, we want that on selecting the **Add** button from the product menu, we should be navigated to a class that displays the information of the products (item name, price, and image) of all the products that are available for sale (from the *MasterProduct* entity) along with a *Search Bar* at the top. Let us name that class as `SearchProductController` class. On adding, the `SearchProductController` class, the navigation between the views of the classes will be set as follows: **DisplayCustomerController | ProductInfoController | SearchProductController | AddProductController**.

Displaying the products available for sale

We will create a class with the name `SearchProductController` that will be invoked from the product menu (*ProductInfoController*) and which will retrieve all the rows from the *MasterProduct* entity to display the list of products available for the same. Not only this, the class will also display a *Search Bar* at the top allowing us to quickly search the product. On selecting any product from the *SearchProductController*, we will be navigated to the view of *AddProductController* where the product name and its price will be automatically displayed and we just have to enter the quantity of the product sold to the customer.

The steps required in implementing the search facility for the products sold to the customers are as follows:

1. Adding the `SearchProductController` class.
2. Designing the view of the `SearchProductController`.
3. Coding in the `SearchProductController` class.
4. Invoking the `SearchProductController` from the *Product* menu.
5. Displaying name, price, and image of the selected product.

Adding the SearchProductController class

For implementing the search facility, we will be adding one more class to our application by the name: *SearchProductController*. The `SearchProductController` class will be used for searching the product (from the *MasterProduct* entity) that is sold to the selected customer. It will initially display all the products from the *Master Products* with a *Search Bar* at the top. Typing a text in the *Search Bar* will display the products that contain the text typed in the *Search Bar*. To add the `SearchProductController` to our application, follow the given steps:

1. Right-click on the **Classes** folder and select the **Add | New File** option.

2. Select the template as: **UIViewController** subclass option. Don't forget to select the checkbox: **With XIB for user interface** followed by the **Next** button.

3. Specify the name of the new `UIViewController` subclass with XIB as `SearchProductController.m`.

4. Keep the checkbox: **Also create SearchProductController.h** selected, followed by the **Finish** button.

Three files will be created in the `Classes` group, namely `SearchProductController.h`, `SearchProductController.m`, and `SearchProductController.xib`. Drag the `SearchProductController.xib` from the `Classes` to the `Resources` folder. The code that we will write in the header file of the `SearchProductController` class: `SearchProductController.h` is as shown next:

```
//   SearchProductController.h
//   prob

#import <UIKit/UIKit.h>
#import "probAppDelegate.h"
#import "MasterProduct.h"
#import "AddProductController.h"
#import "Customer.h"

@interface SearchProductController : UIViewController
<NSFetchedResultsControllerDelegate>{
  NSFetchedResultsController *fetchedResultsController;
  Customer *cust;
  IBOutlet UISearchBar *srchbar;
  UITableView *tableView;
  NSMutableArray *mastproducts;
IBOutlet UIBarButtonItem *cancelbutton;
}
```

```
@property (nonatomic, retain) NSFetchedResultsController
*fetchedResultsController;
@property(nonatomic, retain) Customer *cust;
@property(nonatomic, retain) UISearchBar *srchbar;
@property(nonatomic, retain)  IBOutlet UITableView *tableView;
@property(nonatomic, retain) NSMutableArray *mastproducts;
@property(nonatomic, retain) IBOutlet UIBarButtonItem *cancelbutton;

-(IBAction) cancel:(id) sender;
@end
```

In the preceding header file, we define the object of the `Customer` class with the name: `cust`, an instance variable of the `NSFetchedResultsController` class with the name: `fetchedResultsController`, an instance variable of the `UISearchBar` class by the name `srchbar`, and an instance variable of `UITableView` class with the name: `tableView`. An instance variable of the `UIButtonItem` class is also created with the name: `cancelbutton`. These instance variables are defined as outlets so that they can be connected to the respective controls that we will be placing in the View.

All the instance variables are defined as properties with the two attributes: `retain` and `nonatomic` for generating the accessor and mutators without any overhead code (when synthesized) and for keeping the objects retained to the mutators without being flushed from the memory. Also, an action method is declared by the name `cancel` that contains the code (in the implementation file) to take us back to the view of the `ProductInfoController` class.

We will be navigated to the view of the `SearchProductController` class from the `ProductInfoController` class (when the user selects the **Add** button from the toolbar). The `ProductInfoController` class, besides displaying the products sold to the selected customer, displays a toolbar to edit and add the information of products sold to the selected customer.

Designing the view of SearchProductController

To design the view of the `SearchProductController` class, perform the following steps:

1. Open the `SearchProductController.xib` file in Interface Builder.

2. Drag-and-drop the **TableView** control on the View. Also place the **Search Bar** control on the top of **Table View**.

3. Drag-and-drop a **Bar Button Item** control from the **Library** window and drop it in the **Documents** window.

4. Set the title of the **Bar Button Item** to **Cancel**.

5. Connect the three outlets: **srchbar**, **tableView**, and **cancelbutton** to the **Search Bar**, **Table View**, and **Bar Button Item** controls respectively.

For connecting the action method: **cancel** with the Bar Button Item control with the title: **Cancel**, follow the given steps:

1. Select the **Bar Button Item** control from the **Documents** window and open the **Connections Inspector** window.

2. In the **Connections Inspector** window, select the circle to the right of the selector (under the **Sent Actions** heading) and keeping the mouse button pressed, drag it to the **File's Owner** icon in the **Documents** window.

3. An action method will pop up with the name: **cancel**; select it to connect it with the **Bar Button Item** control.

To specify a delegate for the *Search Bar*, as we need to implement its method for searching contents from the Table View, follow the given steps:

1. Select the **Search Bar** control in the View and open the **Connections Inspector**.

2. From the **Connections Inspector** window, select the circle to the right of **delegate** under the **Outlets** heading and keeping the mouse button pressed, drag it to the **File's Owner** icon to inform that the `SearchProductController` class is declared as the delegate of the **Search Bar** control.

The `SearchProductController.xib` file, after doing the preceding operations, will appear as shown in the following screenshot:

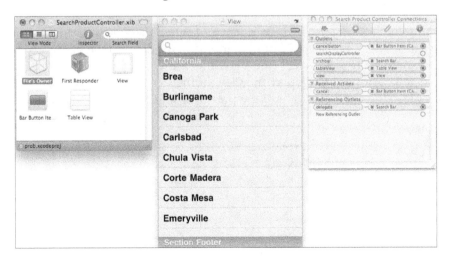

As we have declared the SearchProductController class as the delegate of the *Search Bar* control, we can now implement the delegate methods for the *Search Bar* control in it. So, let's write the code in the *SearchProductController's* implementation file.

Coding in the SearchProductController class

To impart search facility while entering the products sold to the customers, we implement the *Search Bar* control's delegate methods in the SearchProductController class. The complete code of the implementation file of SearchProductController, SearchProductController.m is provided in the code bundle of this chapter. The code that requires explanation is provided next:

```
// SearchProductController.m
// prob

#import "SearchProductController.h"

@implementation SearchProductController
@synthesize srchbar, cust, cancelbutton, tableView, mastproducts,
fetchedResultsController;
```

In the preceding implementation file of the SearchProductController class, we see that all the IBOutlets, srchbar, cust, cancelbutton, tableView, and fetchedResultsController are synthesized for generating the accessor and mutator methods for them.

```
-(IBAction) cancel:(id) sender
{
  [self dismissModalViewControllerAnimated:YES];
}
```

In the action method: cancel (which is invoked when the Bar Button Item control with the title: Cancel is selected from the toolbar), we dismiss the modal view of the SearchProductController class (the View that allows us to select the products sold to the selected customer) to display the view of the ProductInfoController class, which displays the view to add/edit the products sold to the selected customer.

 The SearchProductController class is invoked from the ProductInfoController class.

The view of the *SearchProductController* will display all products of the *MasterProduct* table by default.

```
-(void) searchBar:(UISearchBar *) searchBar textDidChange:(NSString *)
Tosearch{
  if([[searchBar text] length] >0)
    {
    NSPredicate *predicate =[NSPredicate
predicateWithFormat:@"itemname CONTAINS %@", [searchBar text]];
    [fetchedResultsController.fetchRequest setPredicate:predicate];
  }
  else
  {
    [fetchedResultsController.fetchRequest setPredicate:nil];
  }
  NSError *error = nil;
  if (![[self fetchedResultsController] performFetch:&error]) {
    // Handle error
    NSLog(@"Unresolved error %@, %@", error, [error userInfo]);
    exit(-1);  // Fail
  }
  [self.tableView reloadData];
  [searchBar resignFirstResponder];
    return;
}
```

The method `textDidChange:` is invoked every time the text in the *Search Bar's* text field is changed to display the prompt changes in the table's contents as the text is typed in the *Search Bar's* text field. In the `textDidChange:` method, we check if the length of the text in the *Search Bar's* text field is greater than 0. If it is, that means something is typed in the search bar, so then we make use of the `NSPredicate` to write a filter condition (predicate), as follows:

```
"itemname contains search bar text"
```

The filter condition retrieves only those product names from the *MasterProduct* entity table that contains the character(s) typed in the *Search Bar's* text field.

Then the predicate is set to the `fetchrequest` to retrieve only those records from the persistent store that agree to the predicate (filter condition) applied. If the *Search Bar's* text field is blank, the predicate is set to `nil` declaring that there is no filter condition and hence, to fetch all the records from the persistent store.

The performfetch is executed to retrieve the managed object context from the persistent store. We remove the keyboard (when desired products are displayed through table view) by informing the *Search Bar* to resign the first responder status, which will cause the keyboard to go away. Recall that NSPredicate is used for applying the condition on the kind of entities to be retrieved.

```
// Customize the appearance of table view cells.
- (UITableViewCell *)tableView:(UITableView *)tableView cellForRowAtIn
dexPath:(NSIndexPath *)indexPath {

  static NSString *CellIdentifier = @"Cell";

  UITableViewCell *cell = [self.tableView dequeueReusableCellWithIdent
ifier:CellIdentifier];
  if (cell == nil) {
    cell = [[[UITableViewCell alloc] initWithStyle:UITableViewCellStyl
eDefault reuseIdentifier:CellIdentifier] autorelease];
    cell.accessoryType=UITableViewCellAccessoryDisclosureIndicator;
  }

  // Configure the cell.

  NSManagedObject *managedObject = [fetchedResultsController
objectAtIndexPath:indexPath];
  cell.textLabel.text = [[managedObject valueForKey:@"itemname"]
description];
  UIImage *pimage=[managedObject valueForKey:@"image"];
  CGSize size=pimage.size;
  CGFloat ratio = 0;
  if (size.width > size.height) {
    ratio = 44.0 / size.width;
  }
  else {
    ratio = 44.0 / size.height;
  }
  CGRect rect = CGRectMake(0.0, 0.0, ratio * size.width, ratio * size.
height);
  UIGraphicsBeginImageContext(rect.size);
  [pimage drawInRect:rect];
  cell.imageView.image=UIGraphicsGetImageFromCurrentImageContext();
  UIGraphicsEndImageContext();
  return cell;
}
```

In the `cellForRowAtIndexPath` method, we retrieve the managed object from the Fetched Results Controller by just calling `objectAtIndexPath:` on the fetched results controller and pass in the `indexPath` parameter. The `fetchedResultsController` will return the desired objects for each table cell. To display text (item name) in the table cell, we use `valueForKey` (key value method used for retrieving attribute values) to retrieve the contents in the `itemname` attribute of the managed object.

As we want to display the master product image (also) to the left of the master product name in the table view cell, we retrieve the image from the image attribute of the managed object and temporarily assign it to an `UIImage` instance: `pimage`. The image assigned to a `pimage` instance has to be scaled down to accommodate in the table cell.

For displaying the image in the "pimage" instance within the defined size of the frame (of a window), we configure the drawing environment, that is, we create a bitmap-based graphics context using the `UIGraphicsBeginImageContext()` function. In the `UIGraphicsBeginImageContext()` function, we specify the size of the frame within which we want the image to appear. Once the context is created, we retrieve the image based on the contents of the current context (using the `UIGraphicsGetImageFromCurrentimageContext()`) and assign it to the `imageView` of the table cell for display. When our job is over, we clean up the bitmap drawing environment (that we created with `UIGraphicsBeginImageContext()`) and remove the graphics context (from the top of the context stack) using the `UIGraphicsEndImageContext()` function.

```
- (void)tableView:(UITableView *)tableView didSelectRowAtIndexPath:(NS
IndexPath *)indexPath {
  AddProductController *addprodController =[[AddProductController
alloc] initWithNibName:@"AddProductController" bundle:nil];
  MasterProduct *selectedprod=(MasterProduct *)
[fetchedResultsController objectAtIndexPath:indexPath];
  addprodController.mastprod=selectedprod;
  addprodController.cust=cust;
  [self.navigationController pushViewController:addprodController
animated:YES];
  [addprodController release];
}
```

In the `didSelectRowAtIndexPath` method that is invoked when any product is selected from the tableView, we write code to navigate to the View of the `AddProductController` class that displays the information (`itemname`, `price`, and `image`) of the selected product (automatically retrieved from the *MasterProduct's* table) and prompts the user to enter the *quantity* of the selected product that is sold to the customer. We create and initialize an instance of the `AddProductController` class with the name: `addprodController`. We make use of `alloc` to create the view controller object and initialize it. The `init` method specifies the name of the NIB file that has to be loaded by the controller (`AddProductController`) followed by the bundle where the NIB file is expected to be found. The bundle parameter is set to `nil` as we want the method to look for the NIB file in the main bundle. The `initWithNibName` method allows initializing a *UIViewController's* view from a NIB file rather than from the code. This method is preferred when the view of the view controller exists in the NIB and we want to initialize that view controller, that is, we are interested in loading a view from a NIB file. In this method, we also retrieve a managed object context from the `fetchedResultsController`.

The managed object context is retrieved from the `fetchedResultsController` (it is the object that is returned by calling `objectAtIndexPath` on the fetched results controller and passing in the `indexPath` parameter to it) and is assigned to an instance: `selectedprod` of the `MasterProduct` class. That is, the information of the product whose item name is selected from the table view is assigned to the `selectedprod` instance. The contents of the `selectedprod` instance are assigned to the `mastprod` object of `addprodController` (instance of the `AddProductController` class) as we want the information (`itemname`, `price`, and `image`) of the selected product to be displayed via the Text Field and ImageView control placed in the View of the `AddProductController` class. The view controller instance: `addprodController` is then pushed on the navigation stack causing the view of the `AddProductController` to be displayed; this also updates the navigation controls to reflect the changes. The animated attribute is set to `Yes` to display the view (associated with the `AddProductController`) with animation effect.

```
- (NSFetchedResultsController *)fetchedResultsController {
  if (fetchedResultsController != nil) {
    return fetchedResultsController;
  }
  probAppDelegate *appDelegate = (probAppDelegate *)[[UIApplication
sharedApplication] delegate];
  NSManagedObjectContext *context = [appDelegate
managedObjectContext];
  NSFetchRequest *fetchRequest = [[NSFetchRequest alloc] init];
  [fetchRequest setEntity:[NSEntityDescription
entityForName:@"MasterProduct" inManagedObjectContext:context]];
```

```
   NSSortDescriptor *sortDescriptor = [[NSSortDescriptor alloc]
initWithKey:@"itemname" ascending:YES];
   NSArray *sortDescriptors = [[NSArray alloc]
initWithObjects:sortDescriptor, nil];
   [fetchRequest setSortDescriptors:sortDescriptors];
   NSFetchedResultsController *aFetchedResultsController =
[[NSFetchedResultsController alloc] initWithFetchRequest:fet
chRequest managedObjectContext:context sectionNameKeyPath:nil
cacheName:@"Root"];
   aFetchedResultsController.delegate = self;
   self.fetchedResultsController = aFetchedResultsController;
   [aFetchedResultsController release];
   return fetchedResultsController;
}
(...)
@end
```

In the `fetchedResultsController` method, we retrieve the managed object context from the application delegate.

Now, on selecting the **Add** button from the toolbar of the product menu, we should be navigated to the view of the `SearchProductController` class that will display the information (`itemname`, `price`, and `image`) of all the products available for sale from the *MasterProduct* entity along with the search facility. So, let's go ahead and see how the `SearchProductController` can be invoked from the product menu.

Invoking the SearchProductController from the Product menu

As we want to navigate to the view of the `SearchProductController` class on selecting the **Add** button from the product menu, we need to modify the code of the `addproduct` method of the implementation file of the `ProductInfoController` class, that is, `ProductInfoController.m`. Recall that the product menu is displayed through the `ProductInfoController` class. The implementation file, `ProductInfoController.m` may be modified to appear as shown next. Only the modified code is shown next. For the complete code, refer to the code bundle of this chapter.

```
//  ProductInfoController.m
//  prob

#import "ProductInfoController.h"

(....)
```

```
-(IBAction) addproduct:(id)sender
{
   SearchProductController *srchprodController
=[[SearchProductController alloc] initWithNibName:@"SearchProductContr
oller" bundle:nil];
   UINavigationController *navController=[[UINavigationController
alloc] initWithRootViewController:srchprodController];
   [self    presentModalViewController:navController animated:YES];
   srchprodController.cust=cust;
}


(...)
// Customize the appearance of table view cells.
- (UITableViewCell *)tableView:(UITableView *)tableView cellForRowAtIn
dexPath:(NSIndexPath *)indexPath {
   static NSString *CellIdentifier = @"Cell";
   UITableViewCell *cell = [self.tableView dequeueReusableCellWithIdent
ifier:CellIdentifier];
   if (cell == nil) {
      cell = [[[UITableViewCell alloc] initWithStyle:UITableViewCellStyl
eValue1 reuseIdentifier:CellIdentifier] autorelease];
   }

   Product *prd=[products objectAtIndex:indexPath.row];
   cell.textLabel.text=prd.itemname;
   NSString *str=[NSString stringWithFormat:@"%d",
[prd.quantity intValue]];
   cell.detailTextLabel.text=str;
   return cell;
}


(....)


@end
```

If compared to the contents of the file: ProductInfoController.m (in the
*Chapter 8, Entering, Saving, Listing, and Deleting the Records of the Products Sold to
the Customers*), only the methods: addproduct and cellForRowAtIndexPath
are modified. In the addproduct method, we create and initialize an instance of
the SearchProductController class with the name: srchprodController. We
make use of alloc to create the view controller object and initialize it. The init
method specifies the name of the nib file that has to be loaded by the controller
(SearchProductController) followed by the bundle where the nib file is expected
to be found.

The `bundle` parameter is set to `nil` as we want the method to look for the `nib` file in the main bundle. The `initWithNibName` method allows initializing a UIViewController's view from a `nib` file rather than from the code. This method is preferred when view of the view controller exists in `nib` and we want to initialize that view controller, that is, we are interested in loading a view from a `nib` file. Also, the `cust` instance of the `Customer` class containing information of the customer (whose sales information we want to enter) is assigned to the `cust` instance of `srchprodController` (that is, we can access the information of the customer in the view of the `SearchProductController` class).

Also, we add statements (that are highlighted) in the `cellForRowAtIndexPath` to display the quantity of the product that is sold to the customer in the table cell (along with the item name).

The previously modified code will navigate us to the view of the `SearchProductController` class on selecting the **Add** button from the product menu (view of the `ProductInfoController` class). The view of the `SearchProductController` class will fetch the rows from the *MasterProduct* entity to display all products that are available for sale along with their images. On selecting any product from the view of the `SearchProductController` class, we will be navigated to the `AddProductController` class. The `AddProductController` class is supposed to display the product name and price of the selected product prompting us to enter the quantity of the products sold. Apart from the name and price of the selected product, we want the `AddProductController` class to display the image of the selected product.

Displaying name, price, and image of the selected product

For displaying the name, price, and image of the selected product, we need to modify both the header and the implementation file of the `AddProductController` class. Let's begin with the header file. We modify the `AddProductController.h` as shown next (the statements which are highlighted are added). The rest of the file is the same as we saw in *Chapter 8, Entering, Saving, Listing, and Deleting the Records of the Products Sold to the Customers*:

```
// AddProductController.h
// prob

#import <UIKit/UIKit.h>
#import "Customer.h"
#import "Product.h"
#import "SearchProductController.h"
```

```objc
#import "MasterProduct.h"

@interface AddProductController : UIViewController{
    MasterProduct *mastprod;
    IBOutlet UIBarButtonItem *savebutton;
    IBOutlet UITextField *newitemname;
    IBOutlet UITextField *newquantity;
    IBOutlet UITextField *newprice;
    IBOutlet UIImageView *prodimage;
    Customer *cust;
    Product *prod;
}

@property(nonatomic, retain) Customer *cust;
@property(nonatomic, retain) MasterProduct *mastprod;
@property(nonatomic, retain) Product *prod;
@property(nonatomic, retain)  UIBarButtonItem *savebutton;
@property(nonatomic, retain) UITextField *newitemname;
@property(nonatomic, retain) UITextField *newquantity;
@property(nonatomic, retain) UITextField *newprice;
@property(nonatomic, retain) UIImageView *prodimage;

-(IBAction) save:(id)sender;

@end
```

We simply add statements to define an instance of the `Customer` class with the name: `cust` and an instance of the `UIImageView` class with the name: `prodimage`. The `cust` object will be used for storing the information of the customer whose information of products is being stored and the instance: `prodimage` – is for displaying image of the product sold to the customer. The instance `prodimage` is defined as the outlet to be connected to the *UIImageView* control dropped in the View.

We need to add an *UIImageView* control to the view of the `AddProductController` class and also need to remove a Bar Button Item control with title: `Cancel`. The `Cancel` Bar Button Item control will be no more required as the `Back` button of the navigation bar will do the same thing automatically. The steps are as follows:

1. So, let us open the `AddProductController.xib` file in Interface Builder.

2. Drag-and-drop an **UIImageView** control from the **Library** window and drop it on the View.

3. To connect the **prodimage** outlet defined in the header file with the UIImage view control in the View, select the **File's Owner** icon in the **Documents** window and open the **Connections Inspector**. From the **Connection Inspector**, under the heading: **Outlets**, select the circle to the right of outlet: **prodimage** and keeping the mouse button pressed drag it to the **UIImageView** control in the View.

4. Also, delete the Bar Button control with the title: **Cancel** from the **Documents** window.

After doing all the changes as mentioned, the AddProductController.xib file may appear as shown in the following screenshot:

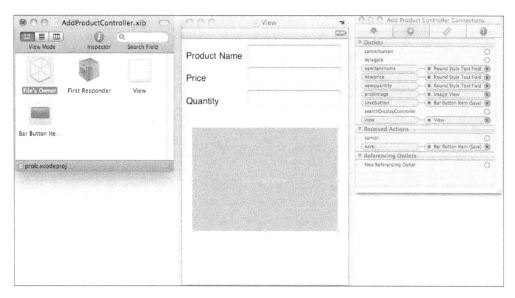

To keep the image confined within the size of the *ImageView* control, we select the checkboxes: **Clip Subviews** and **Autoresize Subviews** from the Attributes Inspector, as shown in the following screenshot:

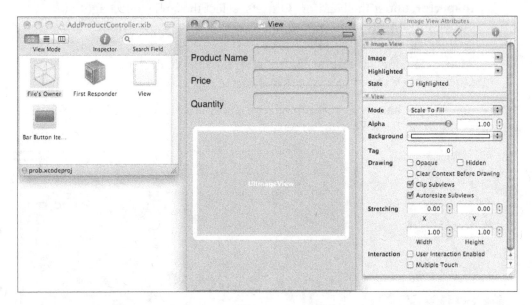

One last thing, that we need to apply to our application is to update the stock, that is, the quantity of the product in the *MasterProduct* entity must be reduced by the quantity sold to the customer. So, let's go ahead and do it!

Updating the stock

The implementation file of the AddProductController class (AddProductController.m) is modified to save the information of the product sold to the selected customer. Not only will the implementation file save the information of the product sold but, will also update the stock; the quantity of the product sold will be reduced from the inventory, that is, from the stock maintained in the *MasterProduct* entity. For example, if the initial quantity of Milk is 100 bottles (in the *MasterProduct* entity) and three bottles are sold to the customer, the quantity of the product left in the *MasterProduct* entity will be 97 bottles. Only the statements that are highlighted are added to the file and rest of the code is same as we saw in *Chapter 8, Entering, Saving, Listing, and Deleting the Records of the Products Sold to the Customers*:

```
// AddProductController.m
// prob

#import "AddProductController.h"
```

```objc
@implementation AddProductController

@synthesize newitemname, newquantity, newprice, prodimage;
@synthesize cust, mastprod, prod, savebutton;

-(IBAction) save:(id)sender{
  NSManagedObjectContext *context = [cust managedObjectContext];
  prod = [NSEntityDescription insertNewObjectForEntityForName:@"Produ
ct" inManagedObjectContext:context];
  prod.itemname=mastprod.itemname;
  prod.price=mastprod.price;
  prod.quantity=[NSNumber numberWithInt:  [newquantity.text intValue]]
;
  [cust addProductObject: prod];
  int balqty=[mastprod.quantity intValue]-[prod.quantity intValue];
  mastprod.quantity=[NSNumber numberWithInt: balqty];
  NSError *error;
  if(![context save:&error]){
    NSLog(@"Unresolved error %@ %@", error, [error userInfo]);
    exit(-1);
}
  [self dismissModalViewControllerAnimated:YES];
}


- (void)viewWillAppear:(BOOL)animated {
  [super viewWillAppear:animated];
    newitemname.text=mastprod.itemname;
  NSString *str=[NSString stringWithFormat:@"%f", [mastprod.price
floatValue]];
  newprice.text=str;
  prodimage.image=mastprod.image;
}

// Implement viewDidLoad to do additional setup after loading the
view, typically from a nib.
- (void)viewDidLoad {
  [super viewDidLoad];
  self.title=@"New Product";
  self.navigationItem.rightBarButtonItem=savebutton;
  NSLog(@"in view did load of addproduct controller");
}

- (void)dealloc {
  [newitemname release];
  [newquantity release];
```

```
    [newprice release];
    [savebutton release];
    [prodimage release];
    [prod release];
    [cust release];
    [mastprod release];
    [super dealloc];
}

@end
```

In the action method: save (that is invoked when the Bar Button Item with title: Save is selected from the toolbar), we write the code to save the information of the product sold to the customer. In this method, we also retrieve a managed object context from the cust object and assign it to the instance: context (of the NSManagedObjectContext class). Then, we insert a new managed object (of the Product entity) into the managed context: context using the class method on NSEntityDescription. Also, we return the instance of the class that represents the Product entity and assign it to the prod object (of the Product class), which will be used to accept the information of the new product sold to the customer. The information of the product (master product) sold to a customer is assigned to the prod object. That is, the itemname and the price attributes of the mastprod (instance of *Master Product*) — the product sold to the customer are assigned to the prod instance — the product sold to the customer. The quantity sold to the customer, that is, entered in the text field control is assigned to the quantity attribute of the prod instance. The quantity attribute of the mastprod instance is reduced by the number equal to the quantity sold to the customer. Finally, the context is saved to the persistent store and dismisses the modal view of the AddProductController class (the view that allows us to enter and save the information of the product sold to the customer) to display the view of the ProductInfoController class, which displays the view to add/edit the products sold to the selected customer.

> The AddProductController class is invoked from the ProductInfoController class.

The viewWillAppear method is for retrieving the information (*item name, price,* and *image*) of the selected product (from the master product object) and displaying in the text field and UIImagerView control placed in the view. Recall that, we just want the user to enter the *quantity* of the product sold to the customer (with the rest of the information to be directly retrieved from the selected product.) This finishes our application.

Running the project

Let's run the application and see how the `SearchProductController` fetches and displays the products available for sale from the *MasterProduct* entity and how the selected product gets displayed in the `AddProductController` along with the product's name, its price, and image, and finally how the quantity of the product is updated in the *MasterProduct* entity after sale. On executing the application, we get the list of customers in the main view. Let's enter information about the products sold to a customer, say *Candace*. On selecting her name from the main menu, we'll see her information being displayed in the view, as shown in the following *image (a)*. At the bottom of the view is the Product Information button, used to add and edit information about the products sold to the selected customer. When we tap this button, we'll see a view with three buttons: **Back**, **Edit**, and **Add**, as shown in the following *image (b)*:

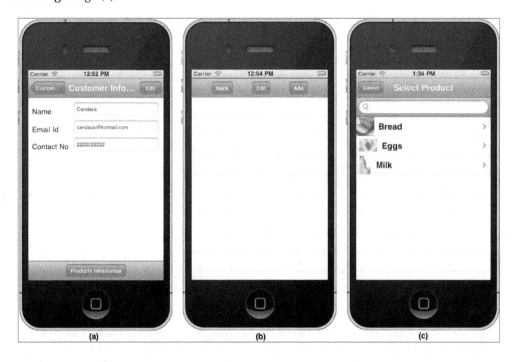

(a)   (b)   (c)

On selecting the **Add** button, we get the list of products that are available for sale along with their thumbnail images shown in the preceding *image (c)*. The list of products is fetched from the `MasterProduct` controller. The *Search Bar* at the top of the view can be used to search for the desired product. Typing the text in the *Search Bar* will filter the products and display only those containing the characters typed into the *Search Bar*. After a product is selected, its name, price, and image will appear and we will be asked to enter the quantity of the selected product sold to the customer.

For example, if we select **Bread** from the list, we'll be asked to enter its quantity, as shown in the following *image (a)*. Let's suppose that *Candace* bought three loaves of bread, so we enter 3 in the **Quantity** text field, as shown in the following *image (b)*, then select the **Save** button from the Navigation bar. We will be returned to the table view shown in the following *image (c)*. Note the value **3** is displayed to the right of **Bread**, which tells us that the quantity of the bread sold to Candace was 3.

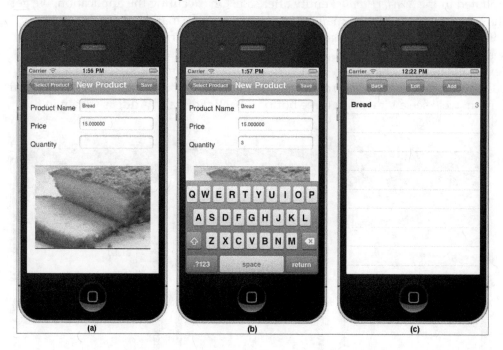

(a)   (b)   (c)

We can again select the **Add** button to add additional products sold to the customer. The following given *image (a)* displays the view when **Eggs** is selected from the available products list. The following given *image (b)* shows how the name, price, and product image automatically appear, asking the user to fill in the quantity sold.

The quantity entered here will be deducted from the product inventory in the *Master Products* entity. After selecting the **Save** button, all products sold to the customer are displayed, as shown in the following *image (c)*. The products will be displayed in sorted alphabetical order.

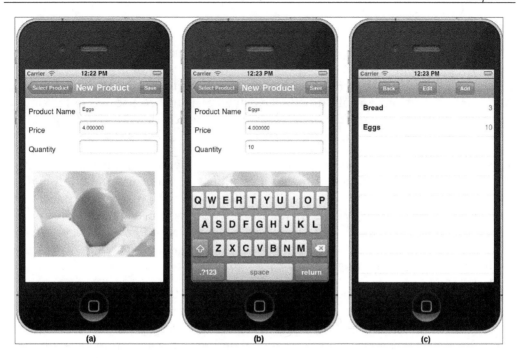

The **Edit** button shown in the preceding *image (c)* is used to delete a product entry sold to the customer.

Automatically updating the quantity of the product in the MasterProduct entity

The quantity sold to a customer is automatically deducted from the master product's quantity in hand. To see if the stock has been updated, first select the **Master Product Information** button from the toolbar at the bottom of the Main view — the first view of the application, we'll see the list of products stored in the *MasterProduct* entity. On selecting a master product, we'll see the page that displays the master product information. We will see that the quantity of the product is reduced by the quantity sold to the customer.

Let's complete the book with a small introduction of migrations and versioning. The concept of migrations and versioning is useful for us to understand in case we make some changes to our data model, that is, if we add or delete some attribute in any of the entities that we created in our application. Modification in the data model is usually required to meet future demands.

Versioning

The concept of migrations and versioning is related to the problems that are caused when we make some changes in our data model. Like if we add or delete some attribute(s) from an existing *Entity* or add one more *Entity* to our data model. In that case, our new version of application will crash when launched because of the simple fact that the existing data in the persistent store on the iPhone will be unusable in the new version of our application.

This problem can be corrected at our end by selecting **Reset Content** and **Settings** option from the iPhone simulator menu or by uninstalling the application from the iPhone and re-installing it. Consequently, the CoreData will create a new persistent store on the basis of the new Data model when the application is launched. But the problem occurs at the client's end, who has the older application, and a new version of the application is sent to them. They cannot uninstall and re-install the application as they will lose their existing data.

To solve such problems, Xcode has a built-in *version-control* mechanism that helps in applying a new version to our revised data model. In this versioning facility, the older data model will be kept (and not erased) and the revised data model is assigned a new version number. This will not only save the user from losing the existing data but will also help in upgrading the older data into the newer version.

Creating a new Data Model version

Let's assume we have an application with the name *demopredicate* that has a data model: **demopredicate.xcdatamodel**. To create a new Data Model version, single click **demopredicate.xcdatamodel** in *Xcode Project* window and select **Design | Data Model | Add Model Version** option. It will add a new version of our data model. We will find that our **demopredicate.xcdatamodel** file gets disappeared from the **Resources** group and is replaced by a new resource with the **demopredicate.xcdatamodeld** with a disclosure triangle next to it, as shown in the following screenshot:

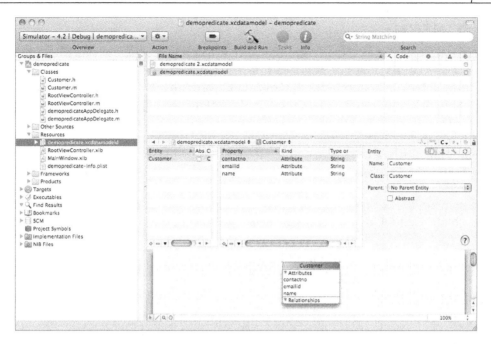

On selecting the disclosure triangle of demopredicate.xcdatamodeld, all the versions of our data model will be displayed and the current data model that is being used by our application will be represented by an icon with green checkmark on it. When we create a new version of our data model, the latest version is represented by the file with the original name, and the older version is represented by a copy that is created with the same name with an incrementally larger number affixed to the end. Like in the preceding screenshot, the file: demopredicate2.xcdatamodel is the original data model.

As we have the older version of our data model safe, we can now make changes to the current version (latest version) as desired. We can always switch to the older data model to see our old existing data. To switch to any data model, that is, to make any data model the current version (to work on), select the data model file from the *Xcode Project* window and select the **Design | Data Model | Set Current Version** option.

Migrations

An exception is thrown if Core Data finds that the persistent store is incompatible with the current data model. To solve this problem, we use a concept called *Migration*, which tells Core Data to move data from the old persistent store to a new one that matches the current data model. Migrations are of two types: *Lightweight* and *Standard*. *Lightweight* migration is easy to achieve (requires no coding) and is used when small modifications are applied to our data model that includes adding or removing attributes from an entity, adding or deleting an existing entity from the data mode, and so on. Whereas *Standard* migration is a bit complicated to implement as it requires creation of a mapping model and coding to inform Core Data to move the data from the old persistent store to the new one. The standard migration is out of scope of this book. We will only discuss lightweight migration in this book.

Implementing lightweight migration to our application

To implement lightweight migration to our application, we have to do some modifications in our application delegate file. So, open the `probAppDelegate.m` file (refer to the *Chapter 4, Designing the Data Model and Building Data Objects for Customers*) and locate the `persistentStoreCoordinator` method, which will have the code as shown next:

```
- (NSPersistentStoreCoordinator *)persistentStoreCoordinator {
  if (persistentStoreCoordinator != nil) {
    return persistentStoreCoordinator;
  }

  NSURL *storeUrl = [NSURL fileURLWithPath: [[self
applicationDocumentsDirectory] stringByAppendingPathComponent:
@"customersdata.sqlite"]];

  NSError *error;
  persistentStoreCoordinator = [[NSPersistentStoreCoordinator alloc]
initWithManagedObjectModel: [self managedObjectModel]];
  if (![persistentStoreCoordinator addPersistentStoreWithType:NSSQLite
StoreType configuration:nil URL:storeUrl options:nil error:&error]) {
    // Handle error
  }
  return persistentStoreCoordinator;
}
```

In the preceding code, while calling the `addPersistentStoreWithType:c onfiguration:URL:options:error:` method, we will pass a `dictionary` into the options argument for adding the newly created persistent store to the persistent store coordinator. In the `dictionary` (that we are going to pass to the options argument), we will use two system-defined constants, `NSMigratePersistentStoresAutomaticallyOption` and `NSInferMappingModelAutomaticallyOption`, as keys in the dictionary, and store an `NSNumber` under both of those keys with a `YES` value. This dictionary will inform the Core Data that we want it to automatically create migrations if any change in the data model version is found. Also, it informs that if a migration is created, use the migrations to migrate the data to a new persistent store based on the current data model.

Let us modify the code of the `persistentStoreCoordinator` method to appear as follows:

```
- (NSPersistentStoreCoordinator *)persistentStoreCoordinator {
if (persistentStoreCoordinator != nil) {
return persistentStoreCoordinator;
}

NSURL *storeUrl = [NSURL fileURLWithPath: [[self
applicationDocumentsDirectory]
stringByAppendingPathComponent: @"customersdata.sqlite"]];

NSDictionary *dicoptions = [NSDictionary dictionaryWithObjectsAndKeys:
[NSNumber boolval:YES], NSMigratePersistentStoresAutomaticallyOption,
[NSNumber boolval:YES], NSInferMappingModelAutomaticallyOption, nil];
NSError *error = nil;

persistentStoreCoordinator = [[NSPersistentStoreCoordinator alloc]
initWithManagedObjectModel: [self managedObjectModel]];
if (![persistentStoreCoordinator addPersistentStoreWithType:NSSQLiteS
toreType
configuration:nil URL:storeUrl options:dicoptions error:&error]) {
NSLog(@"Unresolved error %@, %@", error, [error userInfo]);
abort();
}
return persistentStoreCoordinator;
}
```

With the preceding code, the lightweight migration is implemented to our application and we are ready to make changes to our data model.

In a lightweight migration, Core Data actually analyzes the two data models and creates the migration for us.

Summary

This finishes our book on "Core Data Essentials". The focus of this book was to help you understand the practical aspect of Core Data through an application. Each module of the application followed a step-by-step approach to inspire you to develop your own data-driven application. We've tried our best to keep the code easy to understand in this book and we hope you agree! You now have all the necessary tools for building a data-driven application for iPhone. Have fun creating your own customized programs, and thanks for reading!

Appendix

Attributes: Attributes are the variables within an entity. They are also known as columns of the table in database language terms. For example: name, address, contact number, and so on.

CGRect structure: The CGRect structure is used for holding the location and dimension of the frame of a window on the screen.

CGRectMake function: The `CGRectMake` function is used for defining the frame of a window of an object. With the help of this function, we specify the coordinates of the origin as well as width and height of the frame.

CGSize structure: The CGSize structure represents a size of a rectangle and is used for storing information related to width and height of the object.

CGSizeMake function: The `CGSizeMake` function is used for defining the width and height of an element.

Core Data API: The Core Data API is a stack that consists of three main components, *NSPersistentStoreCoordinator*, *NSManagedObjectModel*, and *NSManagedObjectContext*.

Data Model: The Data Model refers to the information of the entities, attributes, and relationships used in an application.

Data Model Editor: The Data Model Editor is an editor provided by the Core Data framework for creating the entity relationship model quickly.

Delegate: The Delegate is the class that confirms to the protocol and is responsible for implementing the methods of the confirming protocol.

Entity: An individual data object used to store complete information of the person, item, object, and so on. It is also known as a table in the database language.

FetchedResultsController: FetchedResultsController is an instance of the NSFetchedResultsController class and is used for managing the result, that is, the set of entities that are retrieved on the basis of FetchRequest.

FetchRequest: FetchRequest is an instance of the NSFetchRequest class and is used to access the objects in a managed object context.

Image Picker: The Image Picker is used for displaying images allowing the user to choose or pick any image. Photo library, Camera, and Saved photos are the three sources from where Image Picker can pick the images to display.

Interface Builder: The Interface Builder is a visual design tool that makes creation of user interfaces quite easy for iphone applications. Creation of user interface is as easy as dragging and dropping of controls from the Library window to the View window.

iPhone: iPhone is an Internet and multimedia-enabled smartphone designed and marketed by Apple Inc.

iOS SDK: iOS SDK is a software development kit (SDK) released by Apple that contains three important apps: Xcode, Interface Builder, and iPhone Simulator along with several resources. The iPhone SDK helps in writing applications for iPhone, iPod Touch, and also for iPad.

Key Value coding (KVC): KVC is used to store and retrieve data from the managed objects. The key value methods valueForKey: and setValue:forKey: are used for setting and retrieving attribute values from the managed object respectively.

Key Value Observing (KVO): Key Value Observing is the sister API to KVC and is used to inform us if a particular attribute of an object is changed.

Keypath: Keypath is a concept that helps in iterating through object hierarchies using a single string.

Mac OS X: Mac OS X is a series of Unix-based operating systems and graphical user interfaces developed, marketed, and sold by Apple Inc. It is included with all new Macintosh computer systems.

Managed Object Context: The objects that are fetched from the persistent storage are placed in managed object context to perform validations and to keep track of the changes made to the object's attributes.

Managed Objects: Managed objects are instances of the NSManagedObject class or its subclass that represent instances of an entity that are managed by the Core Data framework.

Migration: Migration tells Core Data to move data from the old persistent store to a new one that matches the current data model. Migrations are of two types: Lightweight and Standard.

Model View Controller: MVC where M stands for Model that represents the backend data, V stands for View that represents the user interface elements through which the user can interact with the application and C stands for Controller that represents the application logic that decides which view to display on the basis of actions taken by the user.

NSEntityDescription: NSEntityDescription contains information of the entity, such as its name, its attributes, relationships, and so on.

NSNotification: NSNotification is an object that is broadcasted by an NSNotificationCenter object for its observers.

NSPredicate: NSPredicate is a complex and powerful tool used to filter out the undesired instances of an entity and to display only the desired instances.

Persistence framework: A persistence framework moves the data to and from a permanent data store. It also manages the database and the mapping between the database and the objects.

Persistent Store: The Persistent Store is a data store (repository) that handles mapping between data (in the store) and corresponding objects in a managed object context.

PersistentStoreCoordinator: This is used to store and retrieve Managed Objects from the Persistent Store via ManagedObjectContext.

Predicate Builder: Predicate Builder is a tool that helps in creating predicates, that is, queries for extracting rows from entities.

Properties: The properties describe attributes and relationships of an entity.

Protocol: A protocol is an interface that declares methods without body.

Relationship: A relationship is established between two or more entities to explain how they are mutually associated to each other. The relationship can be of any type, *To-One*, *To-Many*, and *Many to Many*.

Snow Leopard: Mac OS X Snow Leopard is the most advanced operating system built on UNIX. It is an innovative, highly secure, compatible, and easy-to-use operating system.

SQLite: SQLite is a software library that implements a self-contained transactional SQL database engine. It has a small core and is much faster than other databases. It is also the most widely deployed SQL database engine in the world.

TableView: The TableView control is most popularly used to display information in a list format. It is also conveniently used to edit, delete, and insert new information.

Thread: A thread is an individual entity of execution. When a program runs, a thread is created and the operating system allocates processor time to it. A thread has its own individual set of code to be executed independently.

Transformable data type: The transformable data type is a custom data type used to create attributes based on any Objective-C class. It works with *Value Transformers* to store instance of UIColor, UIImage, and so on.

View: A View represents the user interface elements through which the user looks at the contents displayed by the application and can interact with.

Xcode: Xcode is a suite of tools for developing software on Mac OS X and for iOS, developed by Apple. It includes Apple's developer documentation and Interface Builder, an application used to construct graphical user interfaces.

XML files: Extensible Markup Language (XML) is a set of rules for encoding documents in machine-readable form. It was designed to describe data. It allows us to define our own tags.

Index

Symbols

@class Customer statement 191
@end directive 41, 195, 234
@optional compiler directive 67
@optional directive 46
@protocol compiler directive 41
@protocol directive 41, 195, 234
<protocolname> 41
<SecondViewControllerDelegate> 47
-setValue:forKey: method 117
-valueForKey: method 116
(void)addProduct: (NSSet *)value 190
(void)removeProduct: (NSSet *)value 190
(void)removeProductObject: (Product *)
    value 190

A

accessor method 49
action method
  declaring, in
    demodelegateViewController.h header
    file 50
action methods
  defining, in AddNameController.h header
    file 66, 67
  defining, in header file 194, 195
  defining, in SecondViewController.h header
    file 45, 47
action methods, Master Product Information
  defining, in header file 267, 268
add action method 47, 49
Add button 298
AddCustomerController class 147
addcustomerController method 146

addCustomer method 112, 146
AddMasterProductController class 231, 232,
    234
addmastprodController method 240
addmastproduct method 251
addname action method 73
AddNameController class 47, 64, 73, 100-122
AddNameController class View
  defining 67, 69
addnameController method 71, 76, 114
AddNameController.m implementation file
  delegate methods, invoking 70, 71
AddNameController View
  invoking 72, 73
AddNameController View controller
  adding 64, 65
addPersistentStoreWithType:
    configuration:URL: options: error:
    method 303
addprodController method 209
AddProductController class 192, 197, 294,
    296
  view, designing 195-197
addproduct method 209, 210, 253
alloc method 215
allowsReverseTransformation method 224
application
  action method, declaring in
    demodelegateViewController.h header
    file 50
  action methods, defining in
    SecondViewController.h header file
    45, 47
  controls, connecting 47, 51
  creating, delegate used 42-44
  creating, protocol used 42-44

V

valueForKey
  method 170
value transformer, MasterProduct information
  creating 222, 223
value transformer name field, MasterProduct information 222
versioning
  about 300
  new Data Model version, creating 301
View 18, 308
ViewController class
  about 48, 192, 231
  adding 193
  adding, for entering master products information 232

adding, for entering numerical values 44, 45
adding, to display menu 242
using, for customer name addition 98, 99
View Controller class, Master Product Information
adding, to display view 266, 267
importing, in header file 273
viewDidLoad method 61-76, 107, 109, 145, 159, 200, 241, 272
viewDidUnload method 116
viewWillAppear method 261, 296

X

Xcode 9, 90, 308
XML files
  Extensible Markup Language (XML) 308

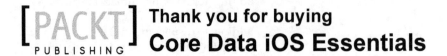

Thank you for buying
Core Data iOS Essentials

About Packt Publishing

Packt, pronounced 'packed', published its first book "*Mastering phpMyAdmin for Effective MySQL Management*" in April 2004 and subsequently continued to specialize in publishing highly focused books on specific technologies and solutions.

Our books and publications share the experiences of your fellow IT professionals in adapting and customizing today's systems, applications, and frameworks. Our solution based books give you the knowledge and power to customize the software and technologies you're using to get the job done. Packt books are more specific and less general than the IT books you have seen in the past. Our unique business model allows us to bring you more focused information, giving you more of what you need to know, and less of what you don't.

Packt is a modern, yet unique publishing company, which focuses on producing quality, cutting-edge books for communities of developers, administrators, and newbies alike. For more information, please visit our website: www.packtpub.com.

Writing for Packt

We welcome all inquiries from people who are interested in authoring. Book proposals should be sent to author@packtpub.com. If your book idea is still at an early stage and you would like to discuss it first before writing a formal book proposal, contact us; one of our commissioning editors will get in touch with you.

We're not just looking for published authors; if you have strong technical skills but no writing experience, our experienced editors can help you develop a writing career, or simply get some additional reward for your expertise.

Cocos2d for iPhone 0.99 Beginner's Guide

ISBN: 978-1-849513-16-6   Paperback: 368 pages

Make mind-blowing 2D games for iPhone with this fast, flexible, and easy-to-use framework!

1. A cool guide to learning cocos2d with iPhone to get you into the iPhone game industry quickly

2. Learn all the aspects of cocos2d while building three different games

3. Add a lot of trendy features such as particles and tilemaps to your games to captivate your players

Unity Game Development Essentials

ISBN: 978-1-847198-18-1   Paperback: 316 pages

Build fully functional, professional 3D games with realistic environments, sound, dynamic effects, and more!

1. Kick start game development, and build ready-to-play 3D games with ease

2. Understand key concepts in game design including scripting, physics, instantiation, particle effects, and more

3. Test & optimize your game to perfection with essential tips-and-tricks

Please check **www.PacktPub.com** for information on our titles